HONG KONG WHISPERS

MICHAEL WOLF ARPAÏS DU BOIS

HANNIBAL

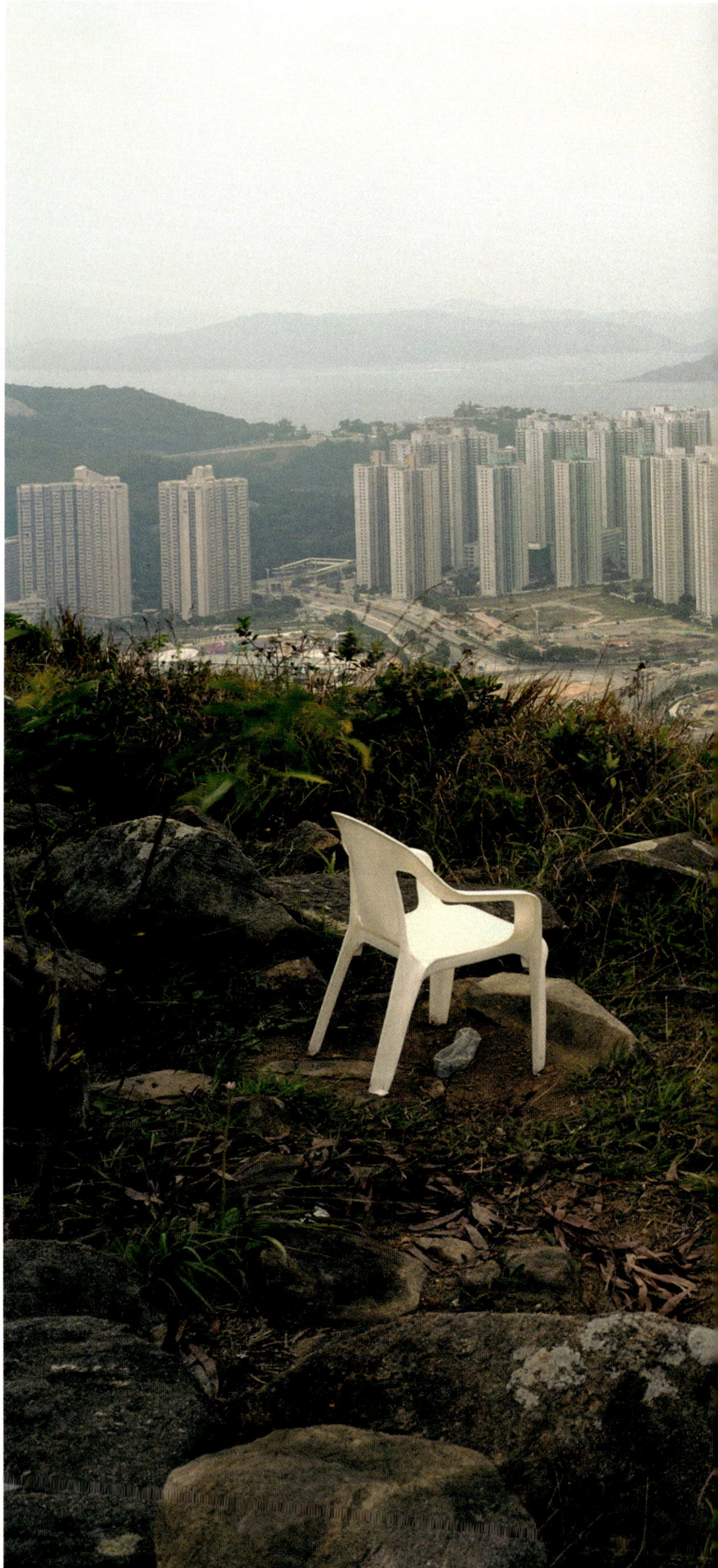

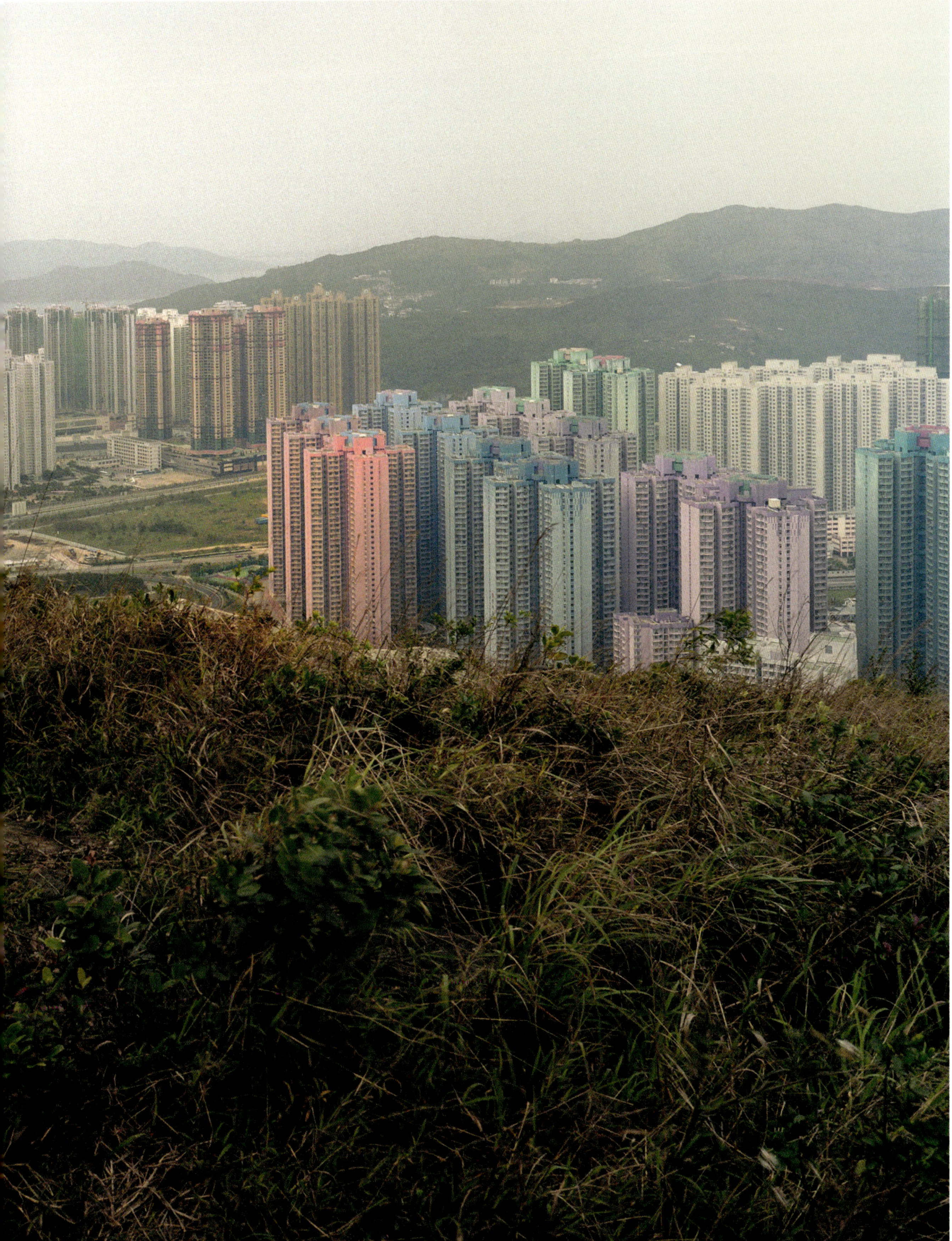

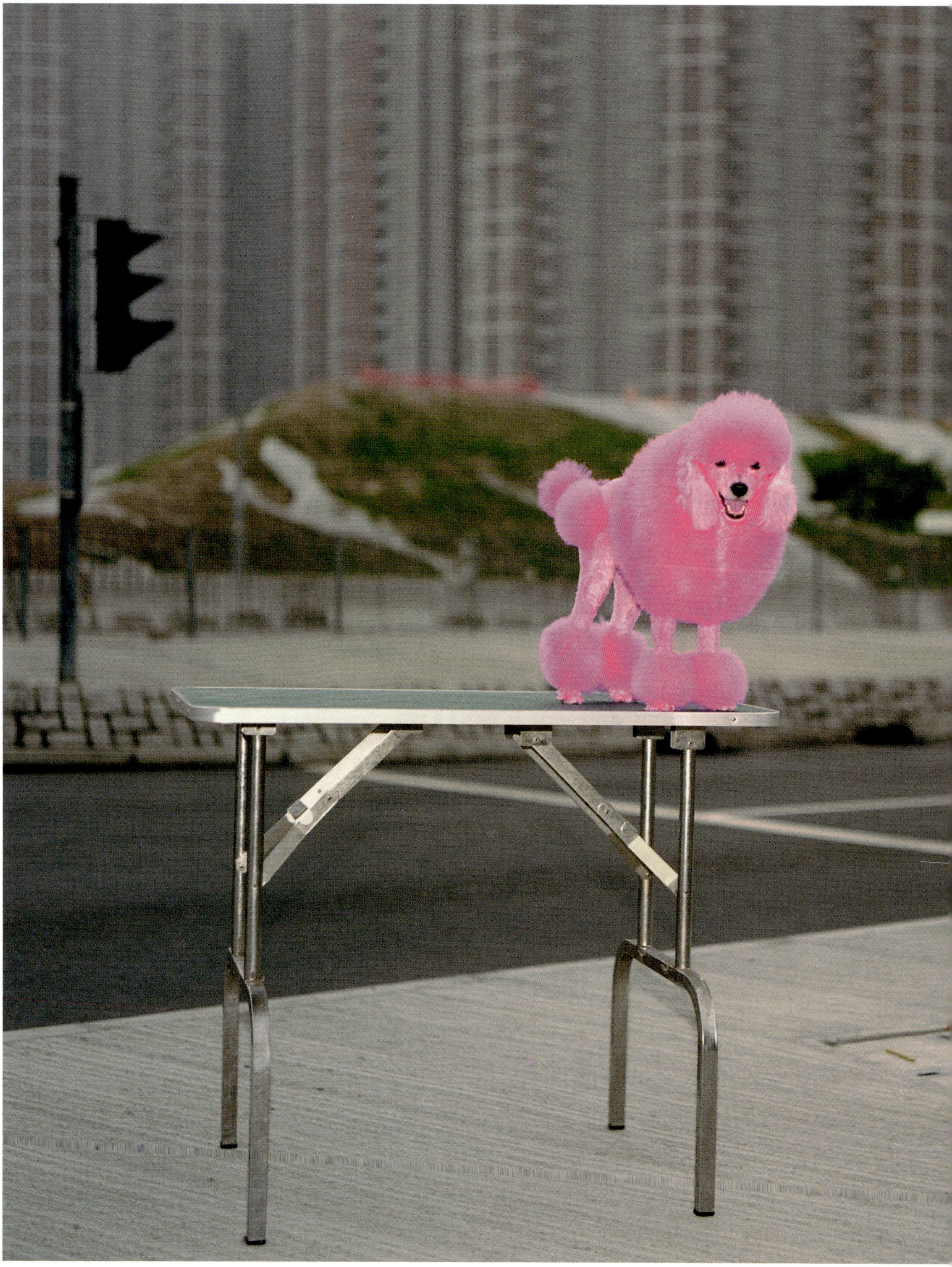

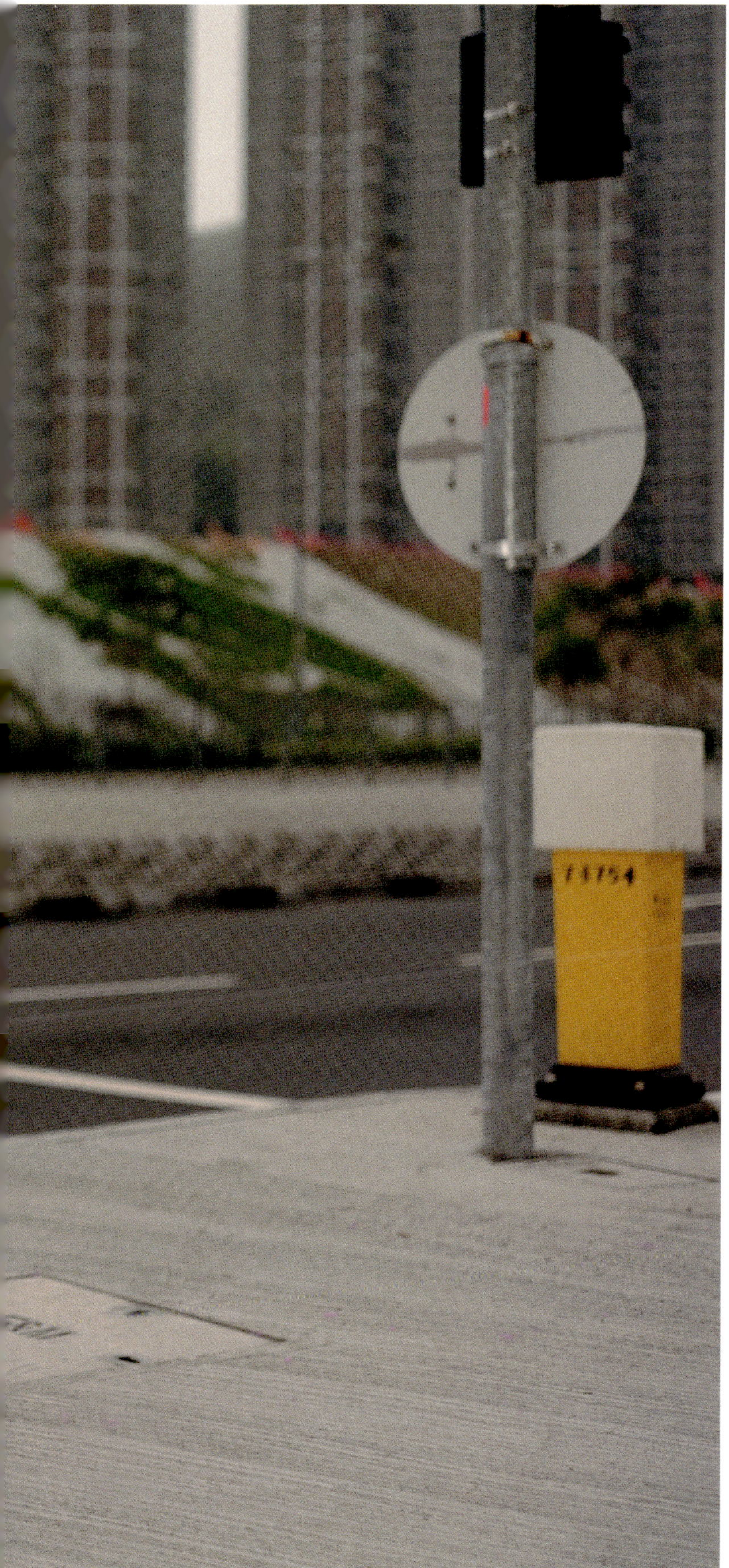

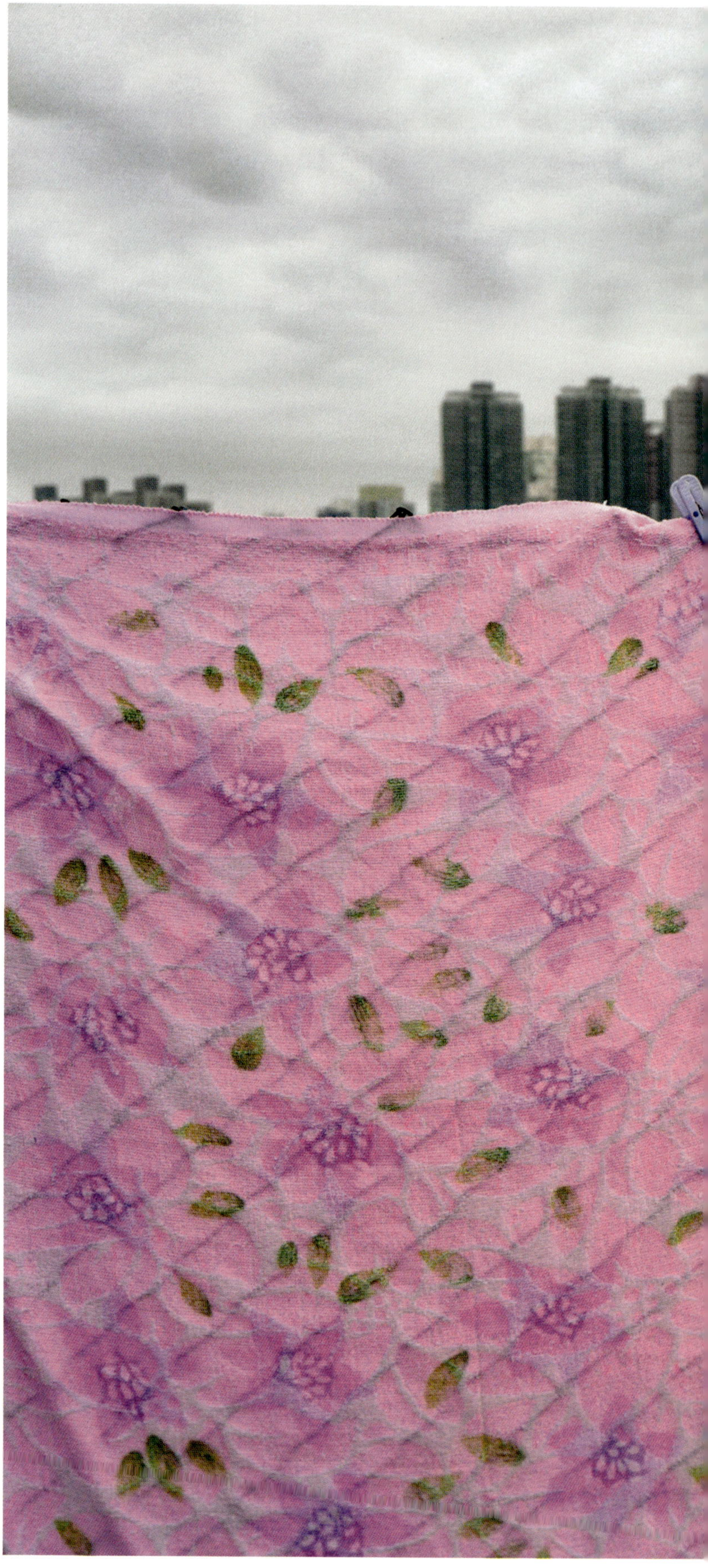

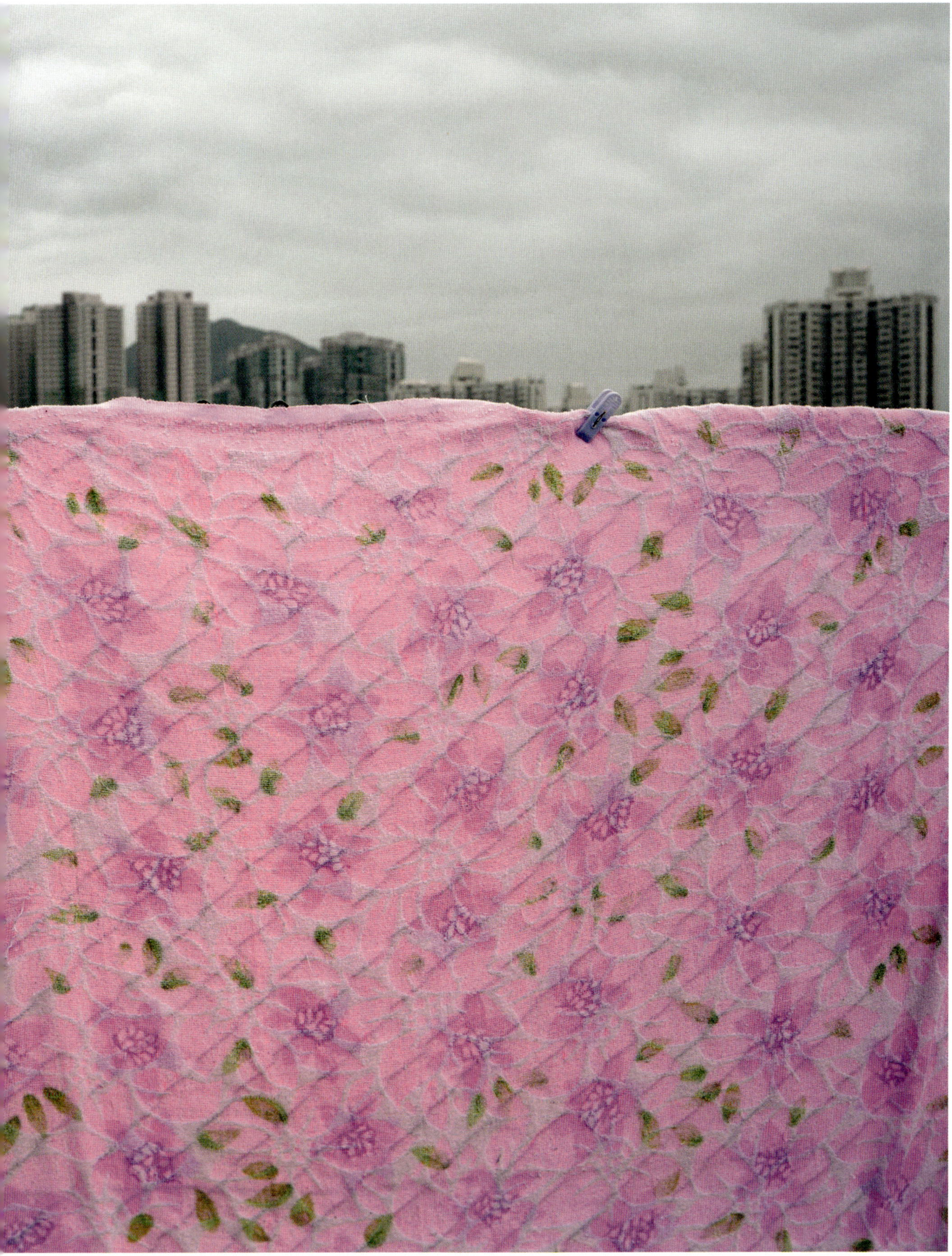

Marc Feustel is an independent writer, editor and curator based in Paris. A specialist in Japanese photography, he is also active as a writer and editor for contemporary art and photography publications including *ca.ra.ma.ru* by Takano Ryudai (Libraryman, 2022), *Boundary Hunt* by Toshio Shibata (Poursuite, 2021) and *BLACKOUT* by Hitoshi Fugo (L'Artiere, 2018). Marc has also contributed essays to several of Michael Wolf's publications, including *Asoue* (2010), *Hong Kong Assemblage Deconstructed* (2015), *Informal Solutions* (2016), *Works* (2017), and *Architecture of Density Hong Kong* (2022). A regular speaker and jury member at photography festivals and events, since 2019 he has been one of the hosts of the Artist Talks at the Paris Photo art fair. He writes regularly about photography and photobooks for publications around the world.

www.marcfeustel.com

INTERSTITIAL INSPIRATION
MARC FEUSTEL

Hong Kong is known for having one of the highest population densities on the planet, with over seven thousand residents per square kilometre, most of whom are concentrated in one-fourth of the city's land. Not only are rents high and living spaces small, but public urban space is also extremely limited, leaving locals with a mere 2.7 square metres per person, just slightly more space than a toilet cubicle.

With parks, sitting areas, and playgrounds at such a premium, residents are forced to make use of parts of the city that are not perceived as spaces unto themselves but rather as gaps in the urban fabric. No matter how small or cramped, these 'interstitial' spaces – sidewalks, stairways, and the network of alleyways surrounding many of the city's older buildings – are essential to urban life and are used by locals in a multitude of fascinating ways. Quite literally hidden in the shadows of tower blocks, it is often unclear to whom they belong, as they can be situated in between two premises or used by different people for different purposes, whether it be as storage units, places in which to sneak a cigarette break, or simply as shortcuts through the city. They are liminal zones, both theoretically and literally situated in the in-between. It is in these urban interstices that photographer Michael Wolf and artist Arpaïs Du Bois found the inspiration for their joint project *Hong Kong Whispers*, which is now being released for the first time, ten years after it was first created.

Having begun his career as an editorial photographer in Germany in the 1980s, Michael moved to Hong Kong in 1994 – a destination he chose based on its proximity to China, although he had yet to visit the city – and worked there for eight years as a contract photographer for the German current-affairs magazine *Stern*. He produced a number of major stories in the region, exploring many aspects of China's rising influence on the global stage.

However, by the turn of the millennium, he had begun to feel that the 'golden age' of photojournalism was behind him. Budgets were tightening, as was the time he was given to produce each story, and frustration was creeping in at not being able to explore the subjects he covered in more depth. In 2002, he decided it was time to scratch the itch that he had felt for some years, and he turned away from editorial work to devote himself to his personal photographic practice.

Despite this new chapter in his professional life, Michael had no desire to leave Hong Kong. If anything, the stimulation and inspiration he received from his adoptive city had been a central source of motivation in following this new path. In Hong Kong, he saw a fascinating microcosm of the challenges of contemporary urban life, which remained his central theme throughout his career. To illustrate just how important the city was to him, when he moved to Paris with his family in 2008, he felt unable to photograph there. The French capital was unchanged and unchanging since Haussmannian times, a kind of urban organism preserved in amber. Unlike Hong Kong, few signs of the city's inner life are visible on its surface. In fact, he was so resistant to photographing the city that he decided to explore Paris through Google's Street View tool, holing himself up with his computer in his Paris apartment to attempt to find a new perspective on the city that could go beyond its historical architecture – an approach that led to multiple bodies of Street View work taken from around the world and an honourable mention at the World Press Photo awards in 2011. Hong Kong's constantly changing urban landscape – not so much in terms of new real-estate developments but rather on the level of the street, which seemed to be in a constant state of transformation – had become essential to his photographic practice.

Beginning in 2001, Michael started devoting himself to personal projects in Hong Kong and China, several of which he had first discovered while pursuing stories for media outlets. After completing several bodies of work in the region, it was with the series *Architecture of Density* that he first made his name as a fine-art photographer. This was the entry point through which I discovered his work. After we met at his first solo show in Paris in 2009, he asked me to write about his latest series. I went on to contribute many essays to his books over the years, but above all, he became a dear friend, always ready to share his enthusiasm for his latest obsession or to drag me with him down a newly discovered rabbit hole.

Architecture of Density employs a formalist, deadpan approach that recalls the work that emerged from the Düsseldorf school of Bernd and Hilla Becher. The series explores Hong Kong's compressed, often brutal architecture, focusing on the sky-scraping residential tower blocks which exemplify the density of Hong Kong life. In the process of shooting these locations, Michael realized that occluding the sky and horizon allowed him to transform these concrete façades into seemingly infinite abstractions. He then further compounded this effect through the large-format prints he made of these images, creating an overwhelming urban landscape that seemed to be drawn from a work of dystopian science fiction rather than from a real city. Although Hong Kong is all but deserted in these images, minute signs of life are visible on their surface, from the tiny pops of colour from the laundry hung out to dry to the odd potted plant resting on a windowsill.

As he photographed these traces of the hundreds – even thousands – of lives contained within each one of his *Architecture of Density* images, Michael found himself wanting to move in closer. Having shot one hundred apartments located in one of Hong Kong's oldest housing complexes over four days for the series *100x100*, he had also begun to regularly explore the network of alleyways that surround many of these tower blocks.

The city's back alleys quickly became Michael's favoured hunting ground. The approach he took to photographing these spaces could be described as street photography – hitting the pavement day in, day out, camera in hand, reacting to the surrounding environment – but unlike most work in this genre, there are remarkably few people present in his images of these spaces. Instead, he focuses on the traces that they

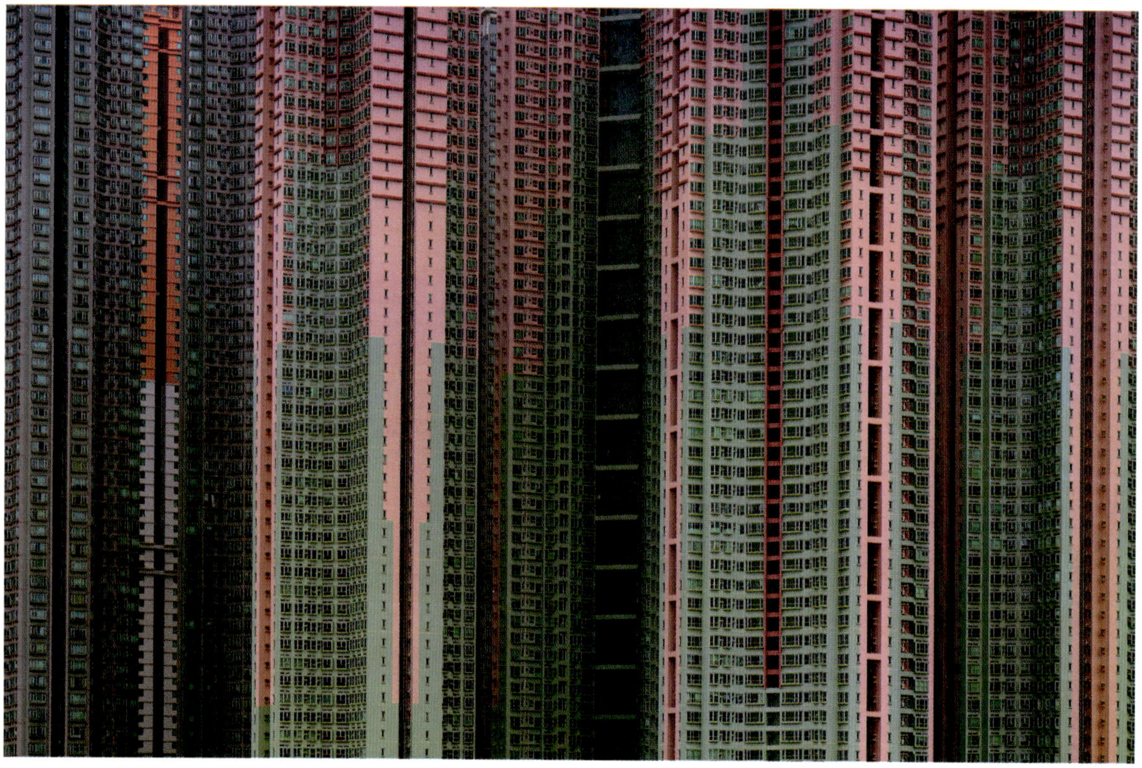

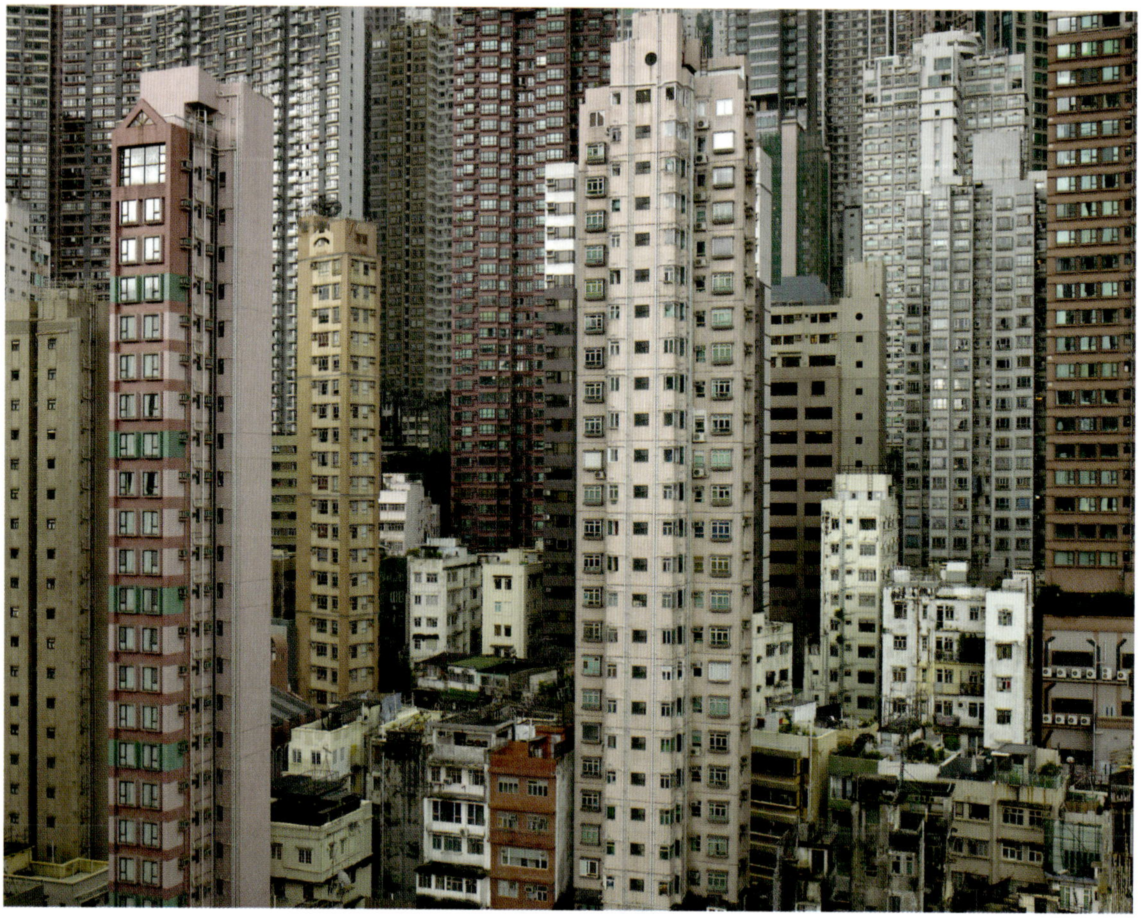

Architecture of Density #39 & #116

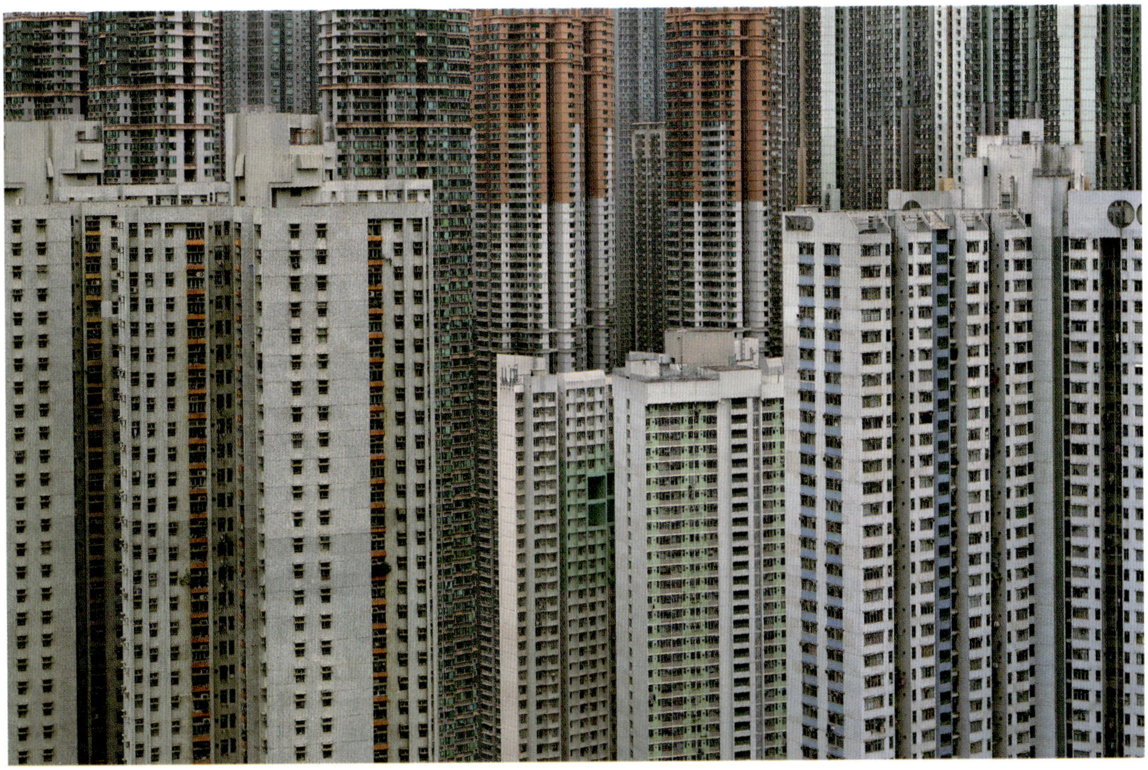

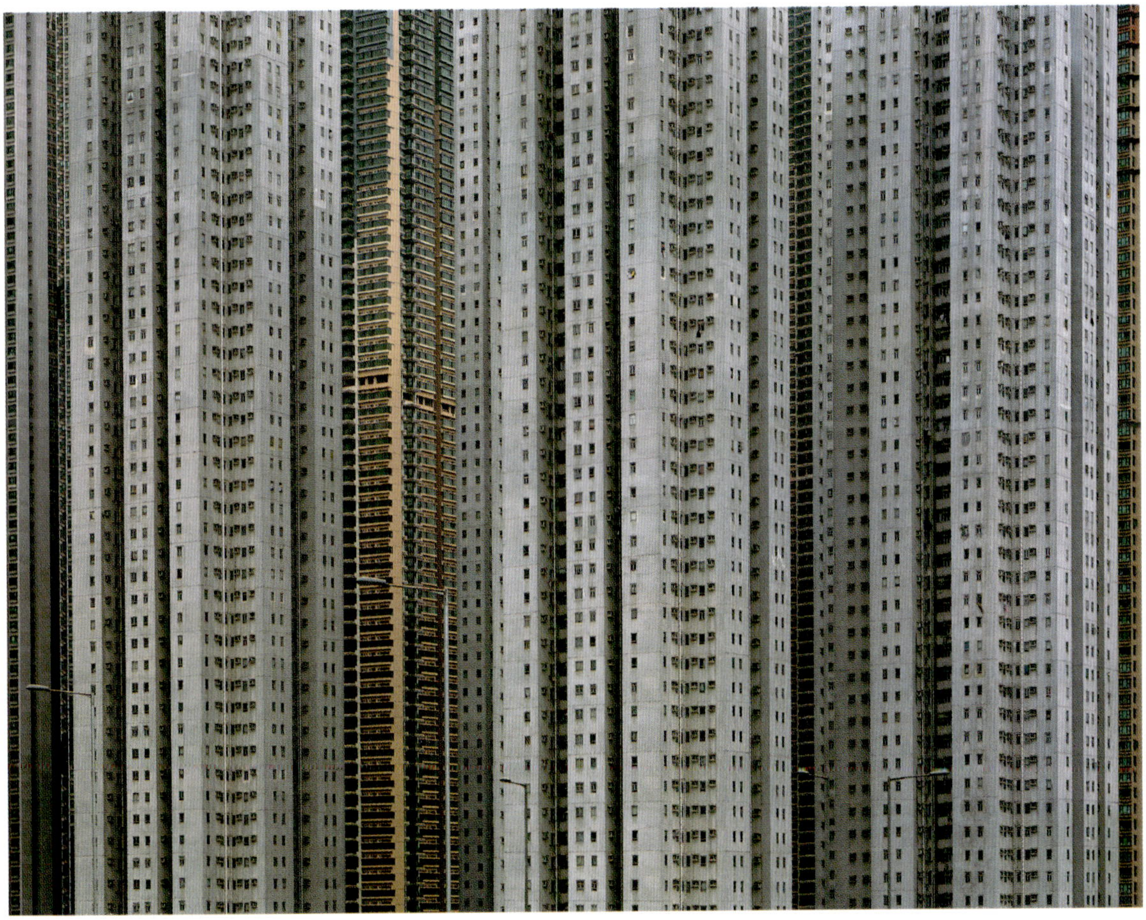

Architecture of Density #45 & #42

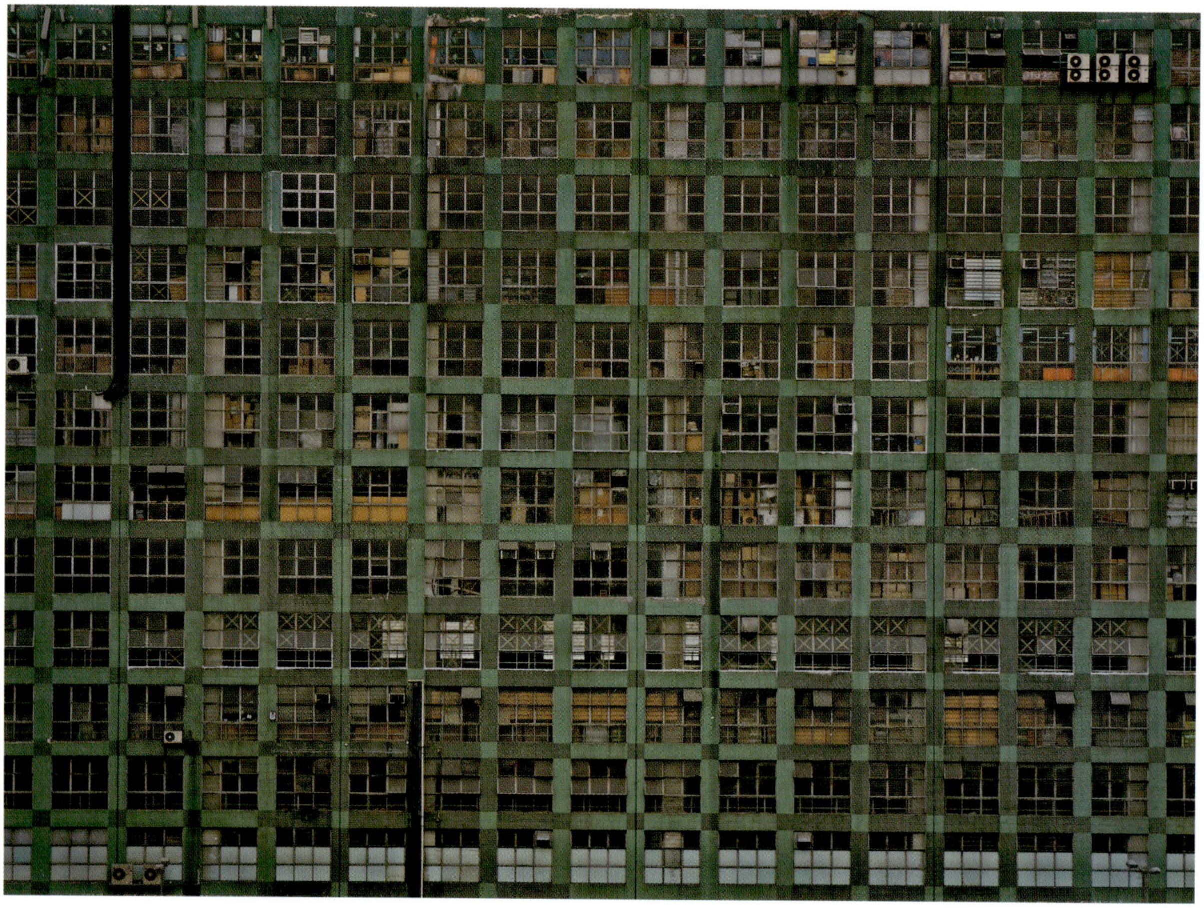

Industrial #04

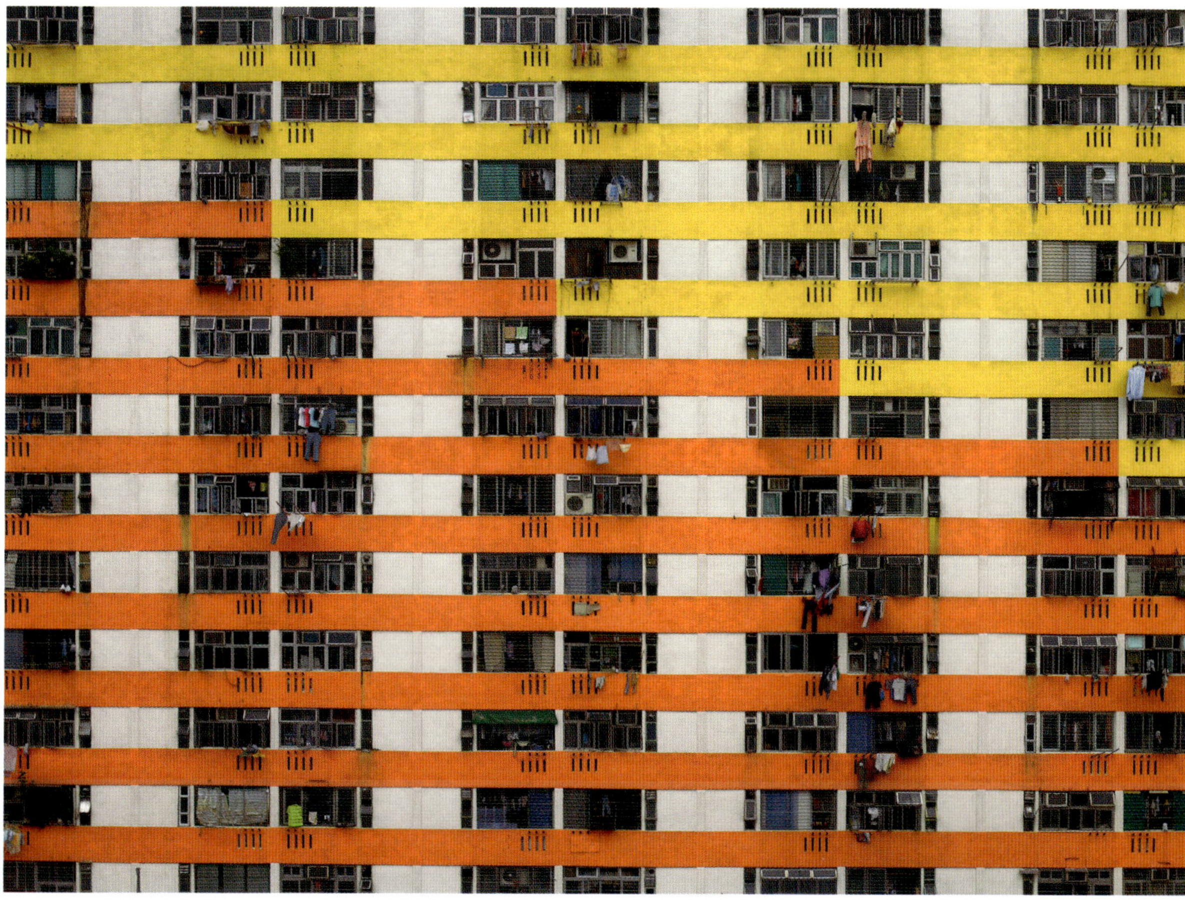

leave behind: workers' gloves drying on a spiral of barbed wire, mops crisscrossed across a doorway, 'bastard chairs' that have been patched up with whatever was on hand, chaotic labyrinths of plumbing and ventilation pipes, and accidental assemblages that combine all these different elements.

Michael amassed an extraordinary collection of material in the back alleys. This body of work is entitled *Informal Solutions*, a reference to the resourcefulness and ingenuity of city dwellers in even the most restricted of public spaces. He was fascinated by the thriftiness on display: the way no materials were thrown away, no matter how basic or worn out, but continuously repurposed. He also celebrated the 'accidental beauty' that he saw there, in spaces that were generally treated as the city's dirty secret. Through a typological approach that studies every aspect of the back alleys in great detail, *Informal Solutions* reveals the surprising diversity of this urban ecosystem. The series had become encyclopaedic, seemingly documenting every possible configuration of these spaces and their uses.

Over time this work acquired a more urgent quality. He became motivated by the need to document a vernacular culture that was on the verge of extinction. The back alleys were increasingly coming under threat as they did not project a desirable image, one in keeping with the country's contemporary ambitions, and the neighbourhoods where they were clustered were increasingly undergoing wholesale redevelopment.

In the early 2010s, having spent a decade developing his artistic practice, Michael moved into a new studio space in Chai Wan, which allowed him to consider new directions for his work. Amongst these ideas, he had begun to feel the urge to invite other artists to Hong Kong, and this new setup gave him the ability to share a studio space and to provide visiting artists with a place to stay. Motivated to share his fascination for this unique city that had already undergone profound changes in the fifteen or so years since it had reverted to China, he was also keen to come into contact with other perspectives and approaches and had invited several artists to come and spend time in his studio in Hong Kong.

While photography is a notoriously solitary pursuit, collaboration was always of great importance to Michael's practice. He had established a very close friendship and working relationship with Hannes Wanderer, the Berlin-based publisher of Peperoni Books. A free-spirited renegade of photobook publishing, Hannes was responsible for producing Michael's series of small books exploring the many different aspects of Hong Kong's back alleys. Together they published nine of these titles – and many other books besides – each focusing on one specific element, from coat hangers to umbrellas or the 'informal seating arrangements' which were the subject of Michael's first book, *Sitting in China*, published in 2022 by Gerhard Steidl. Beyond their publication partnership, Michael and Hannes spent hours on the phone together, as likely to discuss Bob Dylan – both men were experts on the subject – as they were the intricacies of the photobook production process.

Michael was a cultural omnivore, and his interests frequently lay outside the photography world, from music to sculpture, drawing, or painting. He met Arpaïs Du Bois through Roger Szmulewicz, the director of Gallery FIFTY ONE in Antwerp who represents his work. Having seen a solo show of her work during a visit to the gallery in Antwerp, Michael had become extremely taken with her highly sensitive approach. While their oeuvres seem to be cut from entirely different cloths, a mutual admiration for each other's practice and the stories they shared about their family histories brought the two artists together.

Originally from Ghent, Arpaïs Du Bois employs drawing and painting as well as textual elements to create works on paper that are at once playful and poetic, conveying a highly personal and intimate experience of the world. Although her work is often abstract, it is driven by a keen sense of observation and remains deeply connected to the world around her. As a socially engaged artist, her sensitivity also frequently conceals a cutting, critical edge beneath the surface. She questions the structures surrounding us, inviting us to take a step back from the frenetic pace of life to find some sense in an increasingly chaotic reality.

While the two artists have drastically different approaches, they mirror each other in the quotidian diaristic nature of their practice. Michael is involved in a form of visual note-taking, quickly documenting the constant transformations taking place on the city streets surrounding him. Arpaïs's practice, on the other hand, has no documentary ambitions. It is rather inward, a meditative practice through which she is able to process her experience of the world around her.

On Michael's invitation, in early 2014 Arpaïs travelled to Hong Kong to undertake a six-week residency. This was not only her first visit to the city but to Asia too, an intense experience that was entirely new to her. Michael acted as a guide to the Belgian artist during the first days of this residency, explaining the dynamics of the city and introducing her to his favoured photographic playgrounds. During these walks, they spoke at length about the specifics of Hong Kong and China, but also about memory, transmission and the injustice that is evident in these spaces that generally go ignored. Beyond the resilience and ingenuity of the people who use the back alleys, Arpaïs was particularly struck by the forces that would lead someone to repair a plastic bucket for the thousandth time. While they explored the network of back alleys together, the two artists did not identify a specific project or subject beforehand but rather followed their individual approaches in response to these environments. The city spoke to them both in subtly different ways, much like the childhood game of Chinese whispers, in which a message is murmured from one player to another, its meaning altering over time.

While Michael had come to know the city of Hong Kong like the back of his hand, he retained the curious and inquisitive perspective of an outsider. In fact, I always felt that this outsider perspective – a trait we shared and which likely brought us together in the first place – is what characterised his work. Born to German parents in 1954 in Munich, he spent his formative years in Canada and the United States

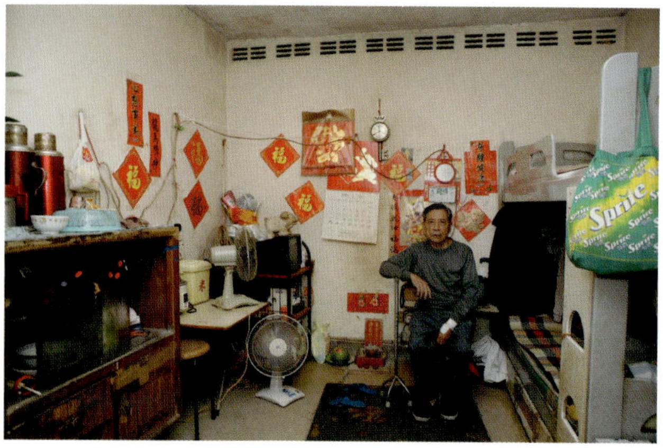

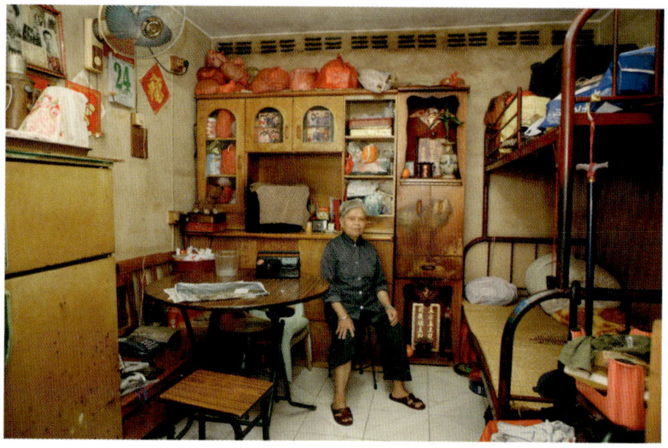

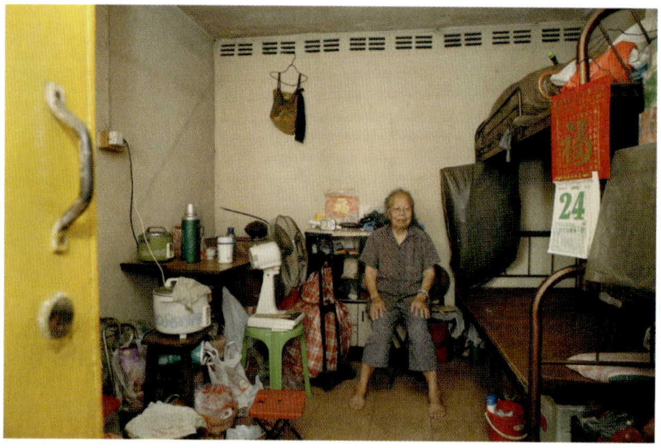

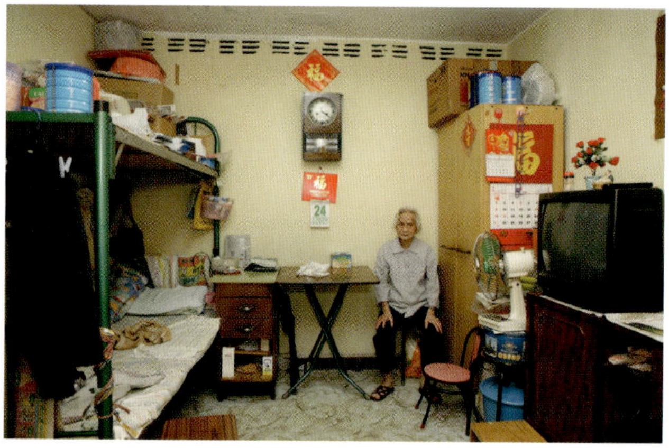
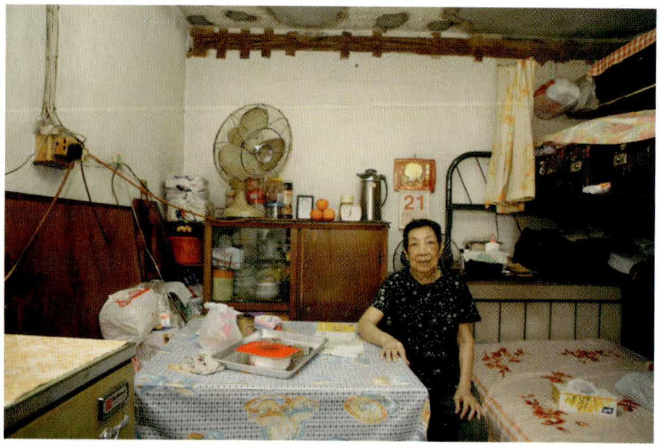

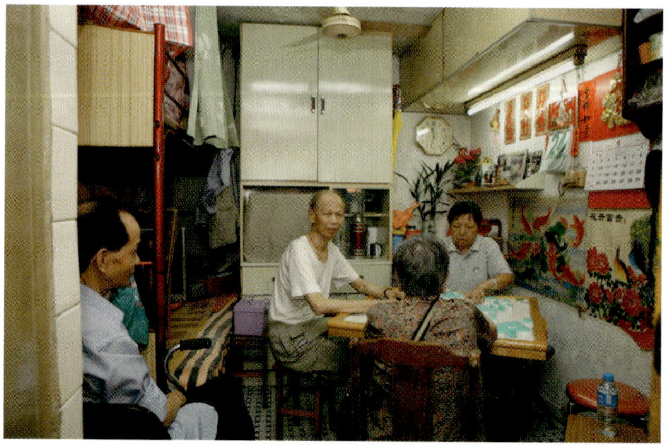
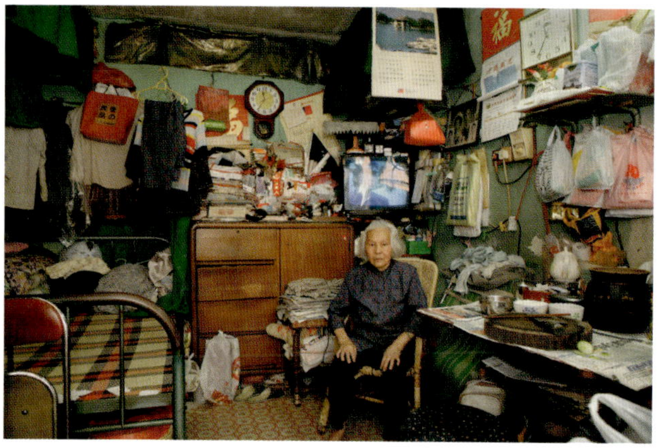
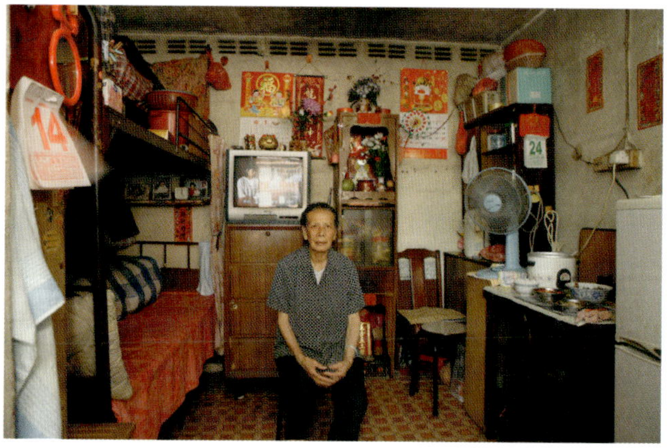

100x100 #90, #7, #16, #12, #13, #15, #17, #02

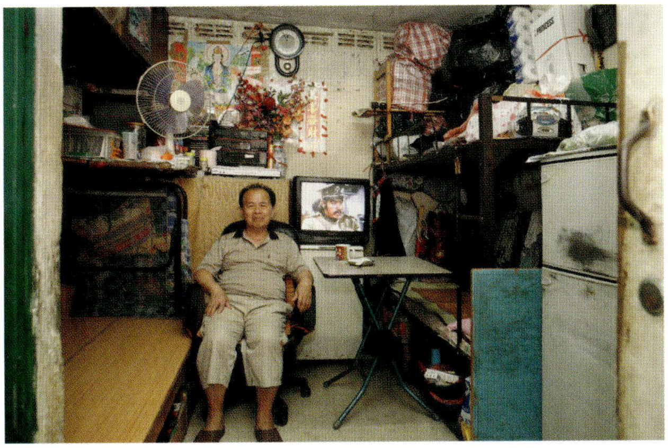
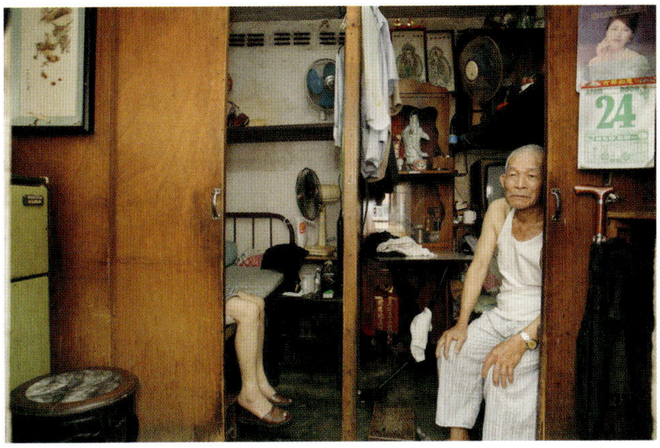
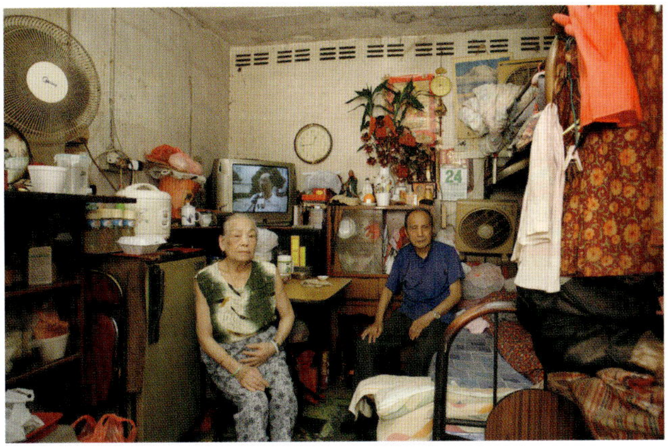
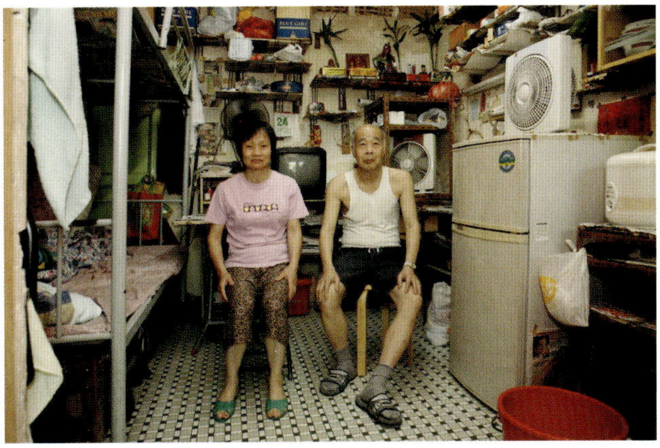
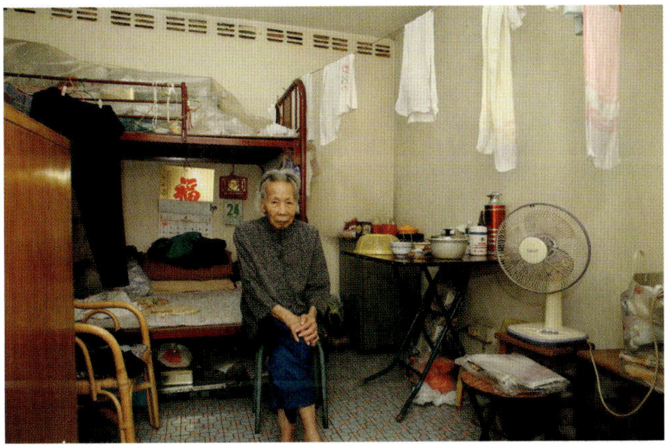
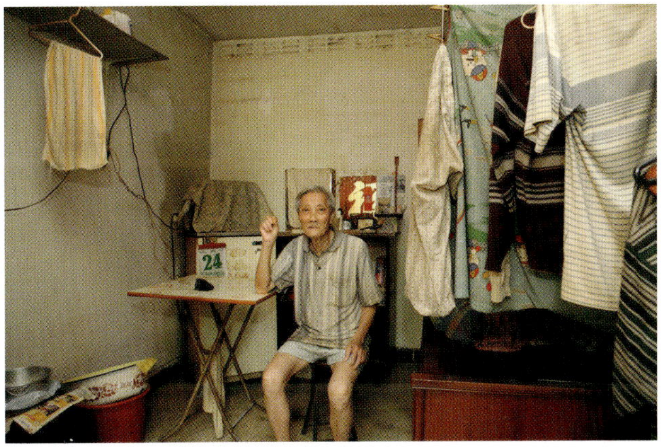
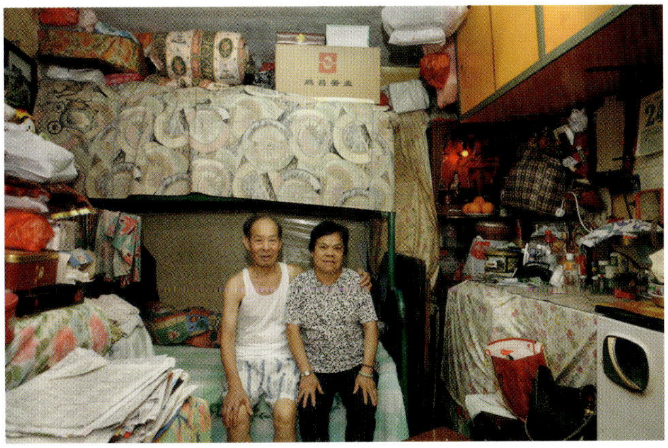
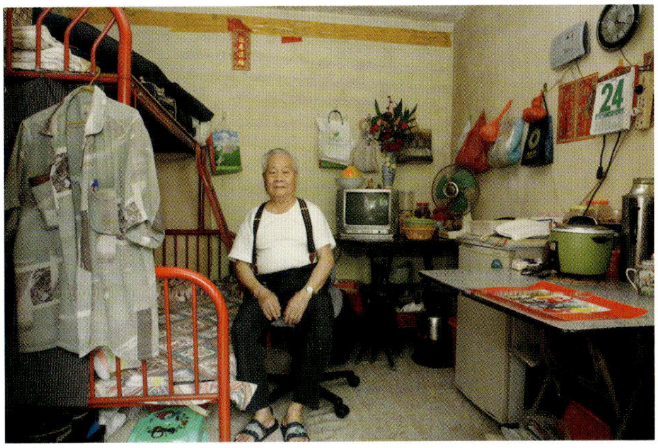

100x100 #22, #25, #29, #31, #35, #39, #50, #53

before returning to Germany in 1972 to study photography with Otto Steinert at the renowned Folkwang School in Essen. Having relocated to Hong Kong in 1994, he then spent the majority of his career – both as an editorial photographer and as an artist – in Asia. That multi-faceted background enabled Michael to develop an extreme sensibility to the world that surrounded him and a fascination for the most seemingly banal or quotidian details.

For *Hong Kong Whispers*, Michael followed the same methodology as for all his *Informal Solutions* work, surveying the alleyways day by day on the lookout for the elements that might catch his eye. His approach is like a form of visual collection, less concerned with the process of photographic composition than with adding new elements to the vast vernacular lexicon he constituted in these spaces. Like many photographers, Michael was an avid, even compulsive collector. Anyone who received an invitation to his home was likely to discover a different esoteric collection every time, from rodent skulls to Chinese propaganda posters, from 'Made in China' plastic toys to his infamous 'bastard chair'. Over time, his collections had even begun to surface in his exhibitions, where he displayed chairs or assemblages of objects taken from the back alleys alongside his photographs.

In the photographs Michael contributed to this project, mops are propped up against a wall, gloves are wedged into fences or pinned to a cascade of interlocking coat hangers to allow them to dry, and thick networks of pipes and ventilation shafts seem to have taken on lives of their own, behaving like creepers inching across the surface of a wall. Elsewhere, pieces of plastic string and plastic bags are bunched together and jammed behind pipes, on hand for whatever packaging or patching-together purpose they may be required for. Organic matter appears too, from a small plant that has somehow found the sustenance and light it requires to emerge from the concrete to a tray full of entrails and a wall of goldfish floating in their numbered plastic bags.

Michael worked swiftly in these alleyways with which he had become so familiar. His images are straightforward and unfussy, less concerned with the individual composition than with gathering more material for his vast visual archive.

Arpaïs's process is quite unlike that of a photographer. The work that she made in Hong Kong was not conceived in response to specific objects or environments in the alleyways themselves – or indeed to Michael's photographs of them. Instead, she produced work after the fact, allowing for the different experiences and sensations of each day to settle and coalesce into a visual idea. Whereas Michael documents specific environments, Arpaïs's approach is more about translating the experience of these spaces and the emotional and sensory impressions that they leave with her. Ten years later, she still recalls the overwhelm she felt at the intensity of this new environment.

Speaking with Arpaïs about this impression, I was reminded of my first visit to Hong Kong as a child no more than a few years old. While such early memories are often unreliable, derived from stories overheard or photographs that become confused with our own visual recollections, I can still recall the sensory overload that the city set off in me. Not only the experience of landing at the city's former international airport, Kai Tak, flying so close to the residential tower blocks which Michael would later photograph that I had the impression I could see people eating breakfast at their kitchen tables, but the sensations I experienced as soon as I left the airport. The weight of the humidity, the proliferating signage and colours, the city's looming verticality, the smells from the Dai Pai Dong street stalls and the food markets...

Despite their apparent abstraction, that overload is present in Arpaïs's drawings. In the evenings, she would allow the impressions that formed throughout the day to resurface. She refers to this diaristic practice as one of distillation, allowing little moments or small fragments of reality to resurface and find a form on the page of her notebooks. Sometimes these forms seem to echo those found in Michael's images, isolating the lines of a fence or piece of string. In other works, they are more abstract, sometimes even formless washes of colour that convey an emotional state. Arpaïs's characteristically sombre, earthy palette remains the same throughout, as if filtering the bright colours of the city streets into more fundamental, even subterranean tones.

In addition to these forms and colours, words are a further essential ingredient in Arpaïs's work. Her use of language mirrors the abstract poetics of her forms, fragments of phrases that allow us to project our own readings onto them. Sometimes her handwritten scrawls directly reference the environment ('corner shrines', 'the joyous permanent construction') while others speak more to the artist's personal experience and state of mind ('walking on the edge of everything', 'when the head ferments').

One might expect the work of a former photojournalist to be more overtly critical or denunciatory, but Michael's images always remain neutral and distanced from their subject. In fact, it is through Arpaïs's drawings that the project acquires a more political bent. She writes of 'cages of posthumous smells', 'the song of a caged bird', and 'the rust of the system'. These fragments invite us to consider the lives of those who occupy these spaces and who leave these myriad traces on their surface. We find ourselves considering their struggle to 'find a way to inhabit the world' and the extreme environments in which they eke out their existences.

Having worked mostly independently throughout Arpaïs's residency, the two artists then came together to find a way of combining the work they had produced into book form. They settled on an approach in which their images would be juxtaposed on each spread on a 1-to-1 scale defined by the size of her notebook drawings.

This was not the first time Arpaïs had produced a collaborative book project with a photographer. In 2011, she had worked with the Japanese photographer Masao Yamamoto, whose images had haunted her for many years. Together, they created *Where We Met*, which combines Yamamoto's poetic, dreamlike photographs with Arpaïs's

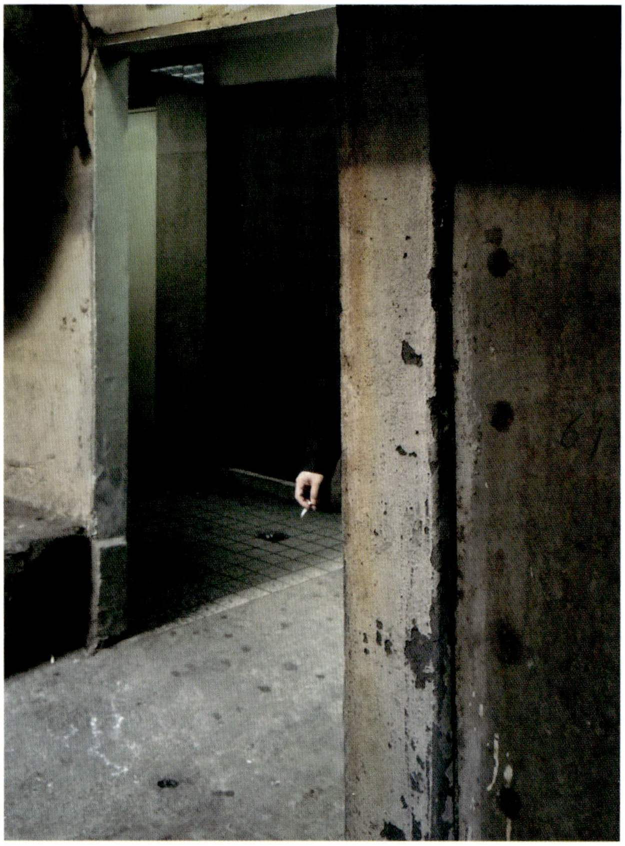

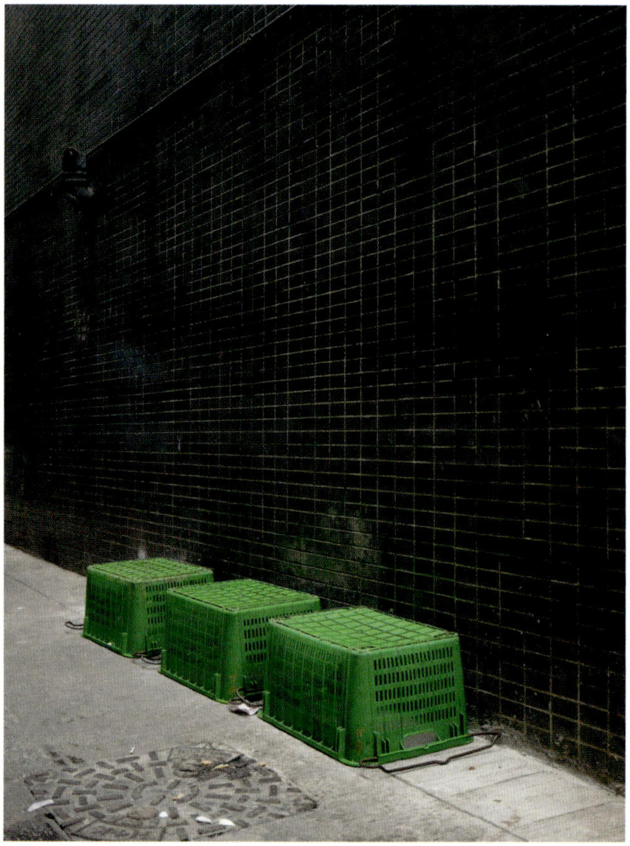

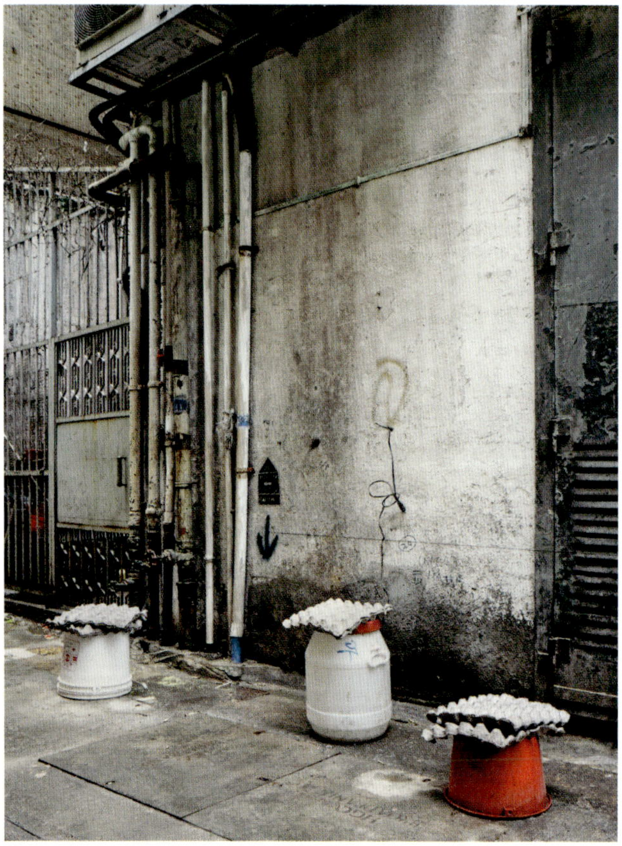

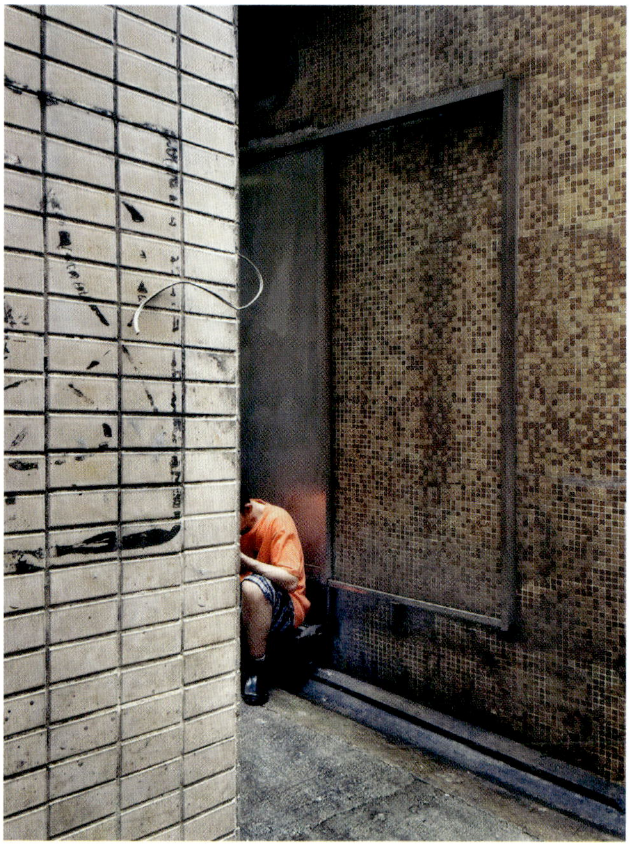

Informal Solutions #28, #19, #73, #147

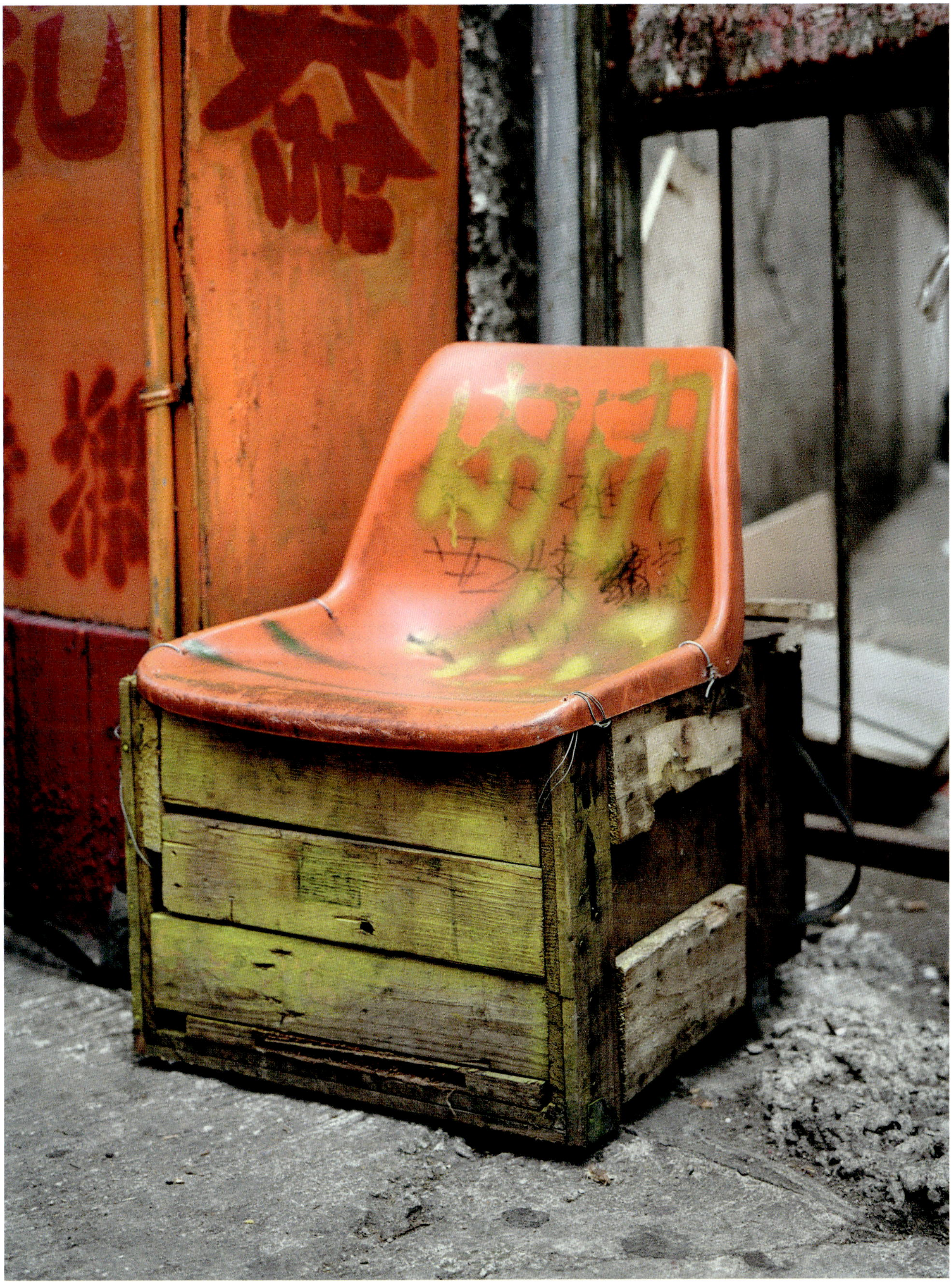

drawings. The book plays with scale and different placements on the page to create a poetic dialogue between the artists' work, resembling the constellation-like installations they both employ in their exhibitions. In a happy twist of fate, the publisher of that project, Gautier Platteau, is now behind the release of this volume.

The nature of this collaboration with Michael was altogether different. While *Where We Met* brought together existing bodies of work and was made without the artists being able to come together in the same location, *Hong Kong Whispers* is the result of a closer collaboration over several weeks in which the artists, fed by their experiences and discussions, produced work side by side in Hong Kong, and also elaborated the sequence and edit of the work together directly afterwards.

Having photocopied the contents of all six of Arpaïs's notebooks, they laid out the images on the floor of the studio alongside prints of Michael's photographs. They agreed on an approach in which their images would be juxtaposed on a 1-to-1 scale on each spread to avoid any sense of hierarchy. Little by little, they assembled pairs of images, frequently selecting photographs that somehow resonated or contrasted with Arpaïs's drawings. The resulting spreads play with different associations, sometimes through parallels based on form and colour, sometimes through oppositions and contrasts. Over two days, they worked together these spreads into a sequence which is reproduced here as the artists developed it together.

The book was intended to be released shortly afterwards, but as is so often the case with collaborative artistic projects of this nature, other personal projects got in the way. *Hong Kong Whispers* came to rest in a drawer, lying in wait for the right opportunity.

This book is now being released, some ten years after Michael Wolf and Arpaïs Du Bois first conceived it and five years after Michael's tragic passing at the age of sixty-four. In many ways, it is an outlier in both artists' practice, a sidestep from their respective artistic trajectories. However, in combining their different universes around the same subject, *Hong Kong Whispers* creates a fascinating dialogue between two contrasting but complementary approaches.

The publication of *Hong Kong Whispers* is all the more important as many of Michael's books have become impossible to find since his main publishing partner Hannes Wanderer passed away suddenly only a few months before Michael. A revised edition of his seminal series *Architecture of Density* was released in 2022 – an important initiative to ensure his work is still accessible – but it is particularly gratifying to see this unpublished project finally released. It reveals an unseen facet of Michael's thinking as an artist and his interest in many fields beyond that of photography. While the collaboration with Arpaïs remained a one-off, Michael had spoken with other artists, and I'm certain he would have found other opportunities to undertake similar projects had his life not been tragically cut short.

The ten years since this work was made have been particularly tumultuous for Hong Kong. The city was shaken by the Umbrella Revolution of late 2014, a mass movement demanding reforms of the electoral system, as well as the largest protests the city has ever seen in 2019–2020 against the excessive use of police force. This was followed by a series of draconian measures put in place during the pandemic in pursuit of a zero-COVID policy. Against this troubled backdrop, urban redevelopment has continued apace, and the back alleys that gave rise to this work have now almost entirely disappeared. Alleyway neighbourhoods are now an endangered urban species, as expansive redevelopment projects and widespread privatization initiatives are eroding the unique urban fabric in cities around the world. *Hong Kong Whispers* is both a document of the extraordinary wealth of the local vernacular of these spaces and a tribute to the creativity that can be found there through the eyes of two singular artists.

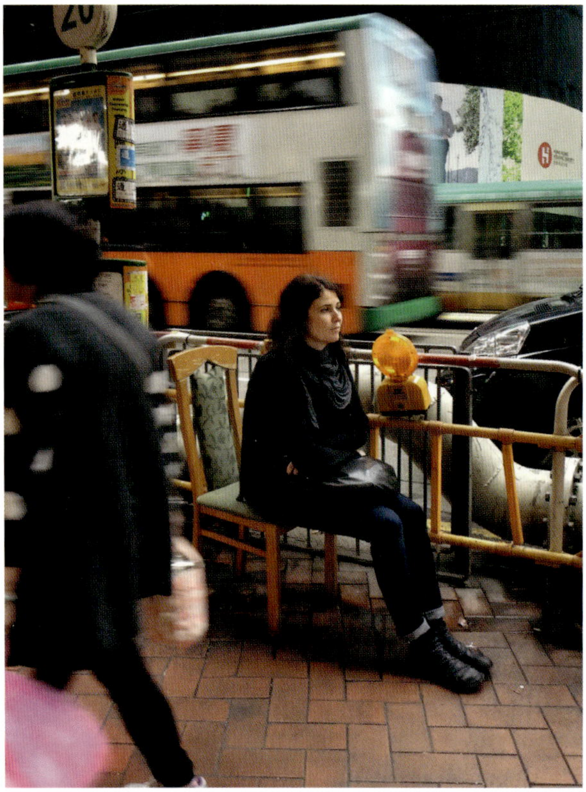

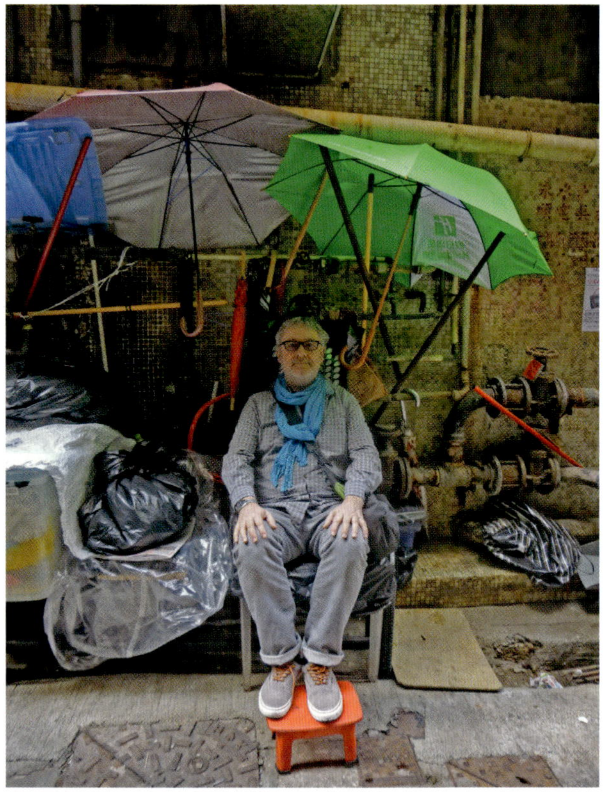

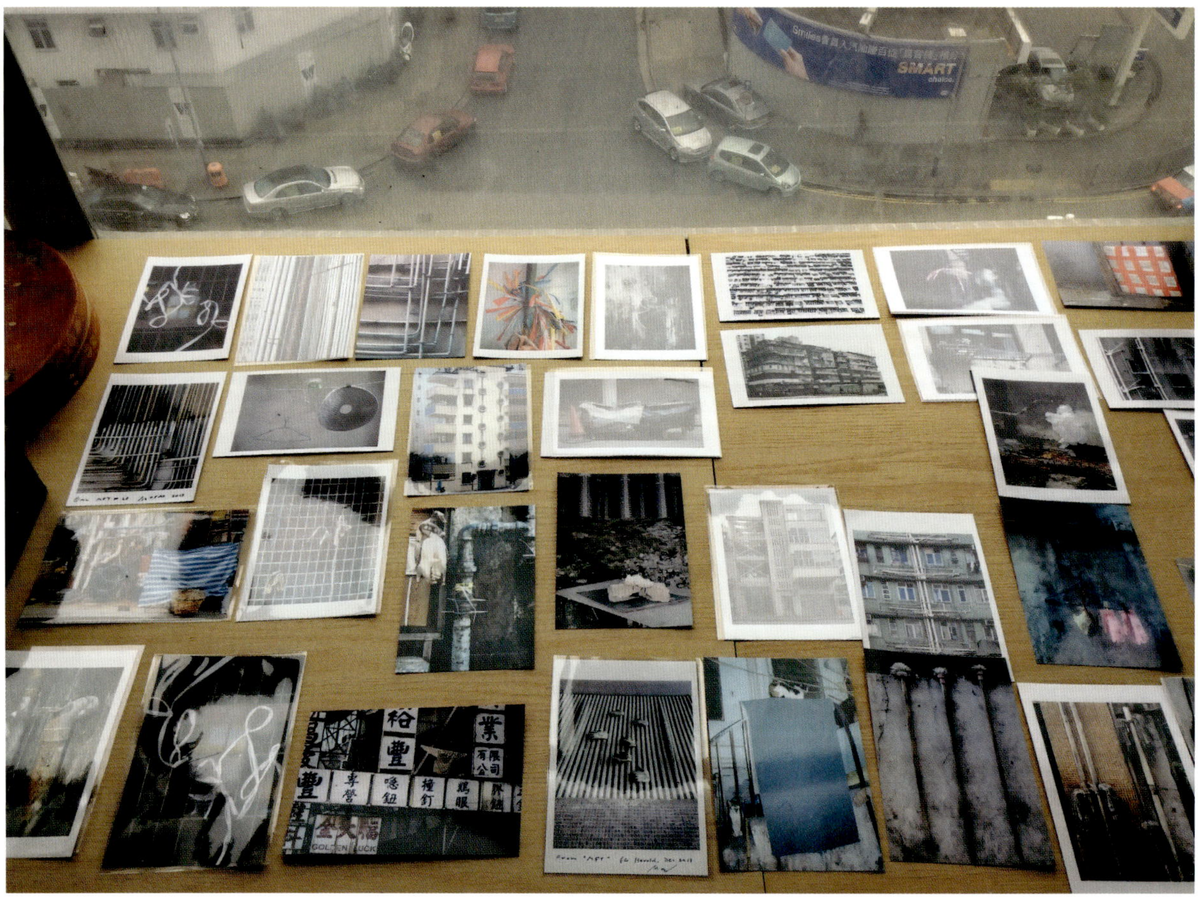
SMART

WONDERFUL PROJECT
ARPAÏS DU BOIS

It is 2012, and Michael and I are turning *Where We Met*[1] inside out. 'Wonderful project,' says Michael. 'We too could consider a collaboration.' We meet again in Paris in late 2013, not long after one of his visits to my Antwerp studio, when he'd casually let slip, while bidding me farewell, 'Hong Kong would be good for you.'

In Paris, I discuss how suffocated I've been feeling lately and how I've been trying to cope through my work in the studio. I urgently need some time out. I decide to take a break of half an academic year from Sint Lucas Antwerp, where I teach. Less casually now, as a fully fledged invitation, Michael says, 'Come over, February onwards is good for me.'

In mid February 2014, I land in Hong Kong. The suffocating feeling of the preceding months (and certainly my apprehension about the density, in every respect, of the city that awaits me) gives way to a state of total surrender, wonder, absorption, overstimulation, and alienation, and at the same time a strange recognition. Together, but more often alone, we dive into the indescribable biotope of the back alleys. When we are exploring together, I can hardly keep pace with Michael, who moves like a lithe cat, runs into buildings, up the stairs, three steps at a time, before fetching up on the roof and coming to a halt there, camera on the attack. A few moments later, knees trembling, I catch up and stand beside him.

On one of the countless floors, about halfway through a long, dark corridor, we pass by the neon glow of a brightly lit room. 'A massive amount of gambling goes on here,' he remarks over his shoulder. (It dawns on me later that evening that I would never, ever, ever have seen this without him.)

We eat, walk, are silent, eat again, talk, and tell stories about what binds us and how each of us relates to such things. We endeavour to find words for a specific light, a colour, a feeling... and we eat again, making detours to sundry stalls for the perfect tofu, that 'something whose precise composition I don't need to know'... And then for days I walk around alone for hours on end, so that once darkness falls and I am thoroughly permeated by the city, I can take note of everything, get the smell of the city again, the feel of it, and parse the white noise crowding my head.

And in the final days of my stay, as we sit on the studio floor assembling a maquette for the book we want to make – ultimately this book – we sip at the promise of this project like the most delicious tea. And then the years pass, as always happens. And – as should not have happened – Michael died in 2019. Sometime during 2023, Barbara [Barbara Wolf, Michael's widow] softly and beautifully breathes new life into the project. And I am so happy that we are thereby bringing Michael back into the now, into the here, into an embrace.

In 2024, ten years after my stay in Hong Kong and five years after Michael's passing, this book is a collection of emotions. I hope, I believe, that Michael would say: 'wonderful project'.

---

1 *Where We Met*, Yamamoto Masao, Arpaïs Du Bois, Lannoo, 2011

par l'abstraction de l'habitat (through the abstraction of the habitat), 2014, 25 × 19 cm, mixed media on paper

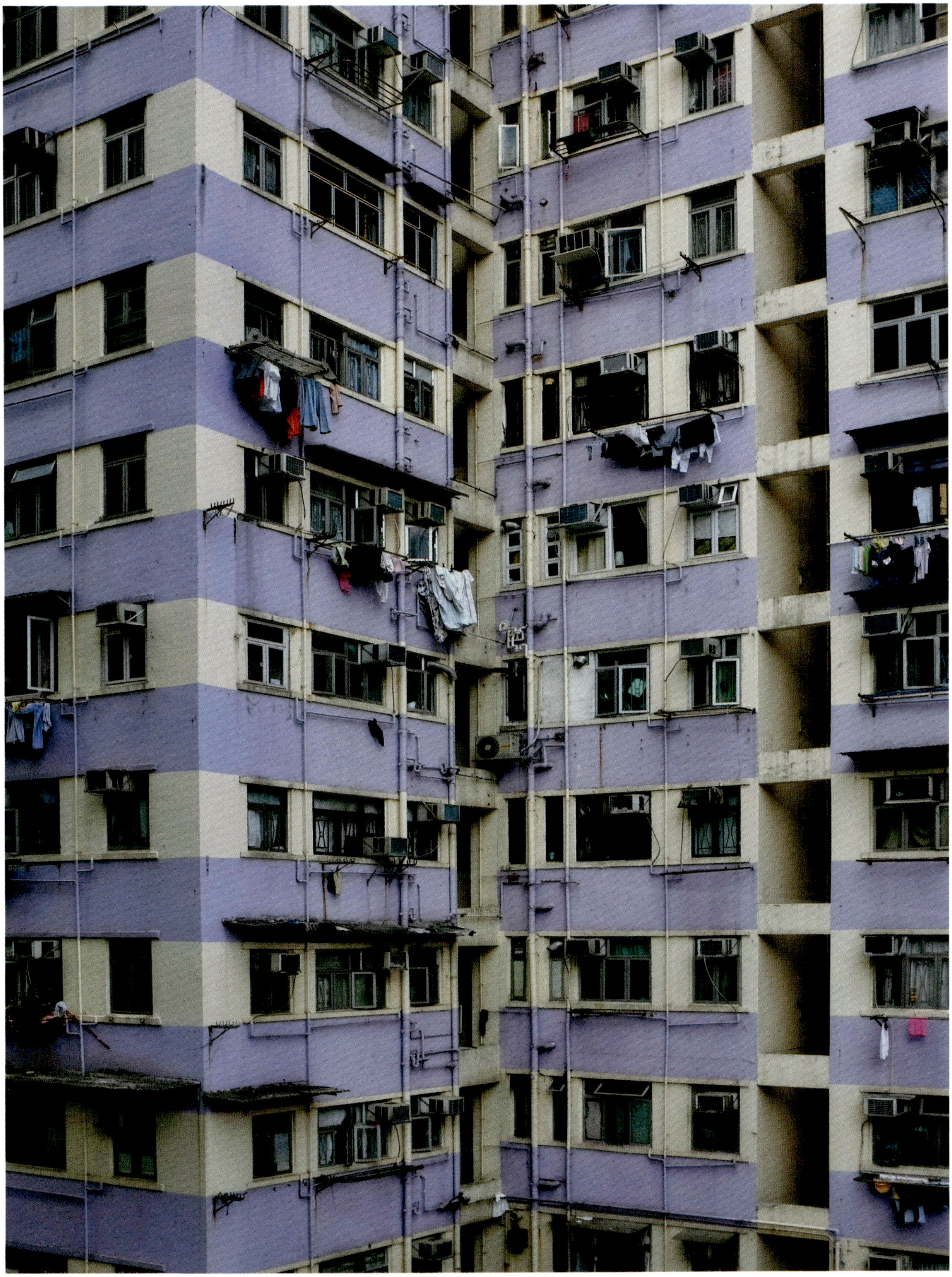

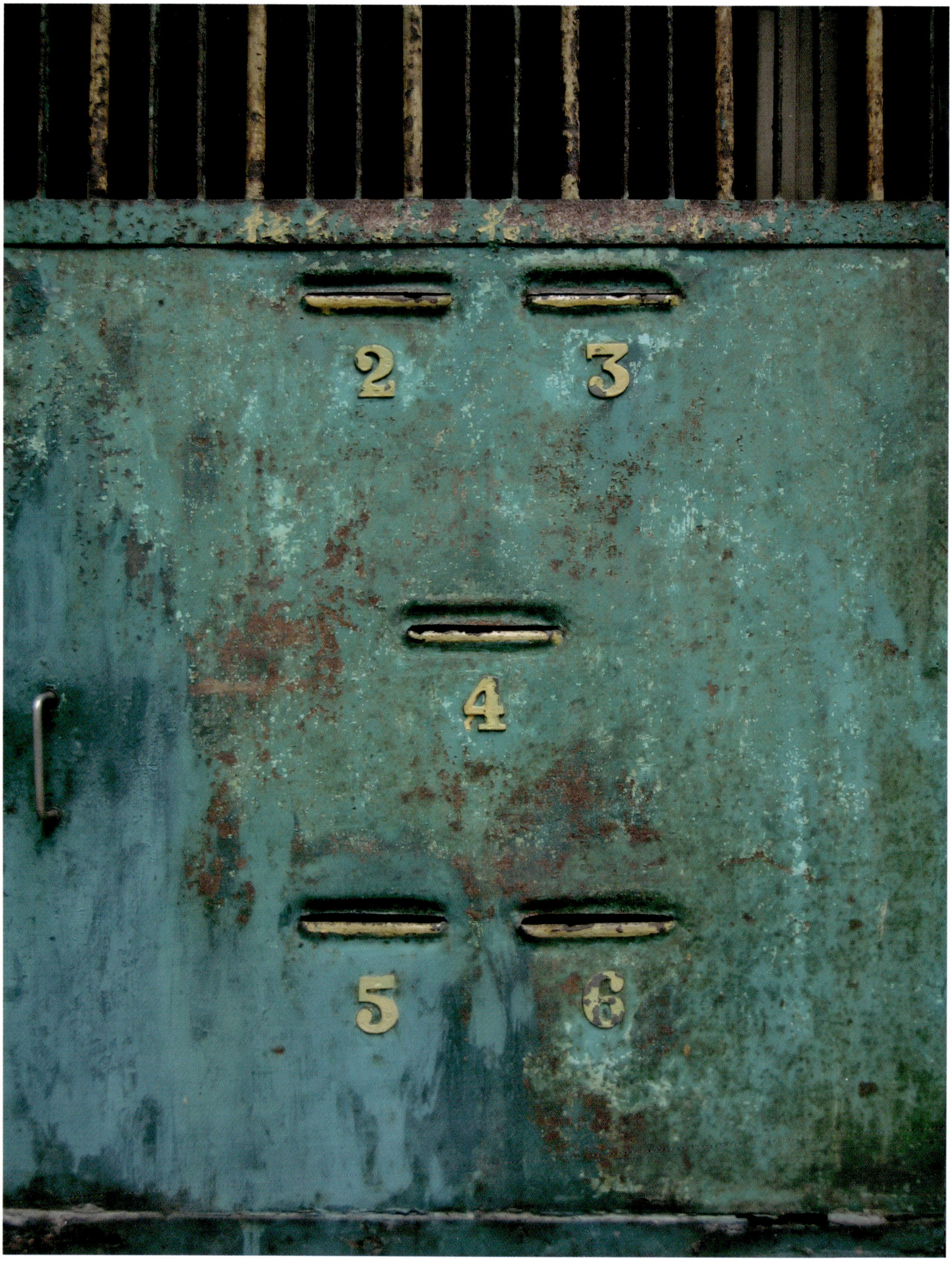
2
3
4
5
6

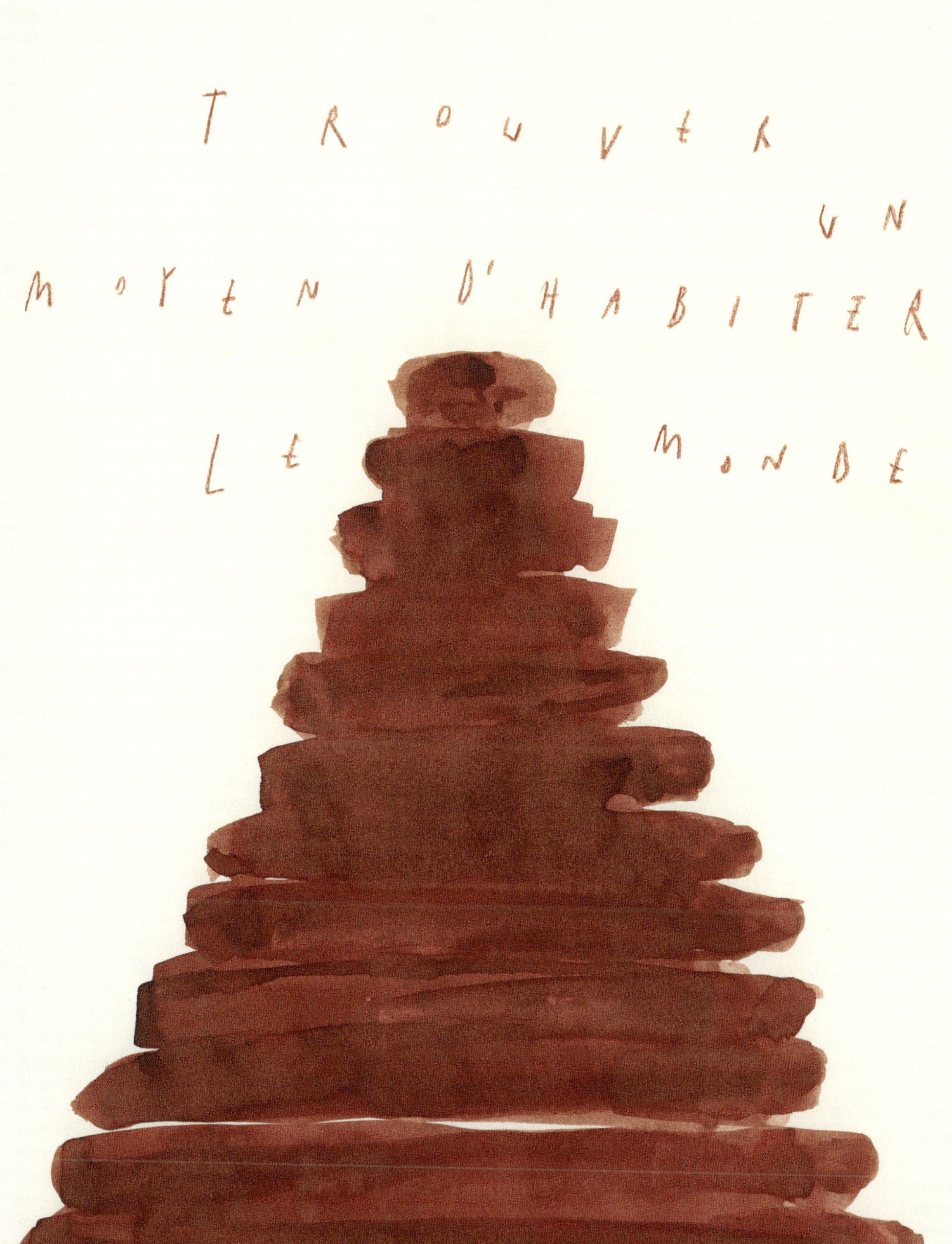

trouver un moyen d'habiter le monde (finding a way to inhabit the world), 2014, 25 × 19 cm, mixed media on paper

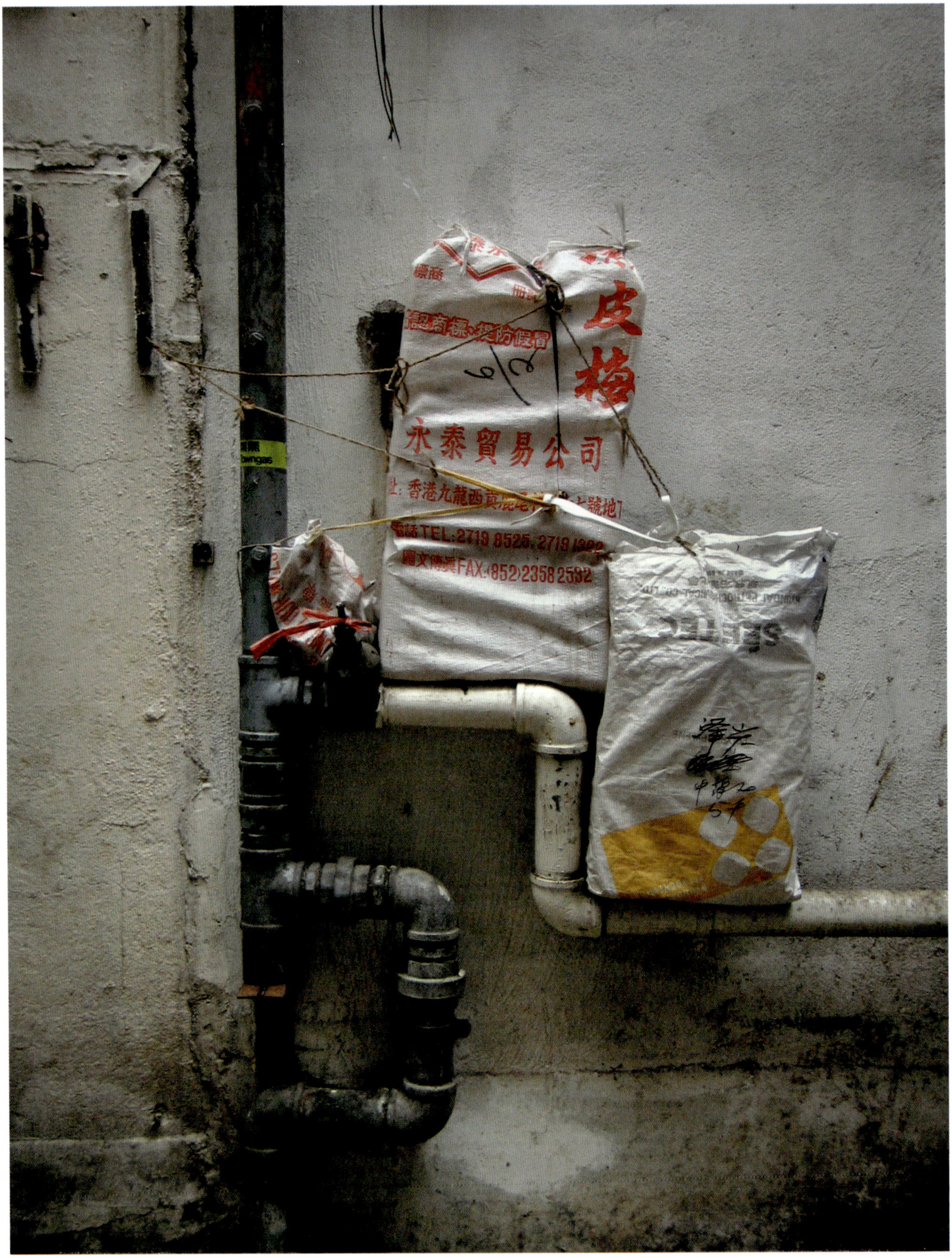
皮梅
永泰貿易公司
FAX.(852)2358 2592

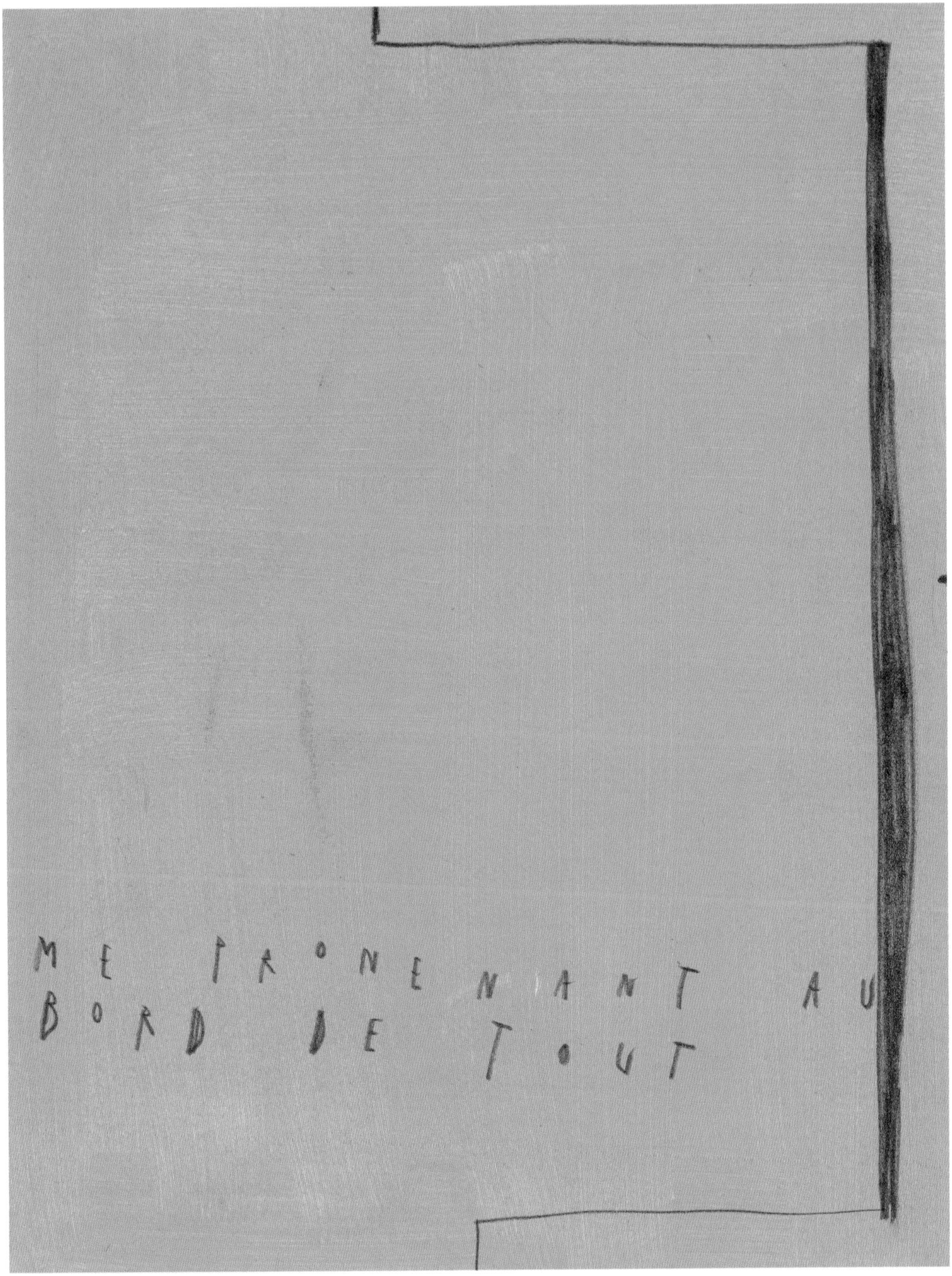

me promenant au bord de tout (strolling along the edge of everything), 2014, 25 × 19 cm, mixed media on paper

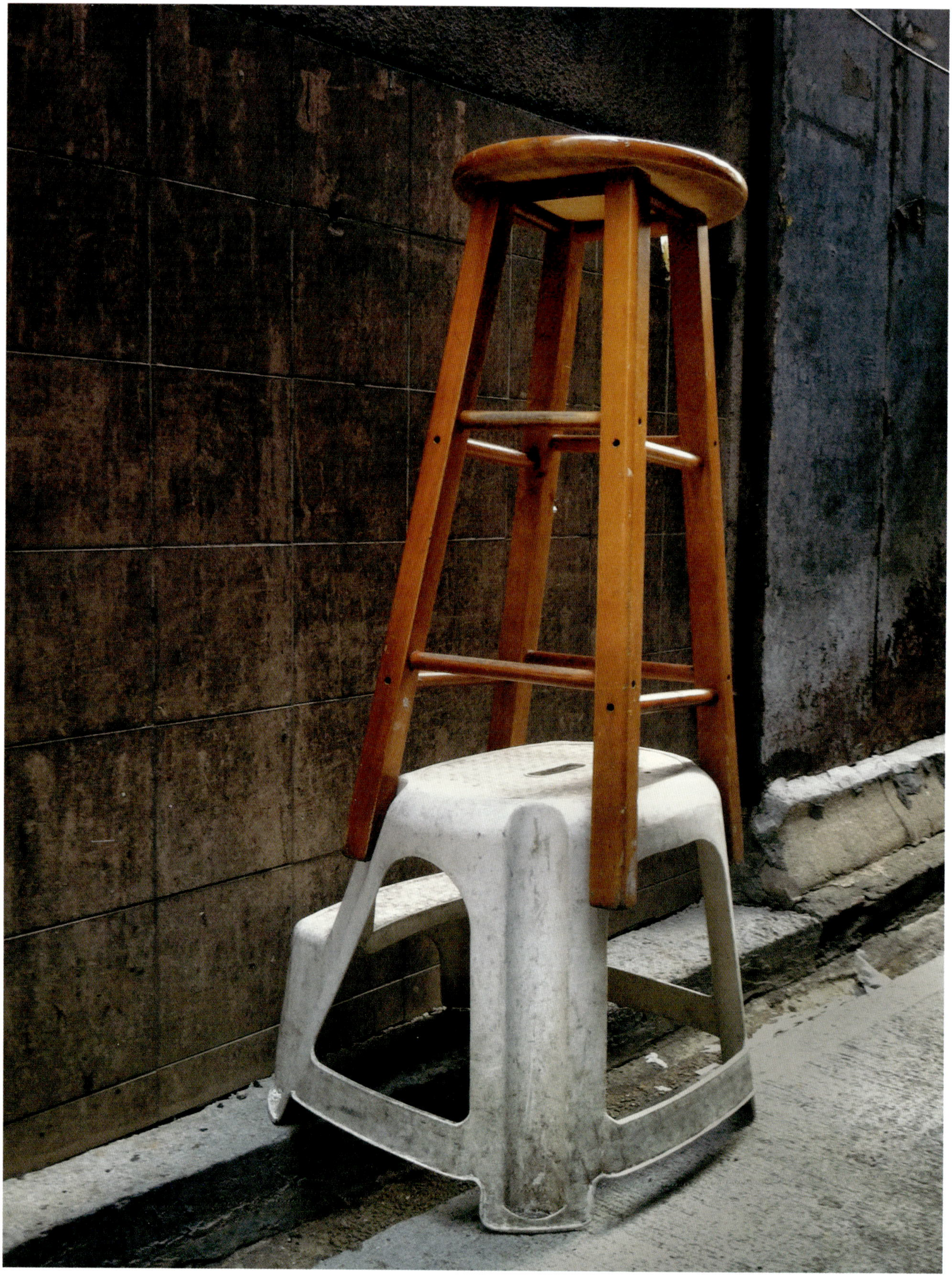

Informal Solutions #93

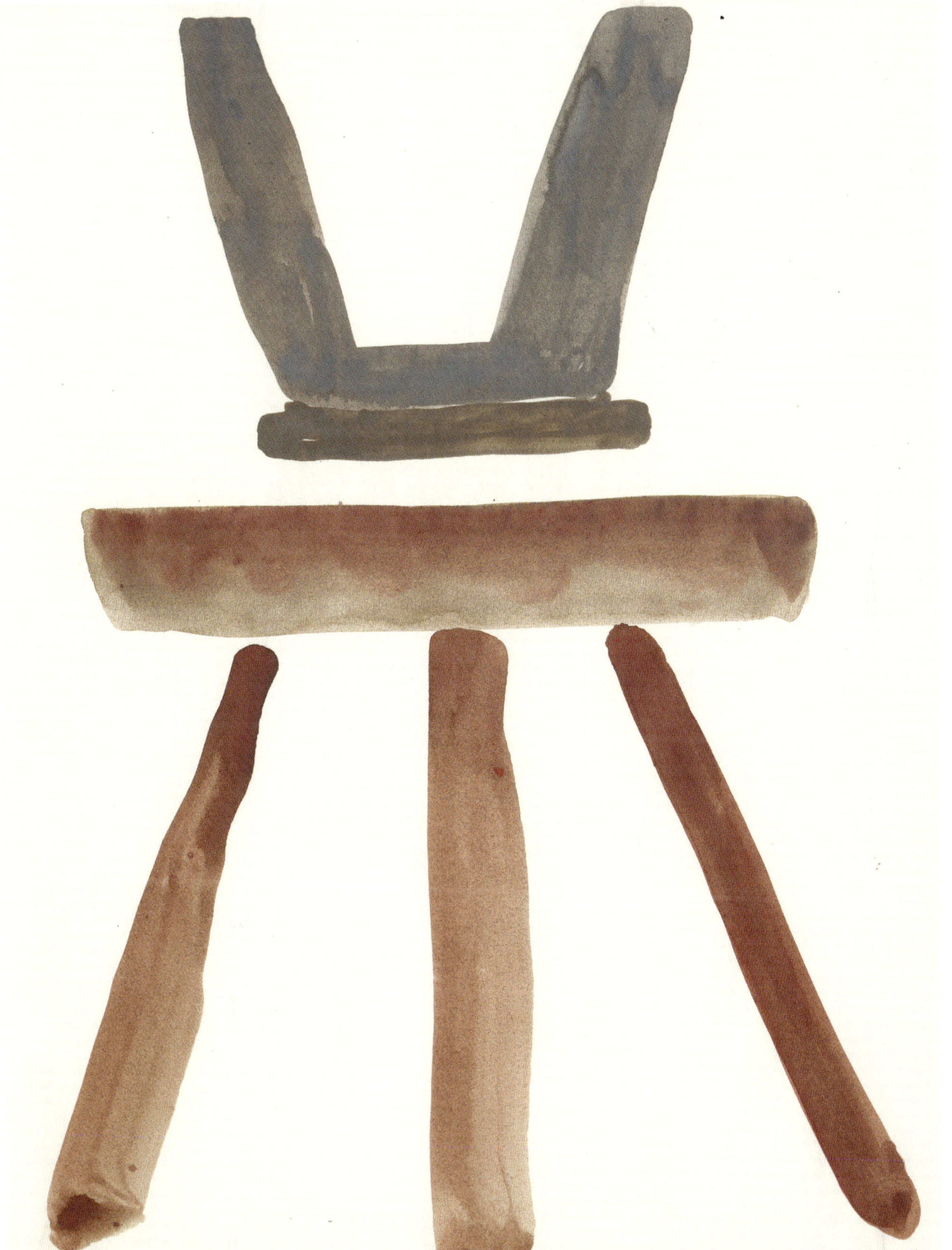

untitled, 2014, 25 × 19 cm, mixed media on paper

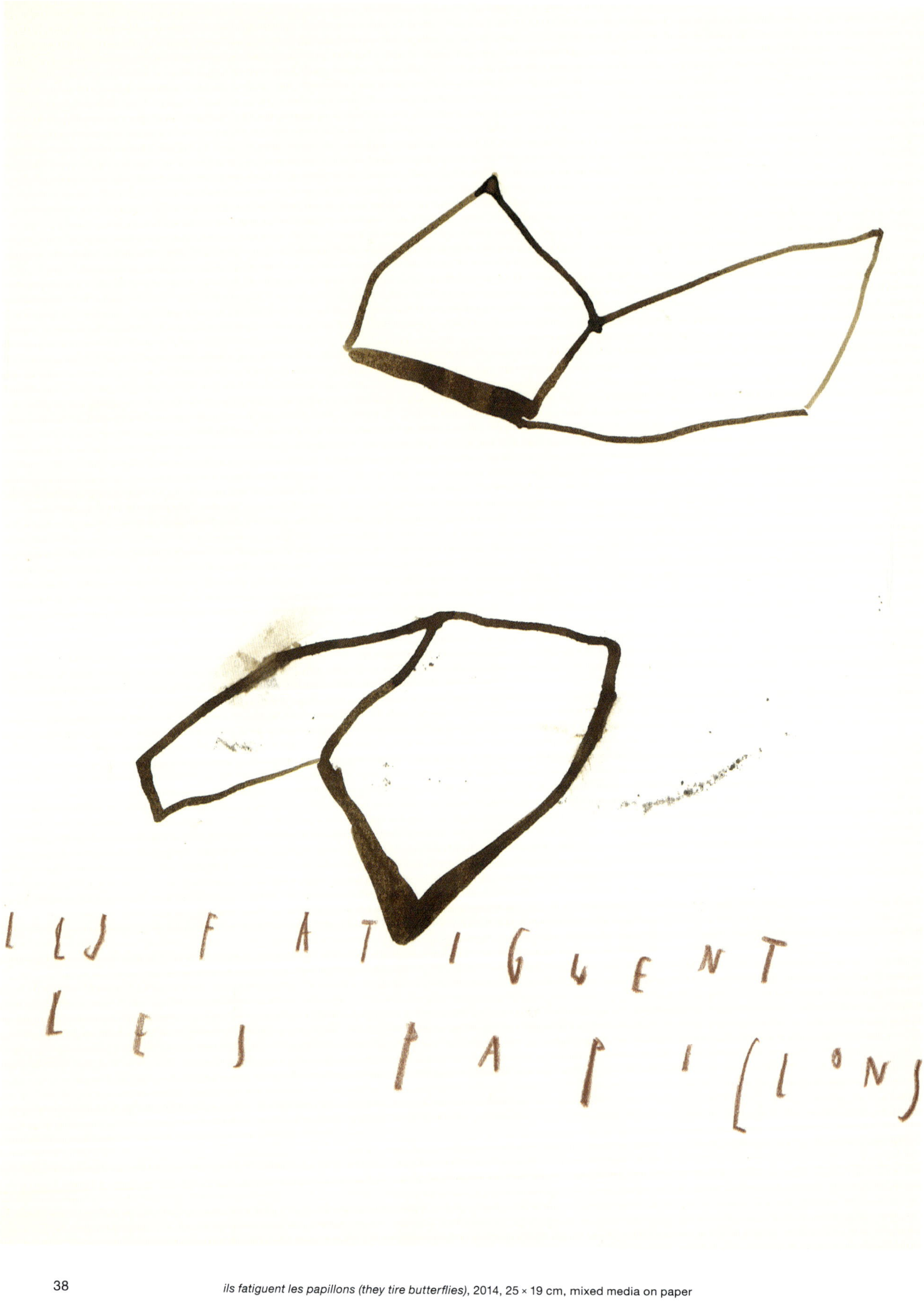

ils fatiguent les papillons (they tire butterflies), 2014, 25 × 19 cm, mixed media on paper

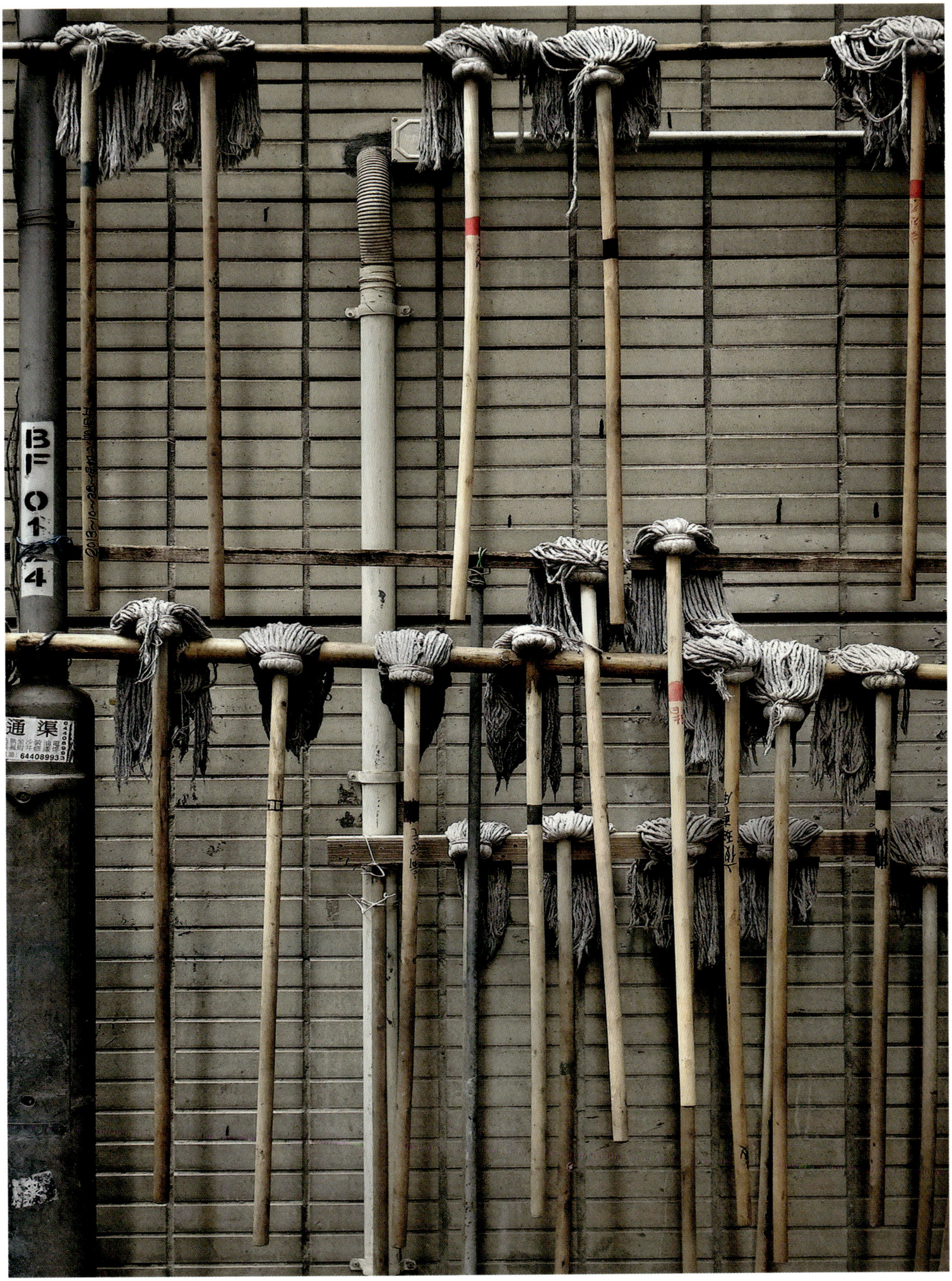
通渠
64408993

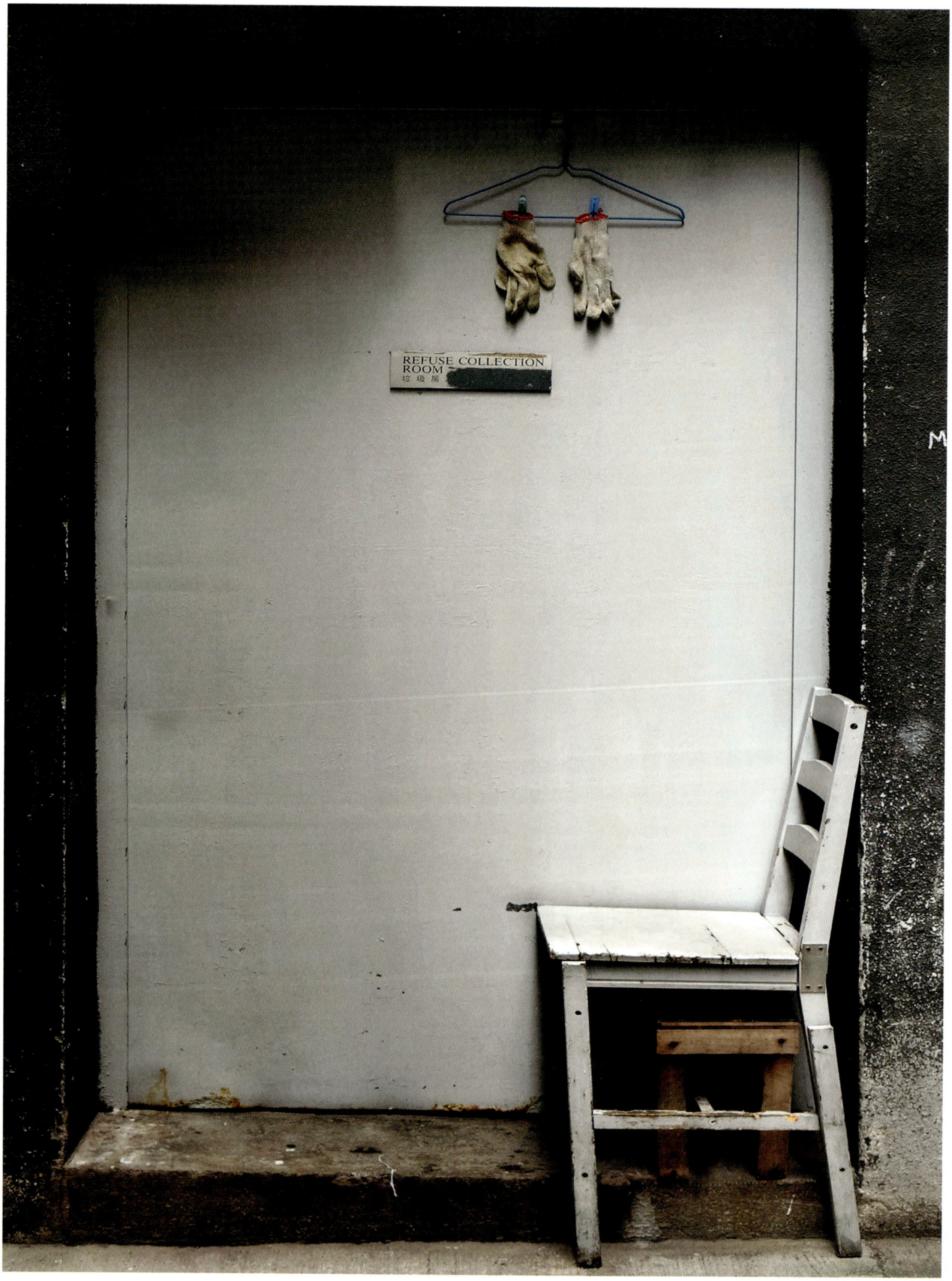
REFUSE COLLECTION
ROOM
垃圾房

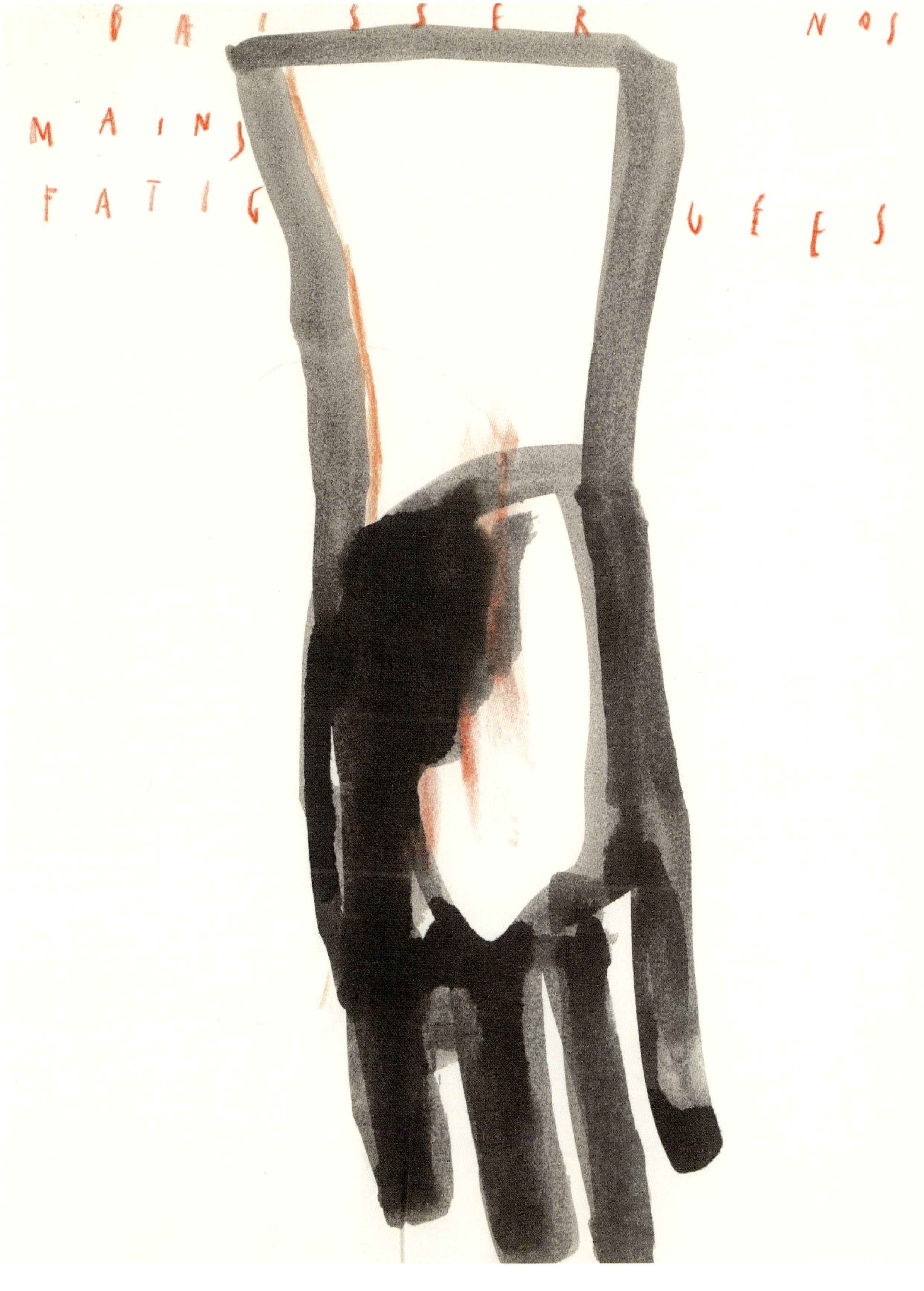

baisser nos mains fatiguées (putting our tired hands down), 2014, 25 × 19 cm, mixed media on paper

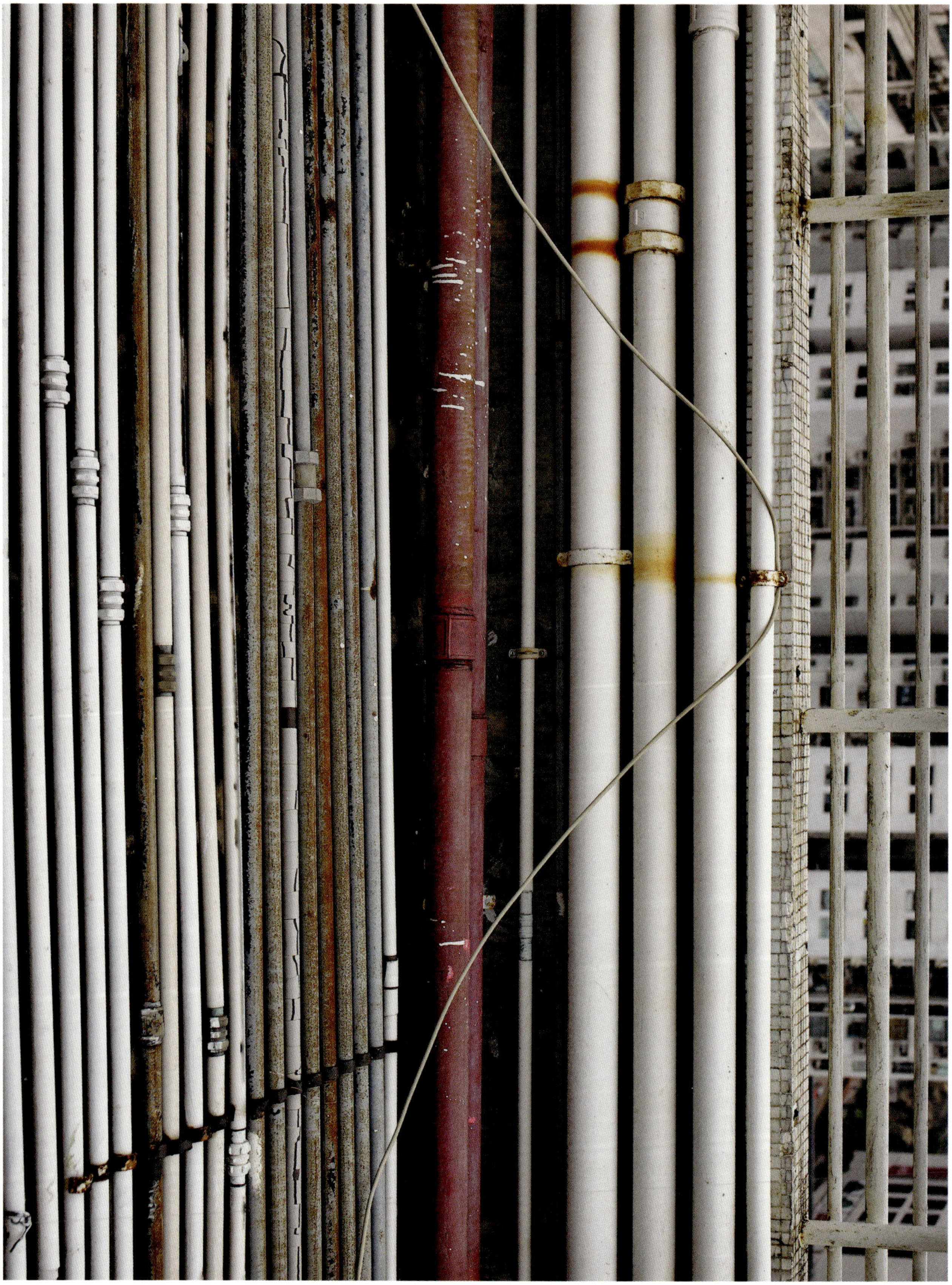

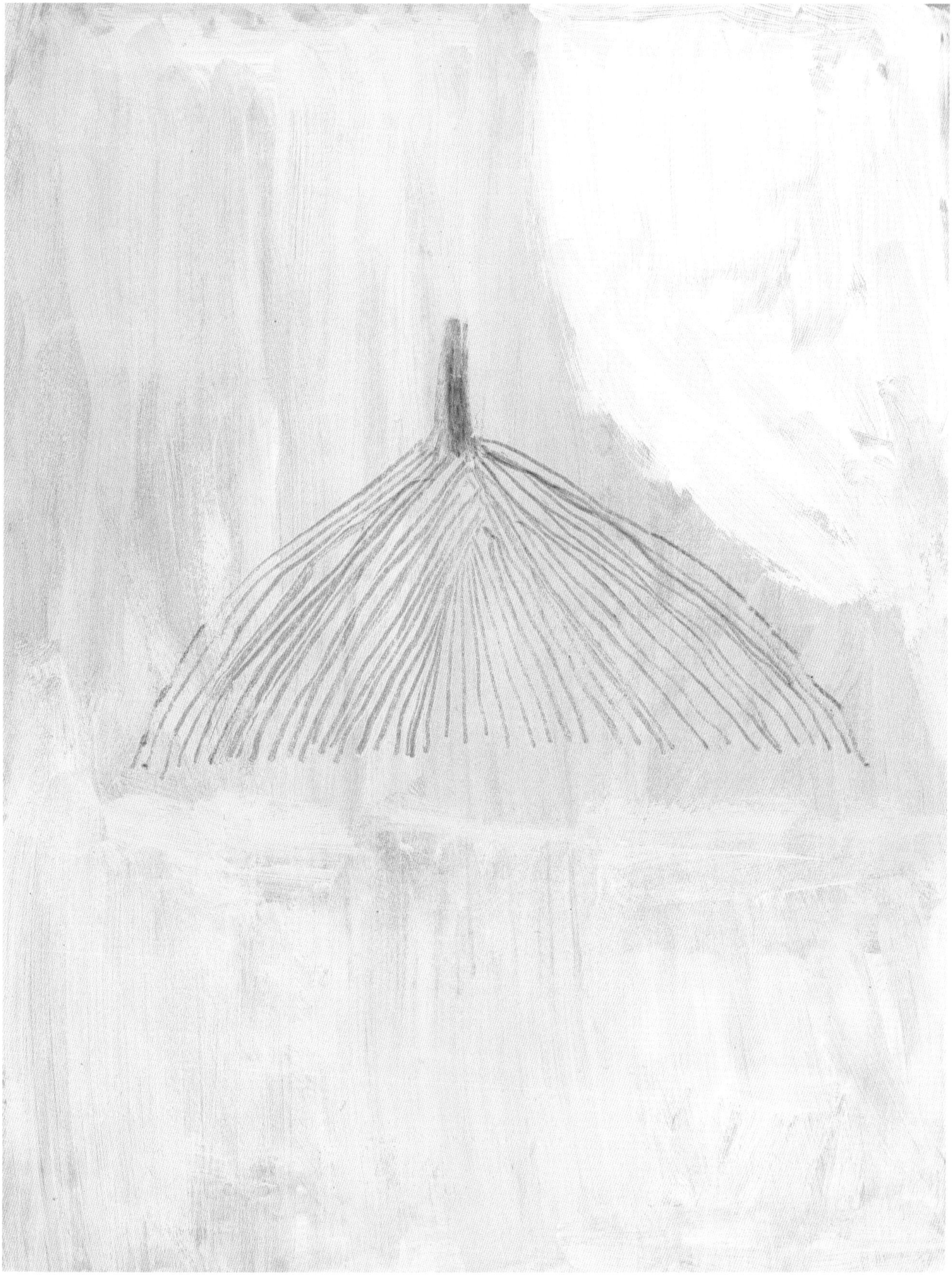

untitled, 2014, 25 × 19 cm, mixed media on paper

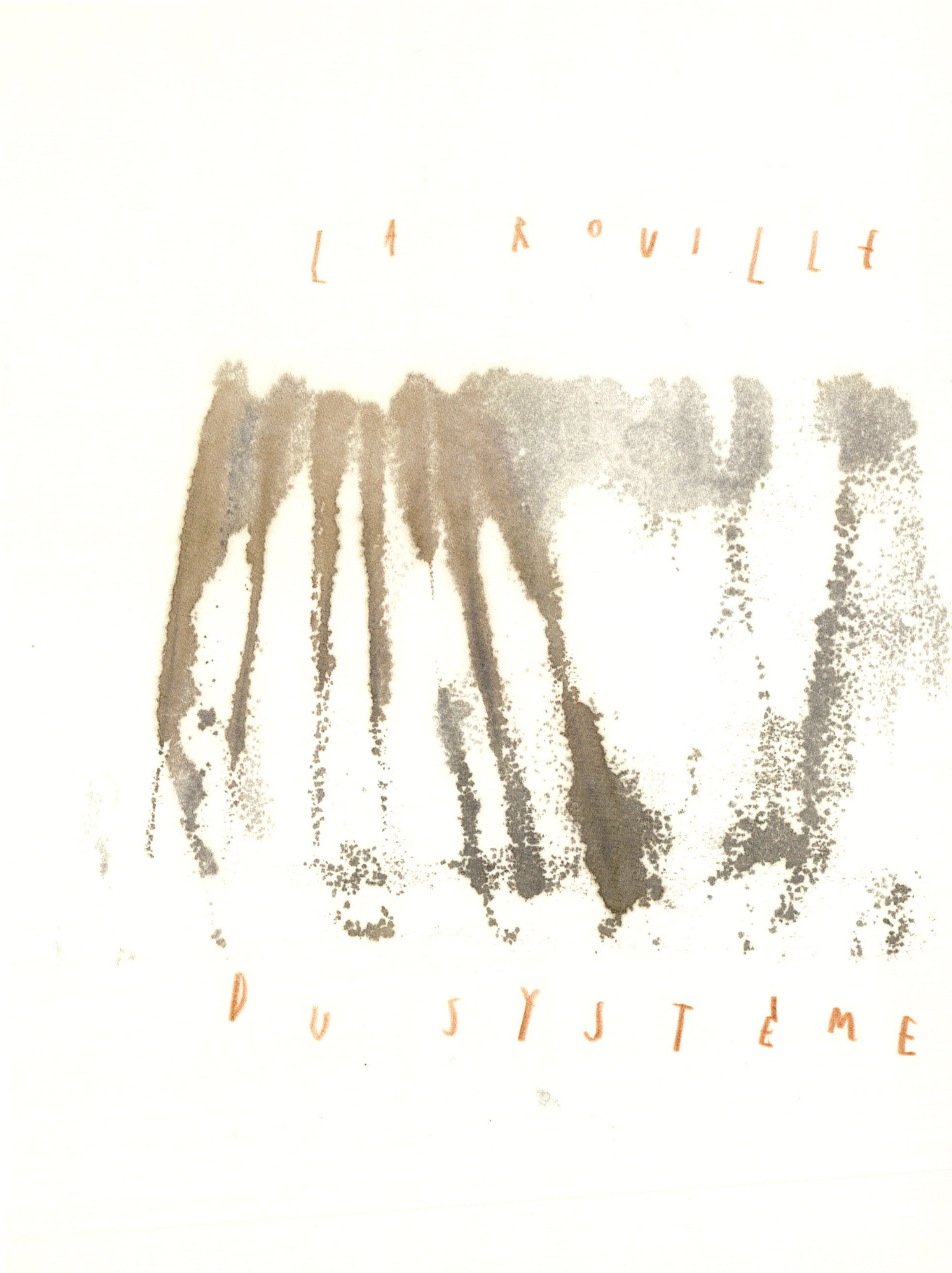

la rouille du système (the system's rust), 2014, 25 × 19 cm, mixed media on paper

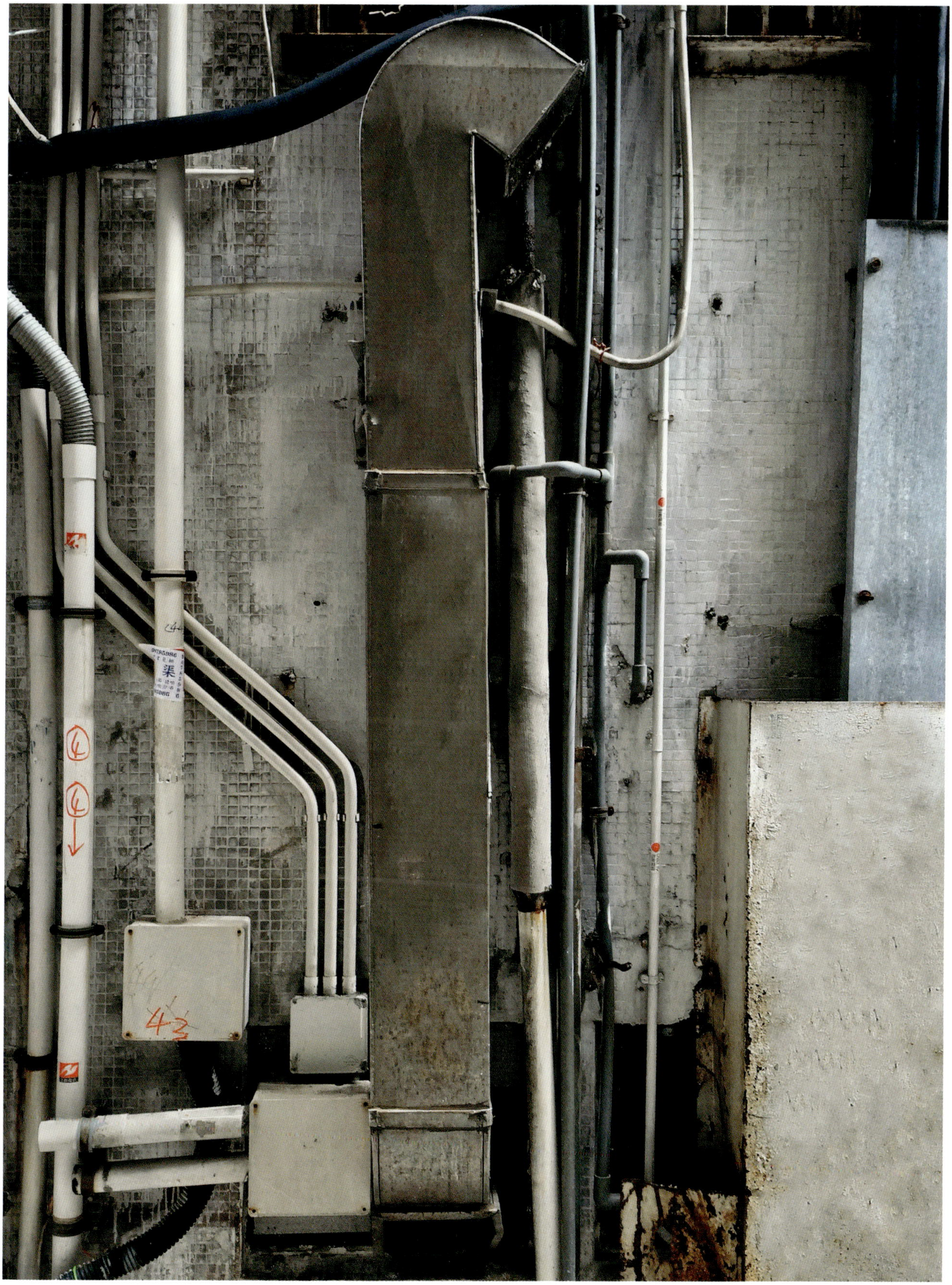
43

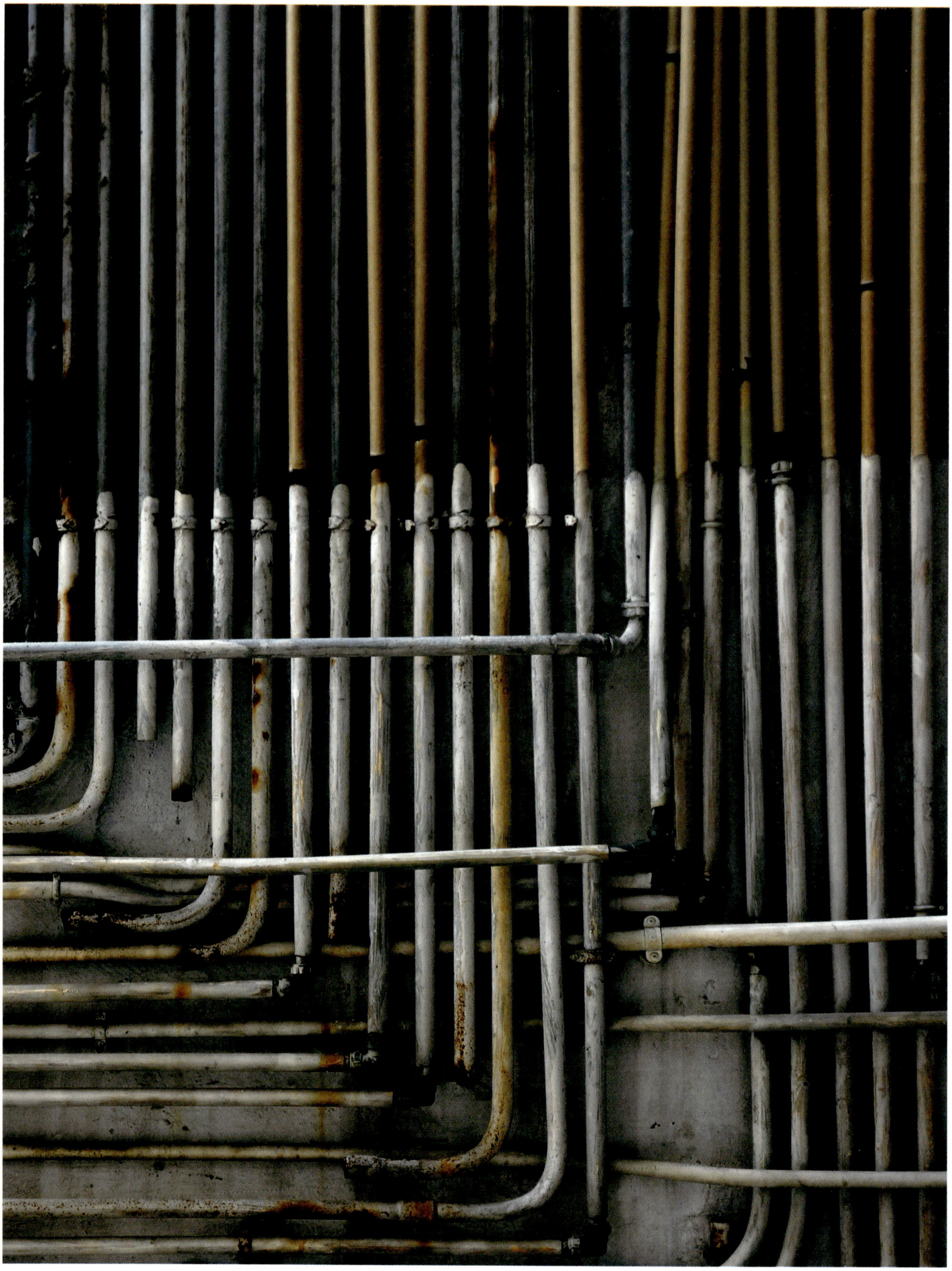

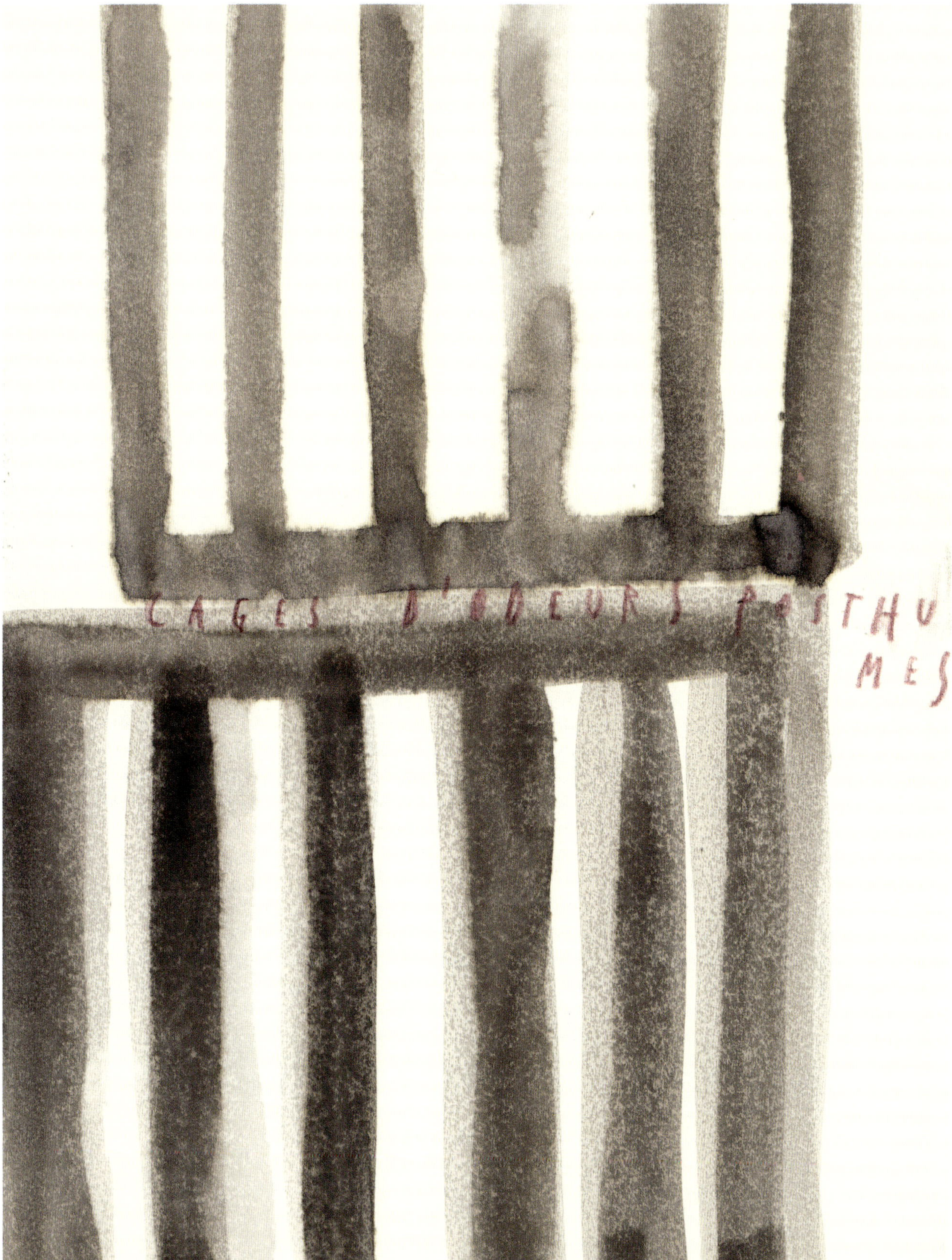

cages d'odeurs posthumes (cage of posthumous smells), 2014, 25 × 19 cm, mixed media on paper

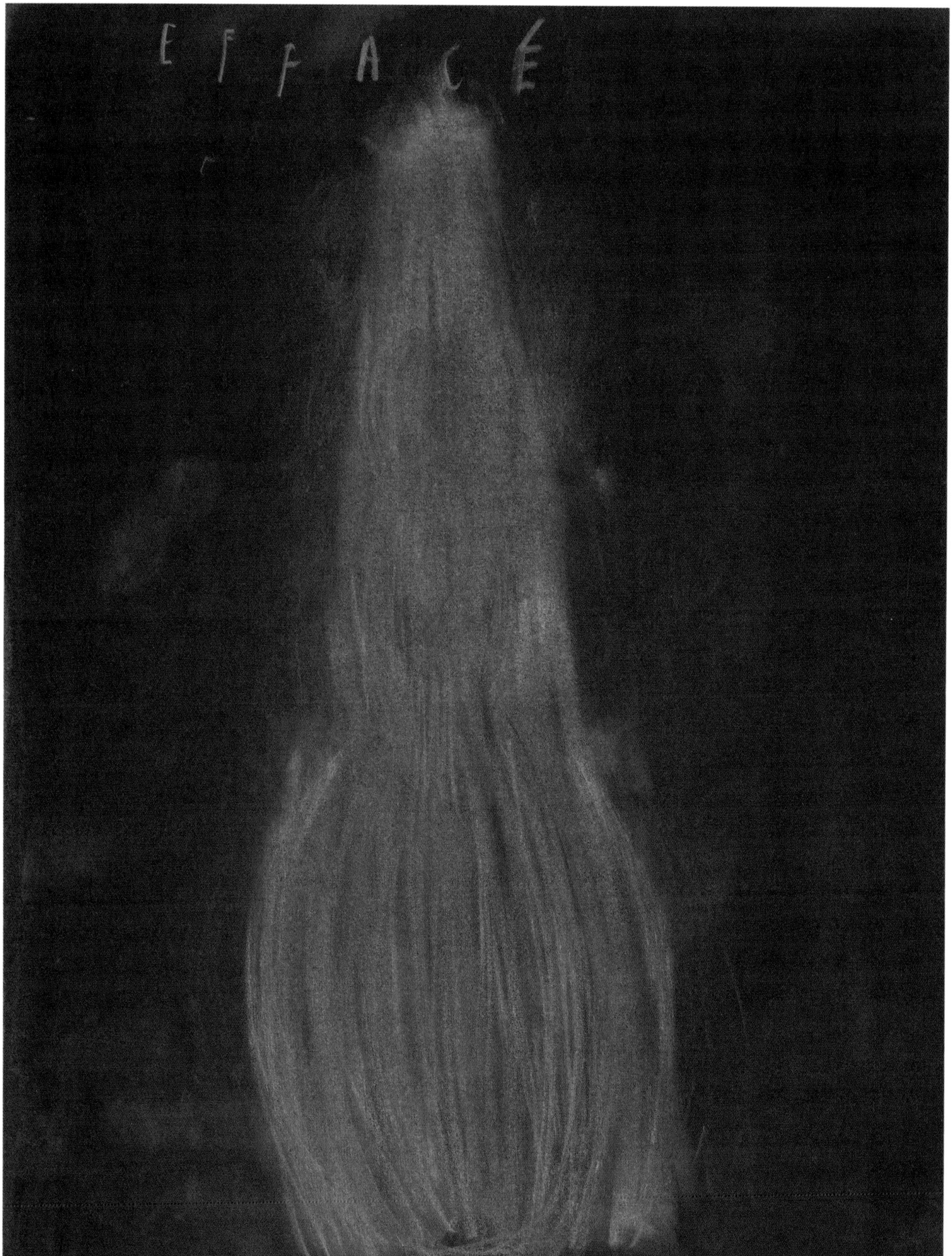

effacé (erased), 2014, 25 × 19 cm, mixed media on paper

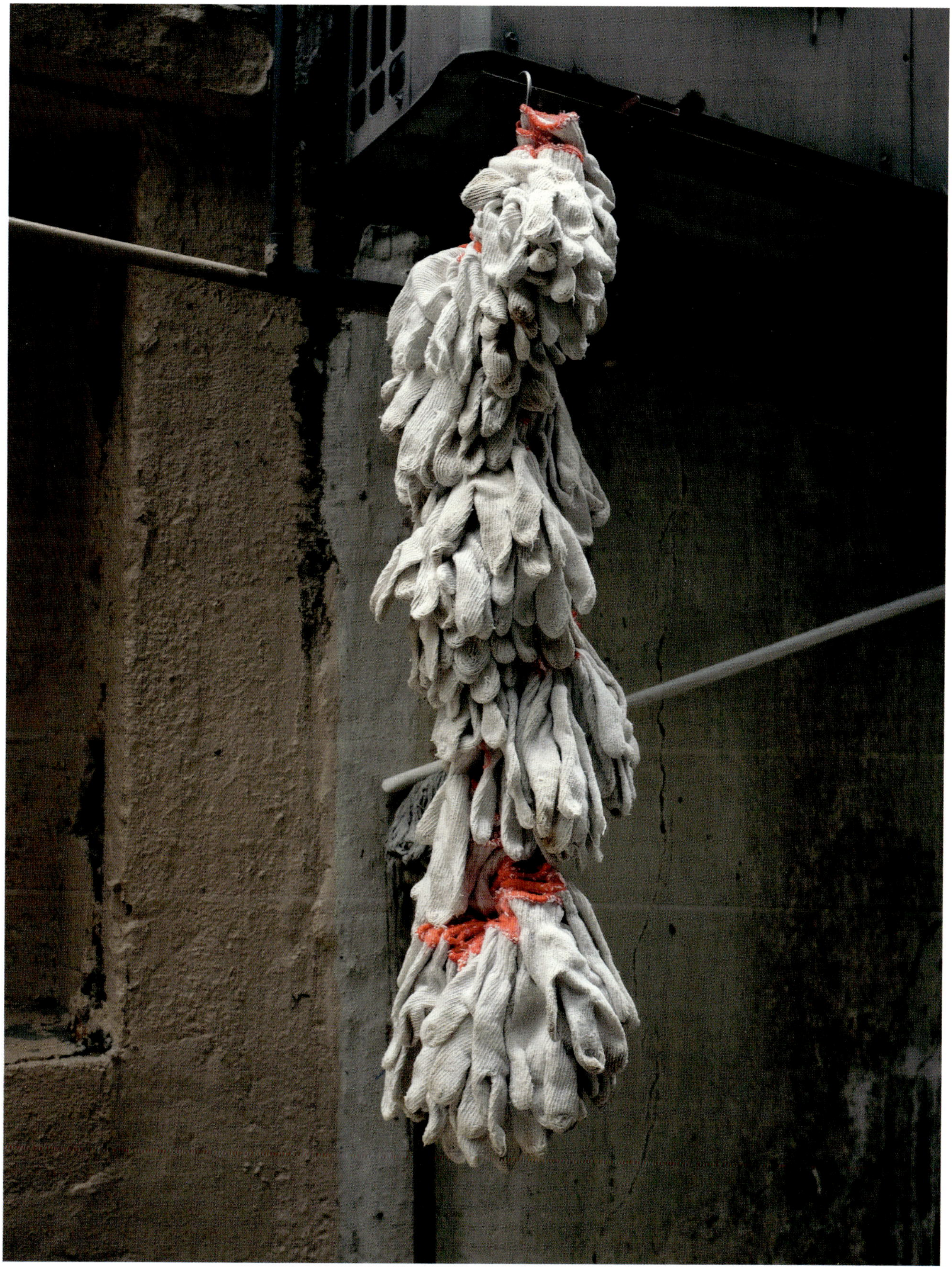

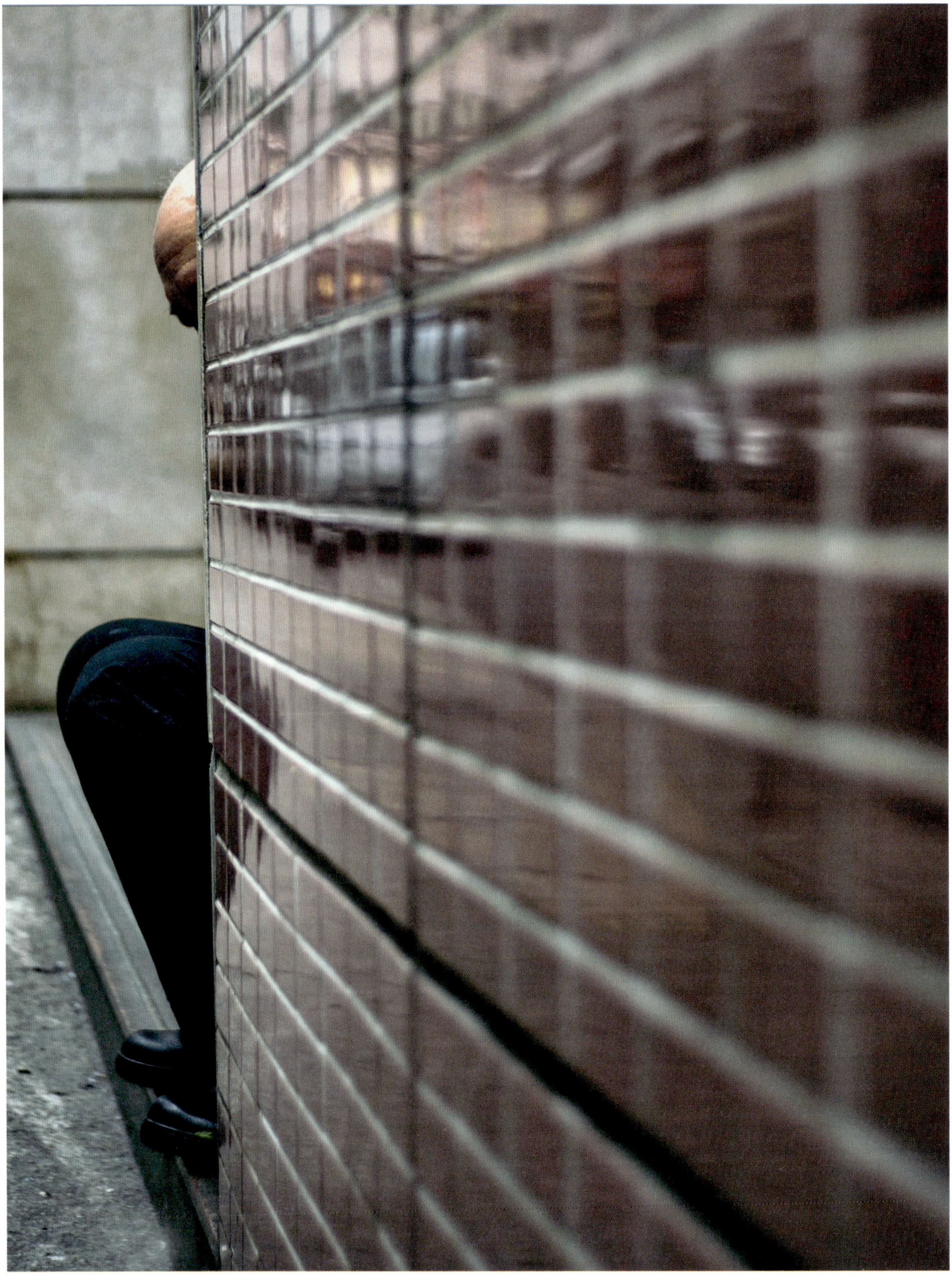

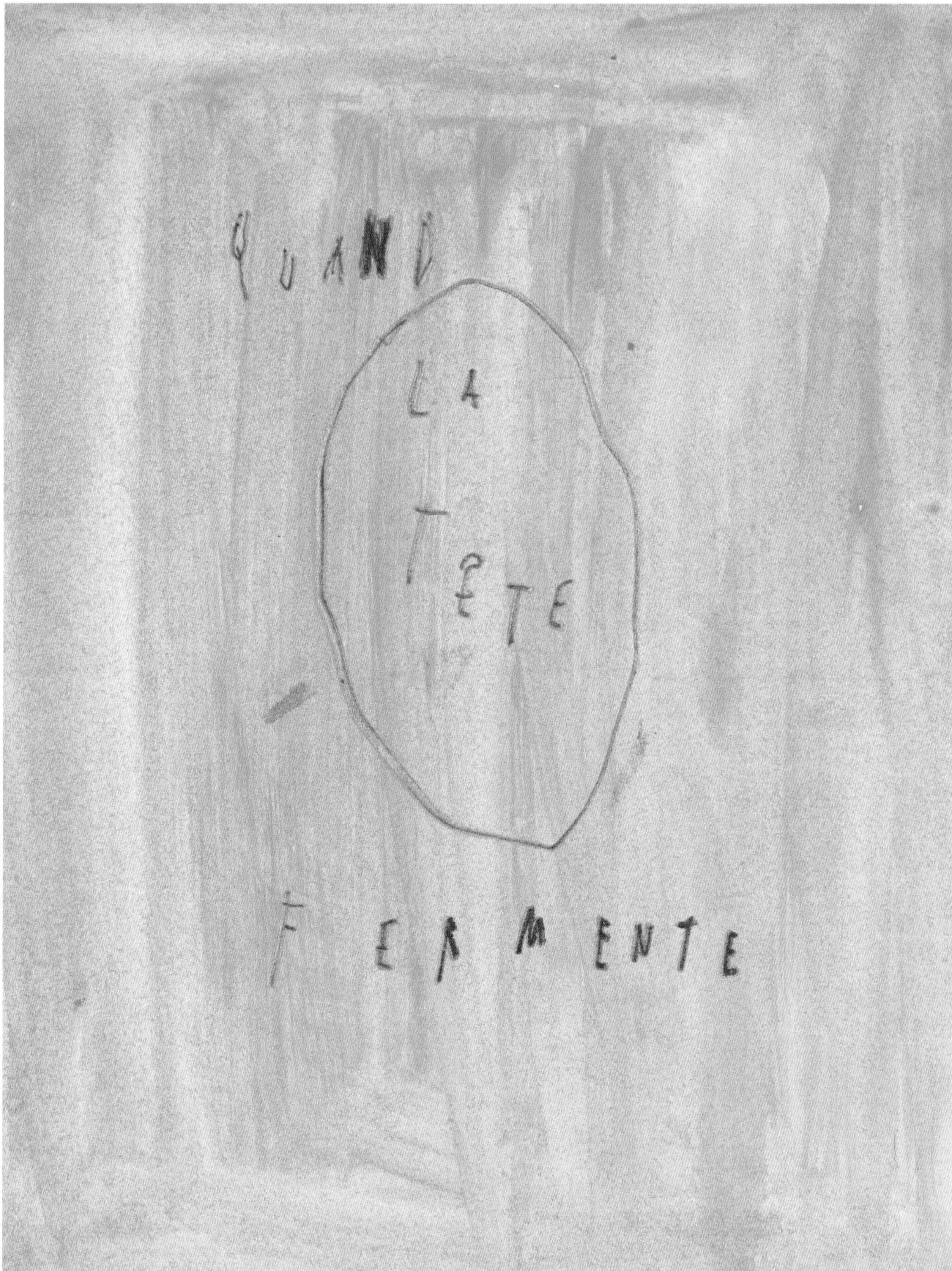

quand la tête fermente (when the head ferments), 2014, 25 × 19 cm, mixed media on paper

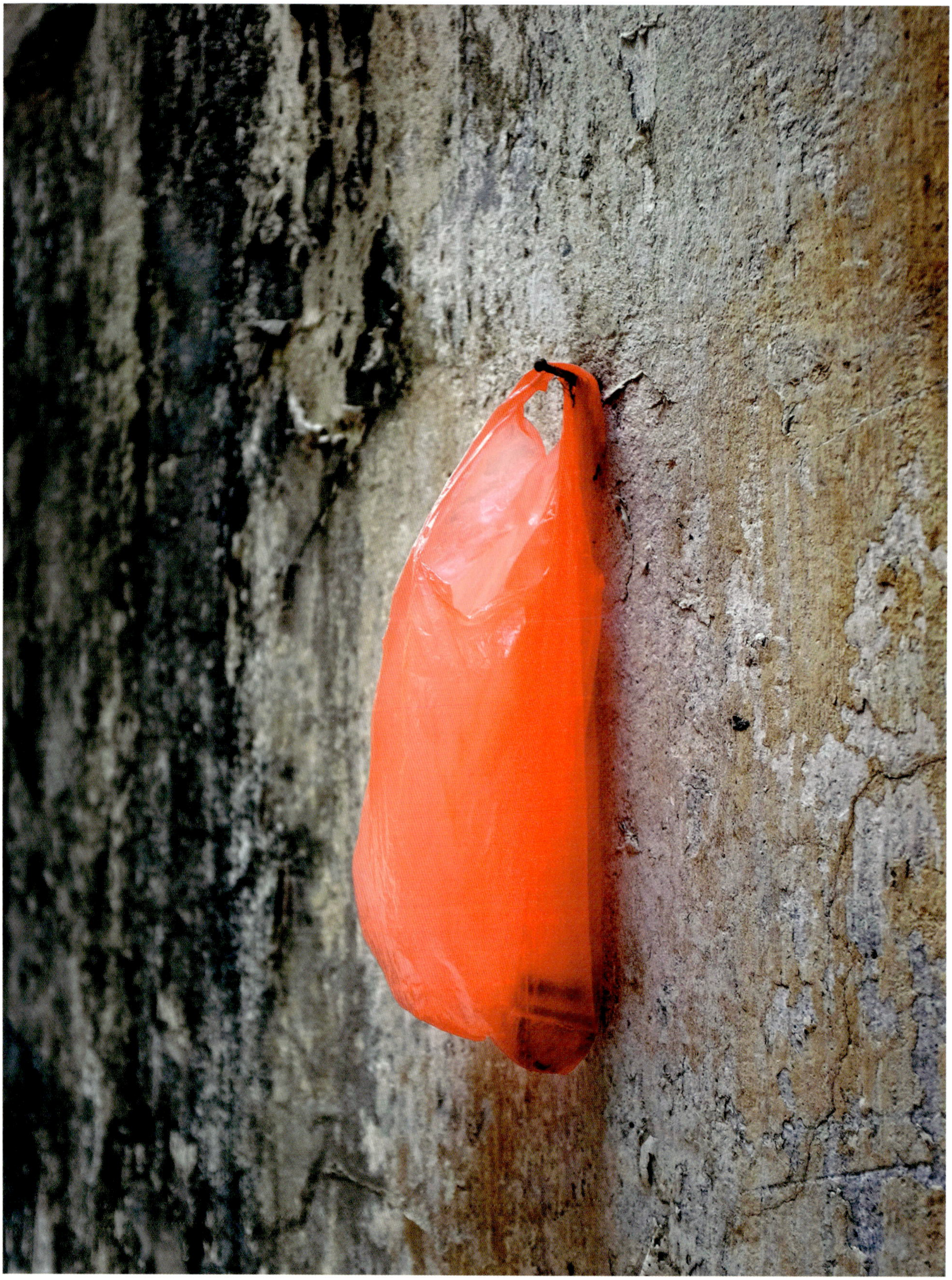

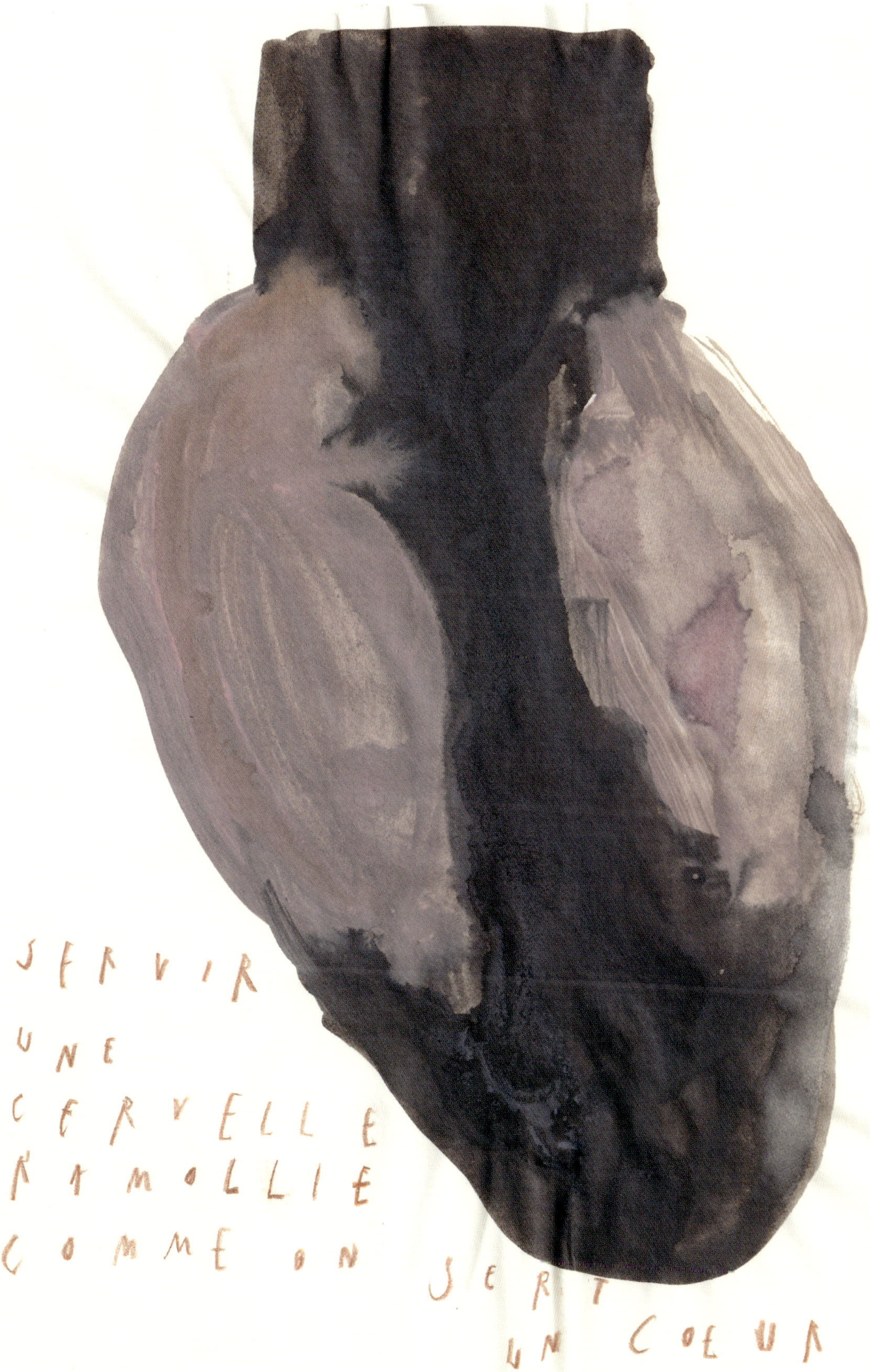

servir une cervelle ramollie comme on sert un cœur (serving a softened brain like you would a heart), 2014, 25 × 19 cm, mixed media on paper

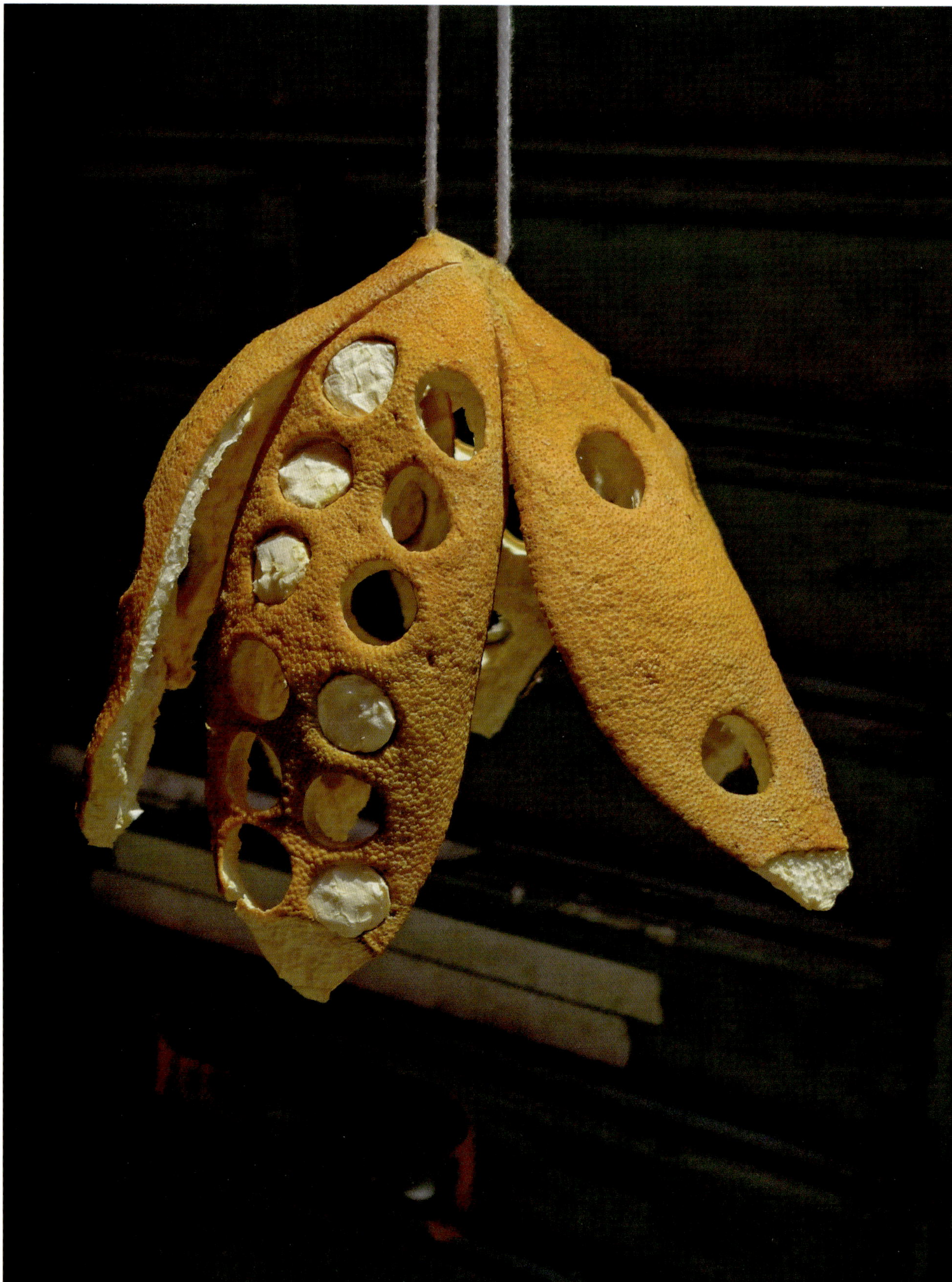

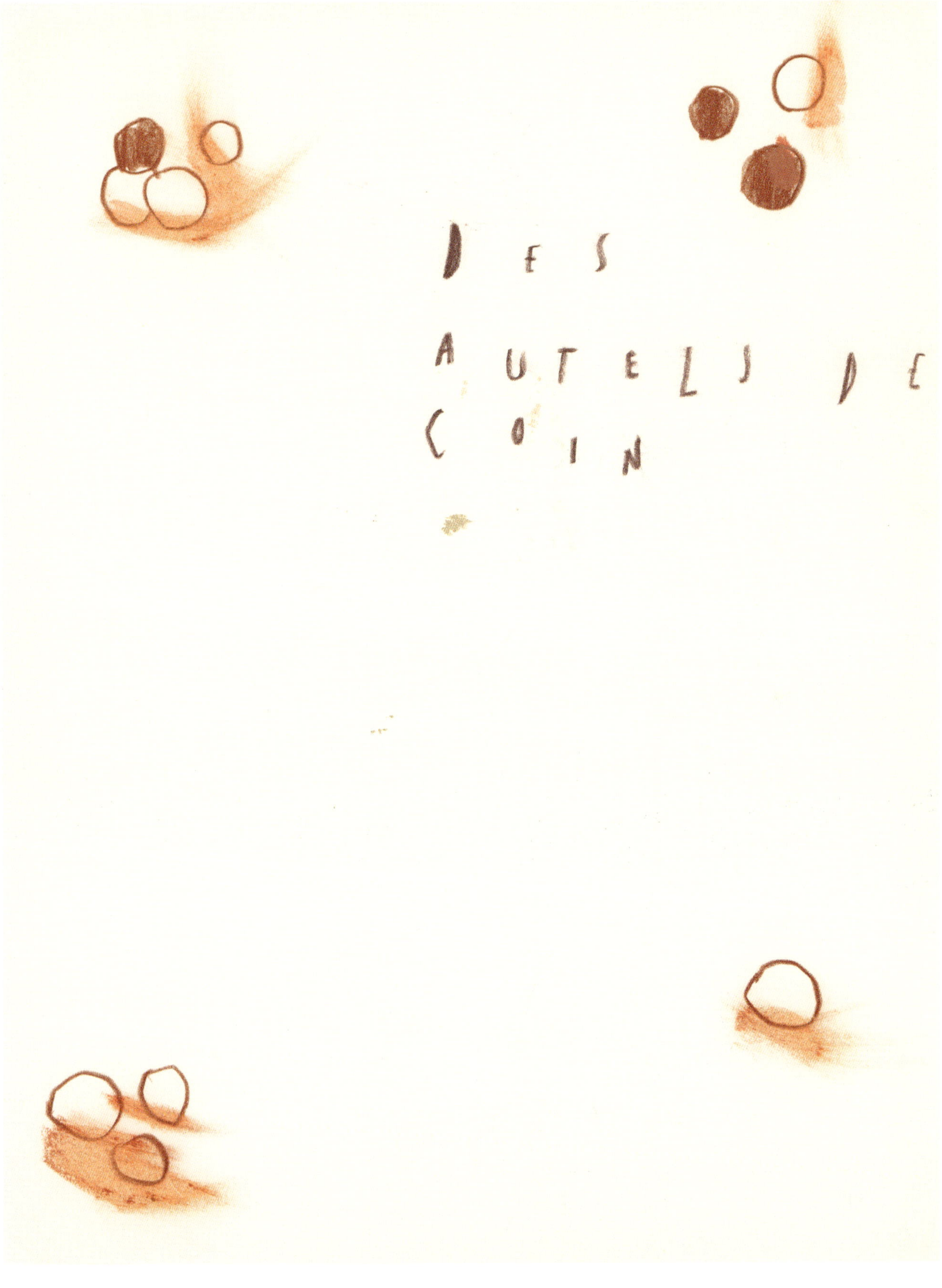

des autels de coin (corner altars), 2014, 25 × 19 cm, mixed media on paper

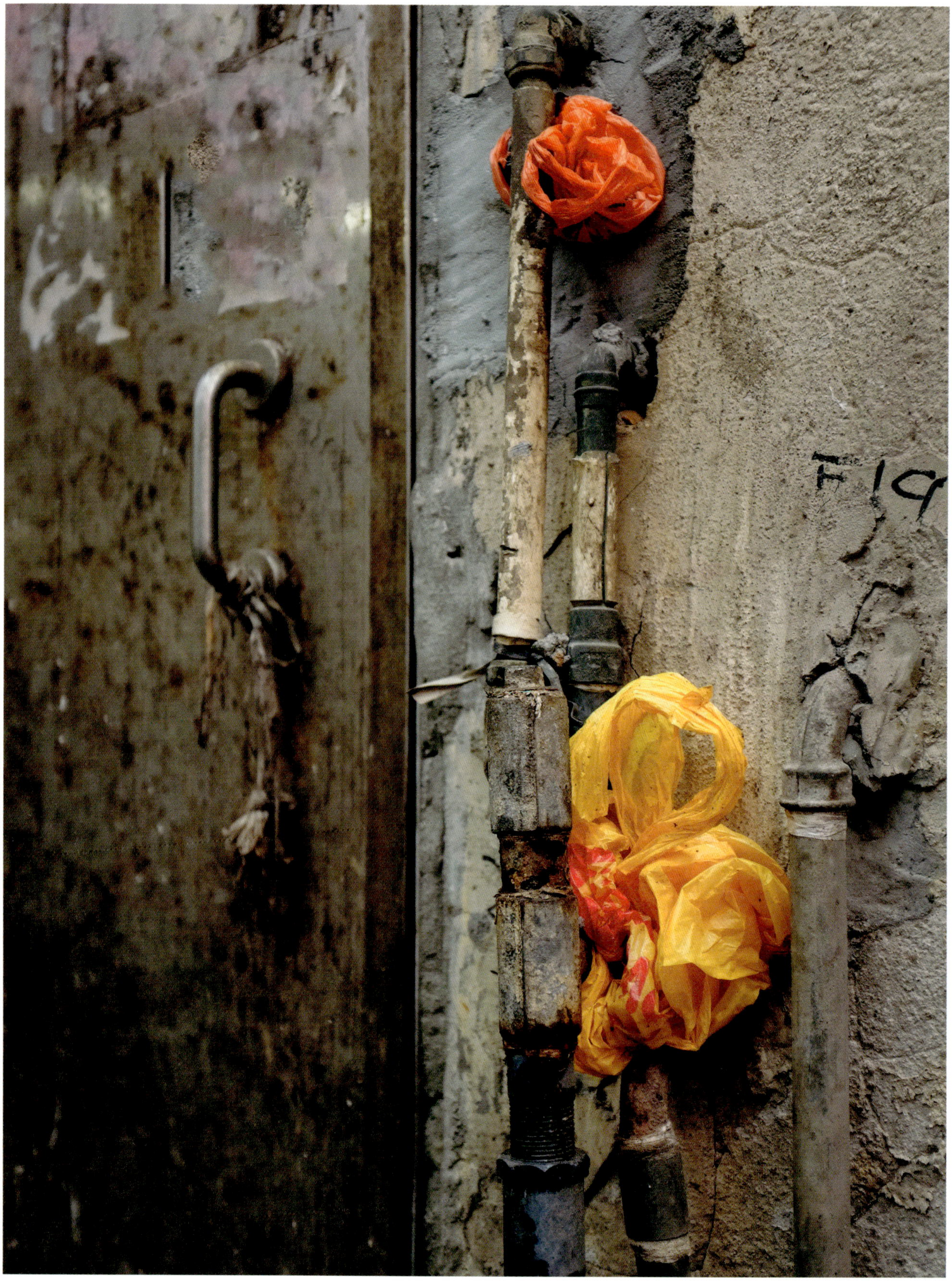

Informal Solutions #103

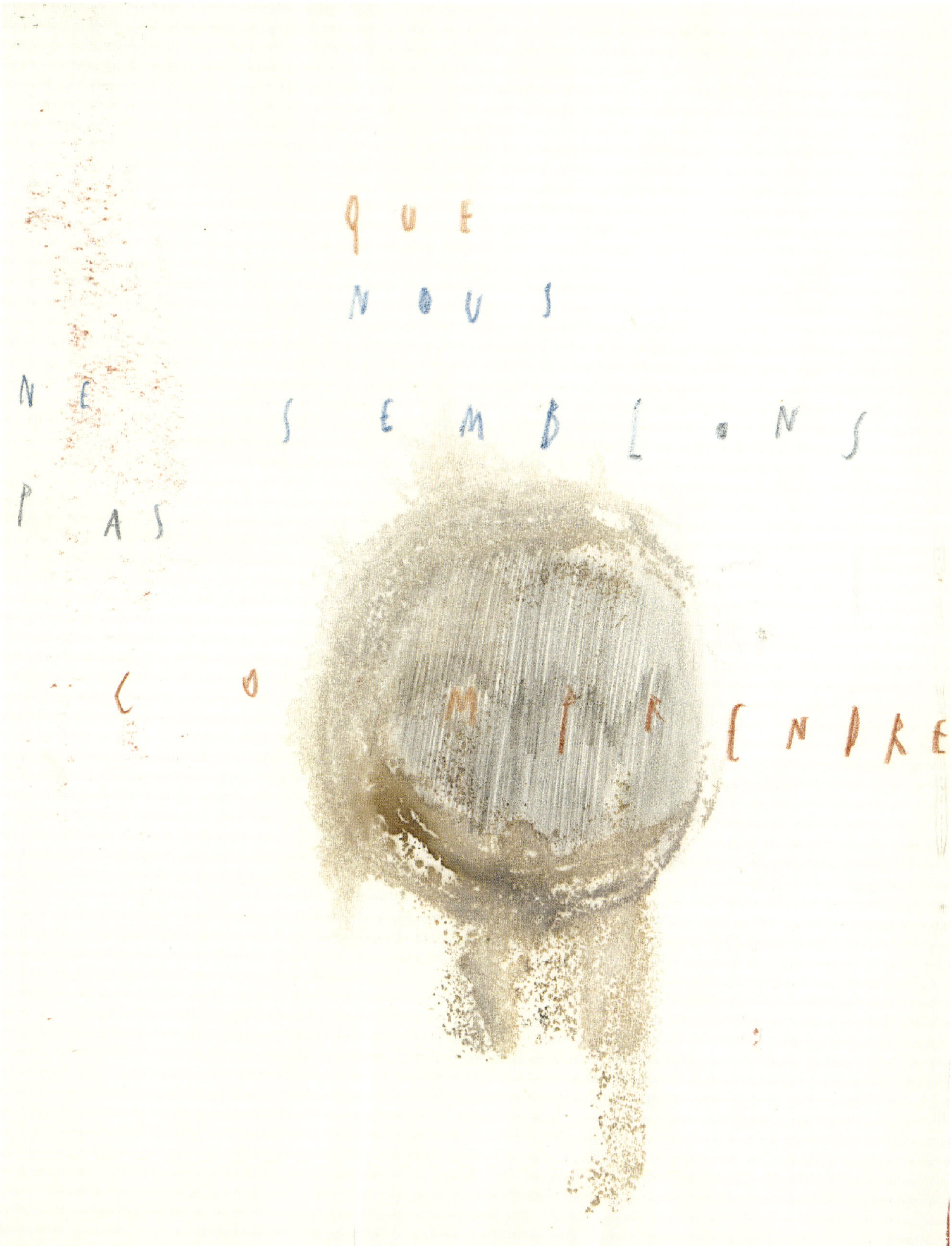

que nous ne semblons pas comprendre (that we don't seem to understand), 2014, 25 × 19 cm, mixed media on paper

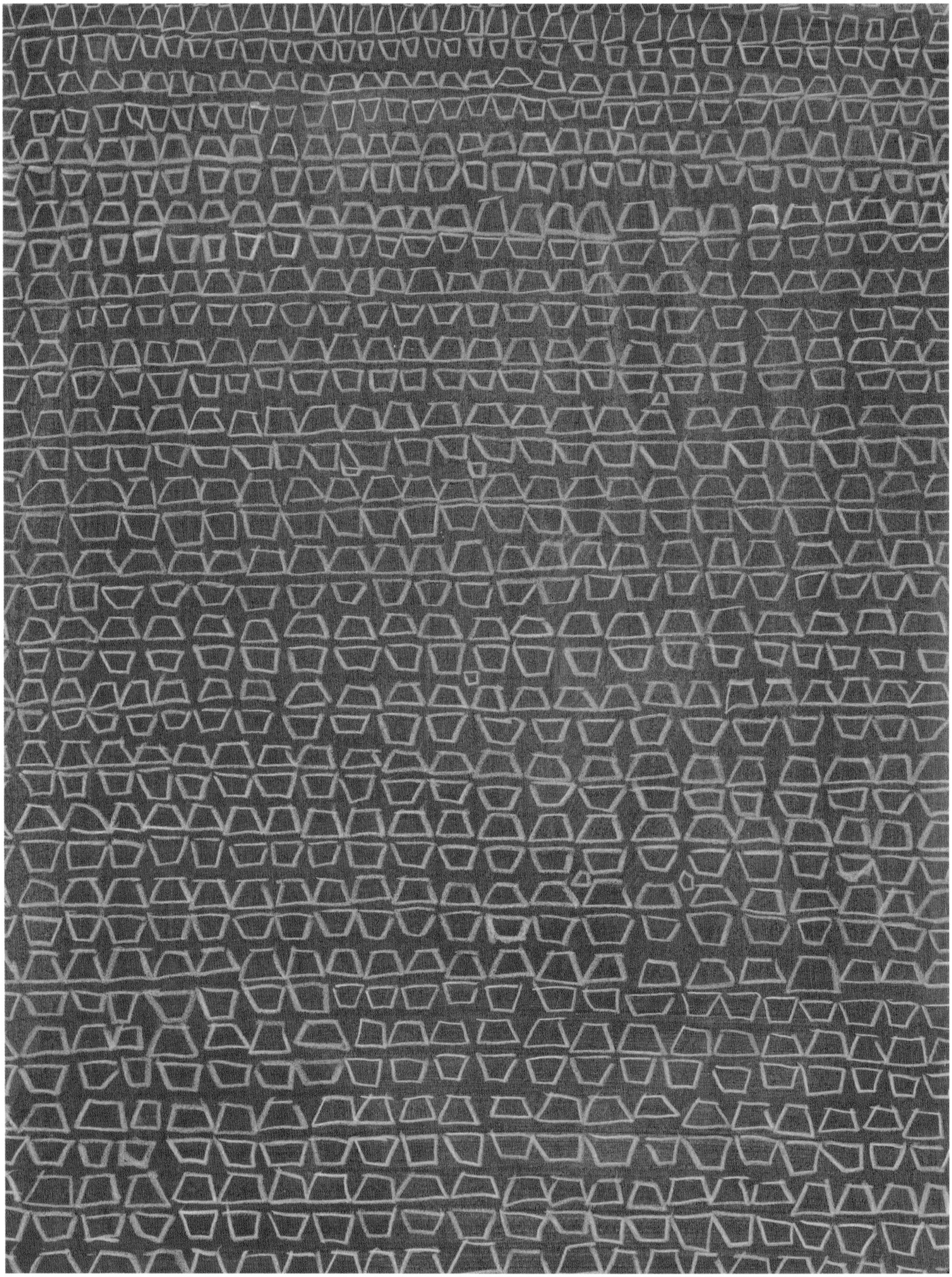

untitled, 2014, 25 × 19 cm, mixed media on paper

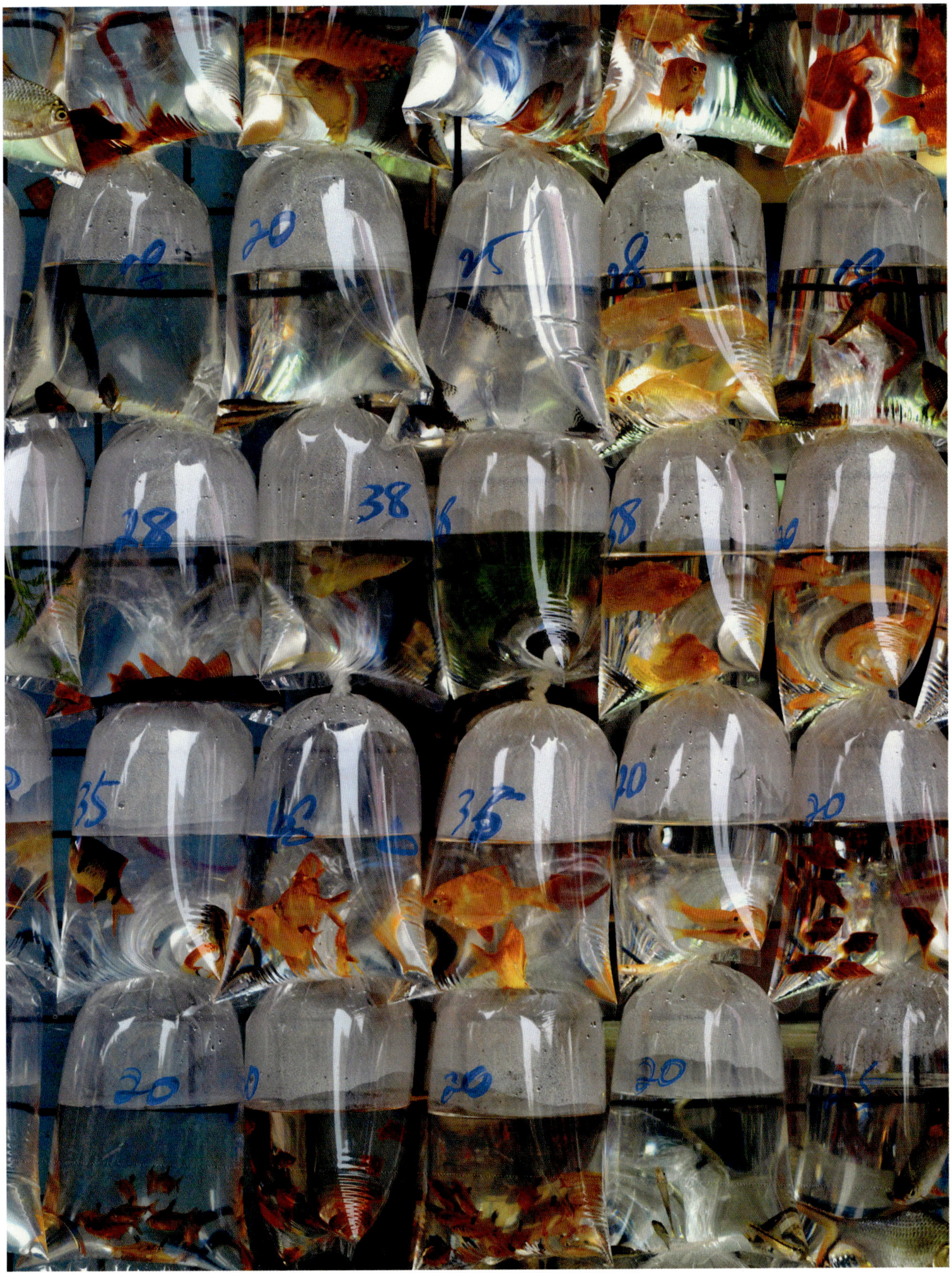

 des points d'eau pour des poissons déjà morts (water points for already dead fish), 2014, 25 × 19 cm, mixed media on paper

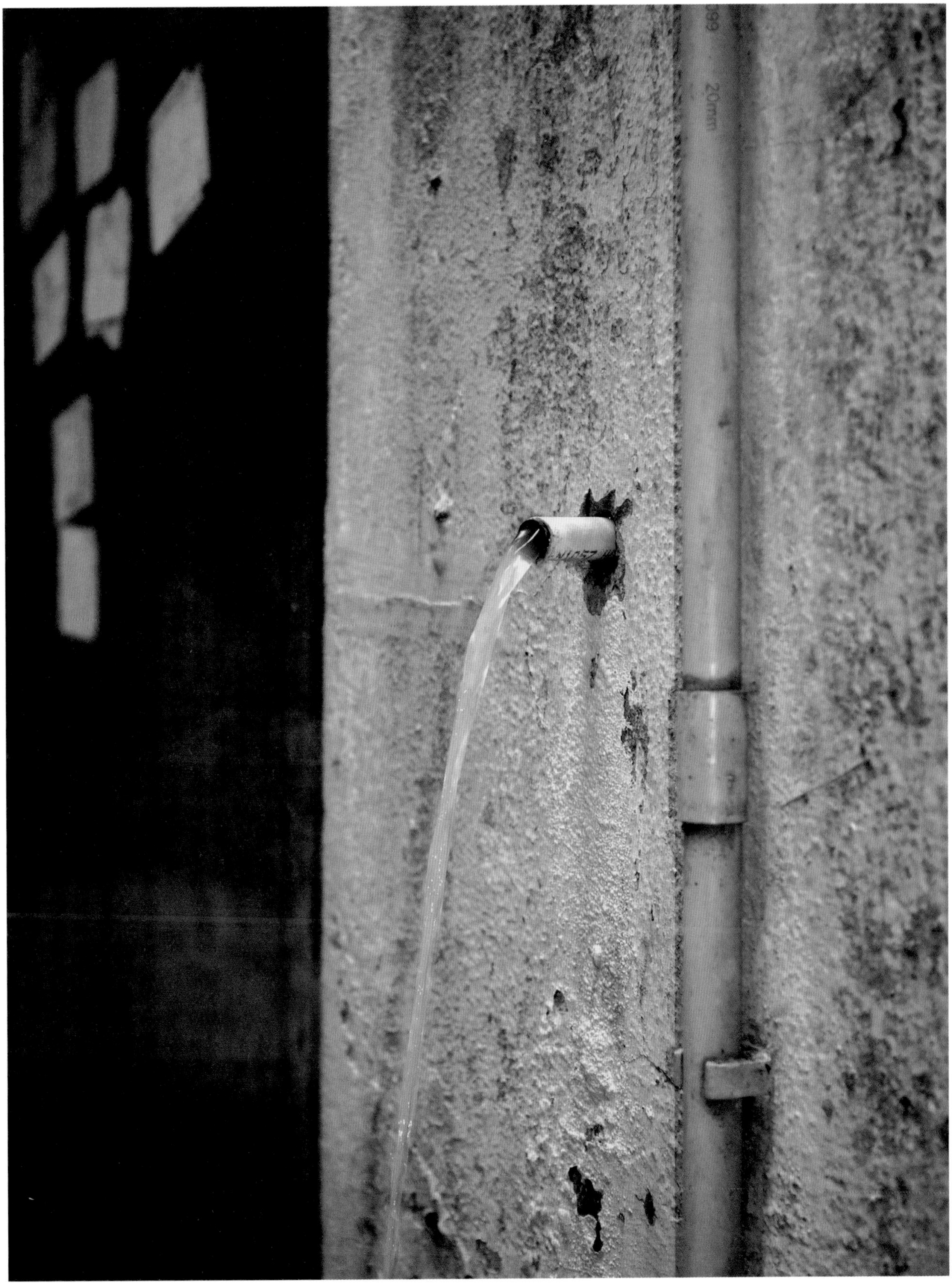

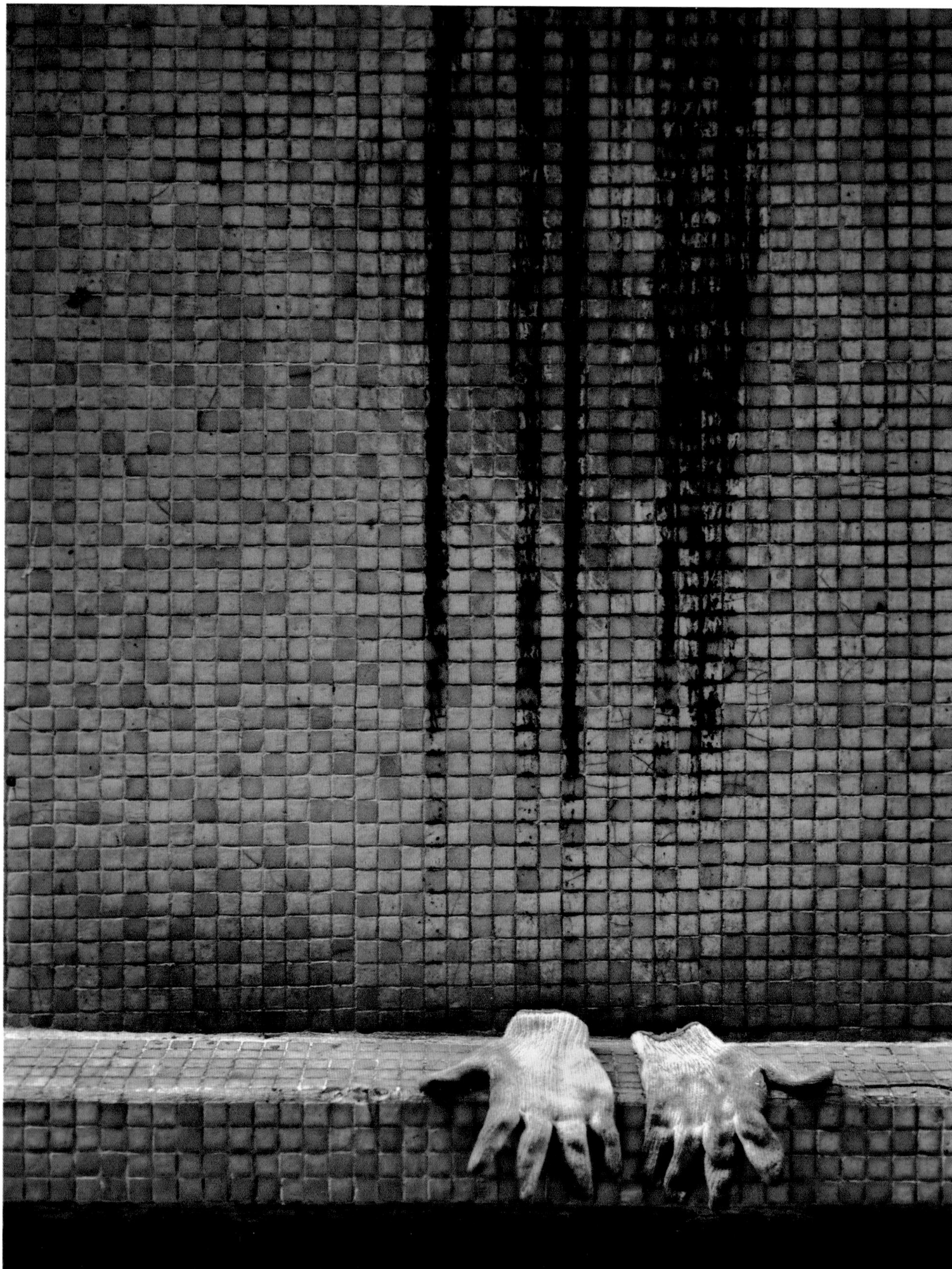

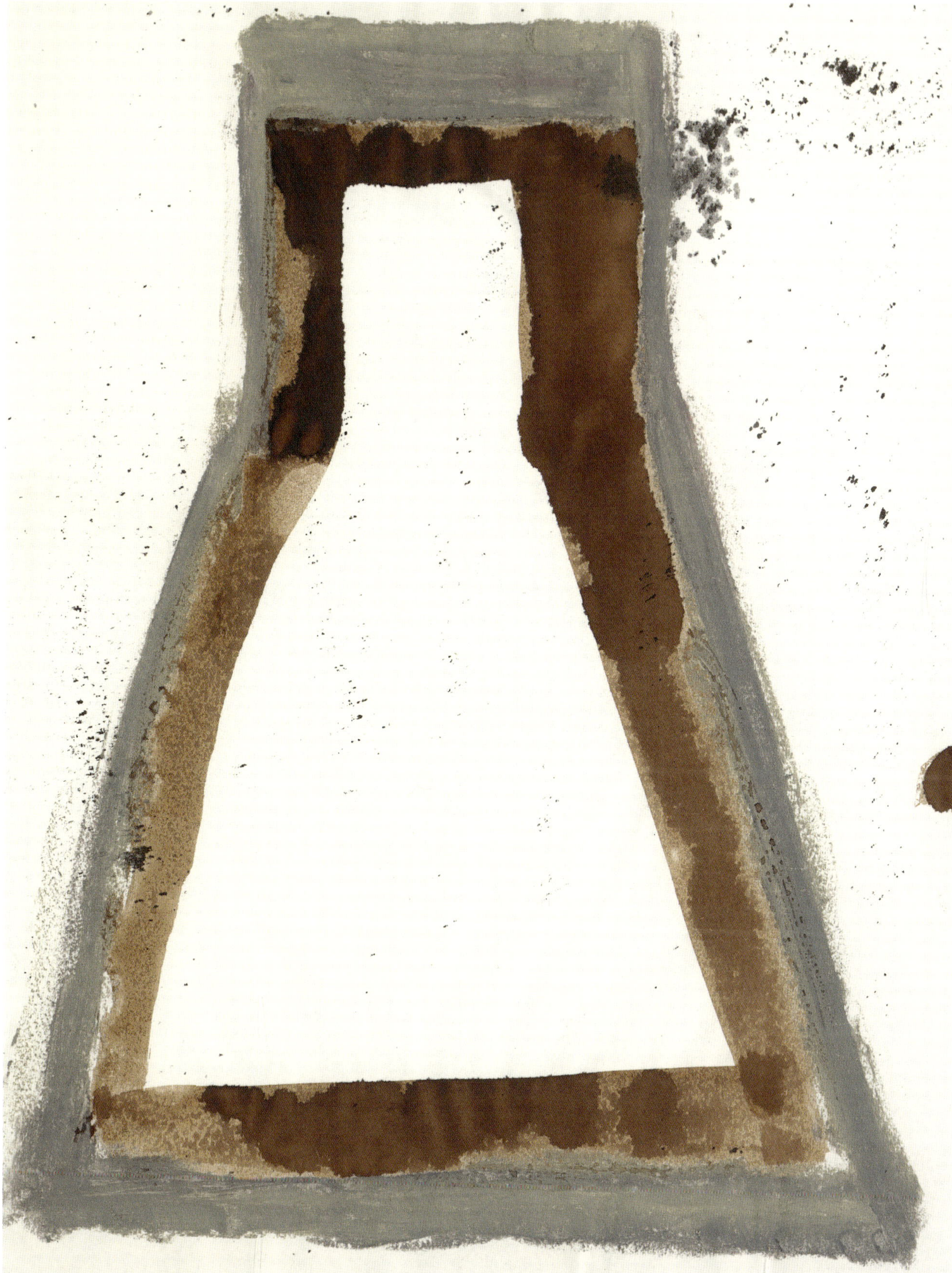

untitled, 2014, 25 × 19 cm, mixed media on paper

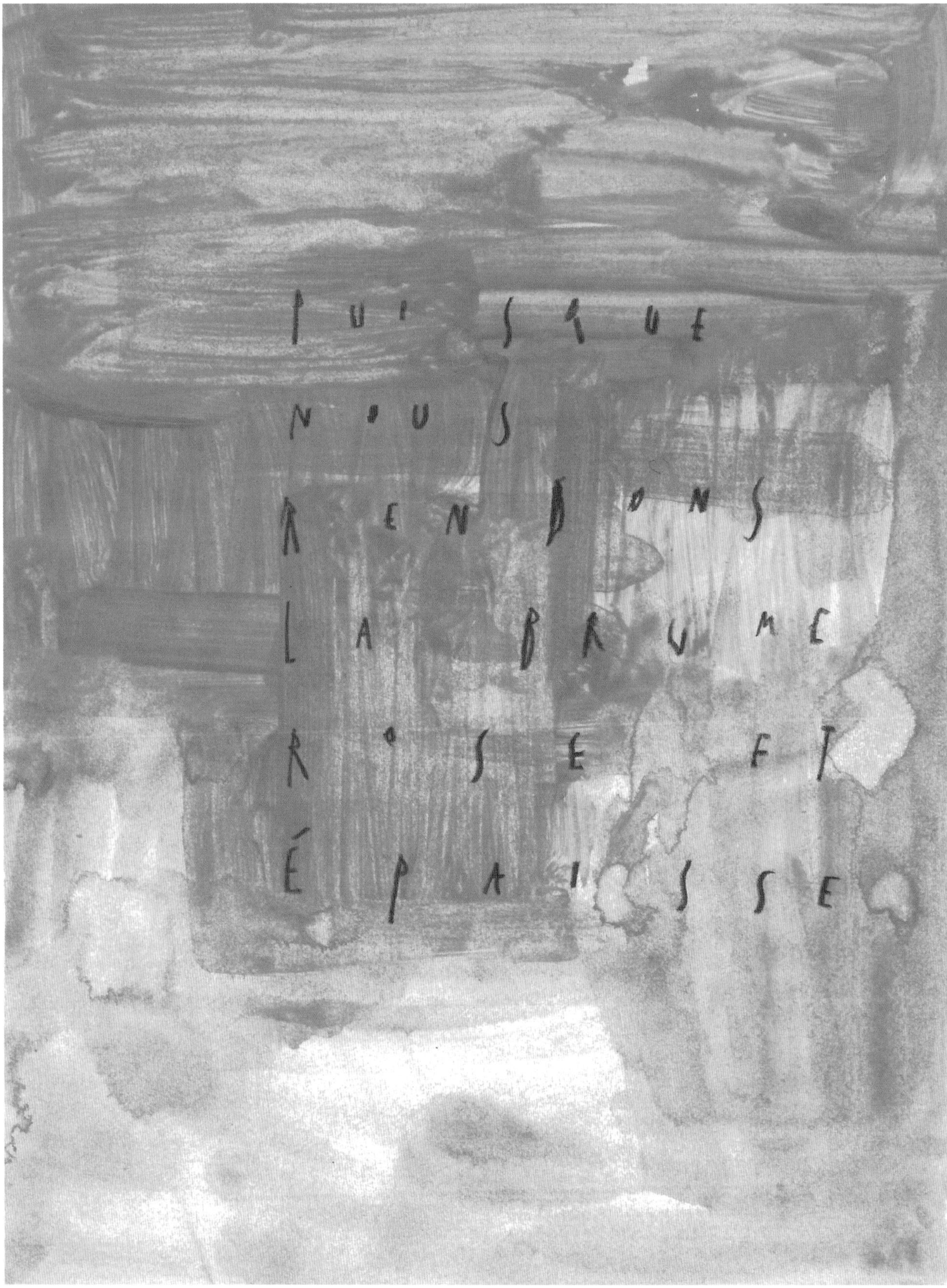

puisque nous rendons la brume rose et épaisse (as we turn the mist pink and thick), 2014, 25 × 19 cm, mixed media on paper

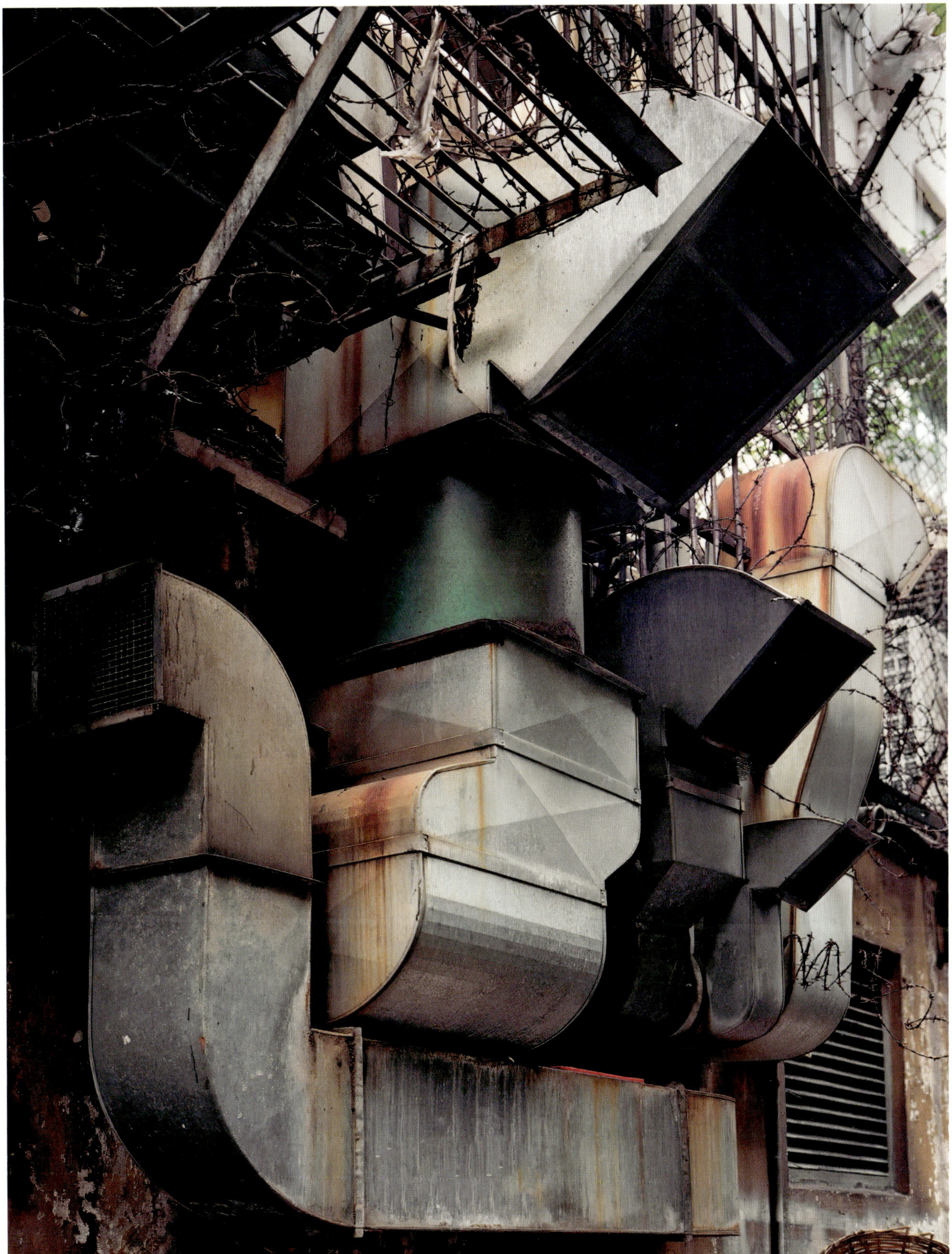

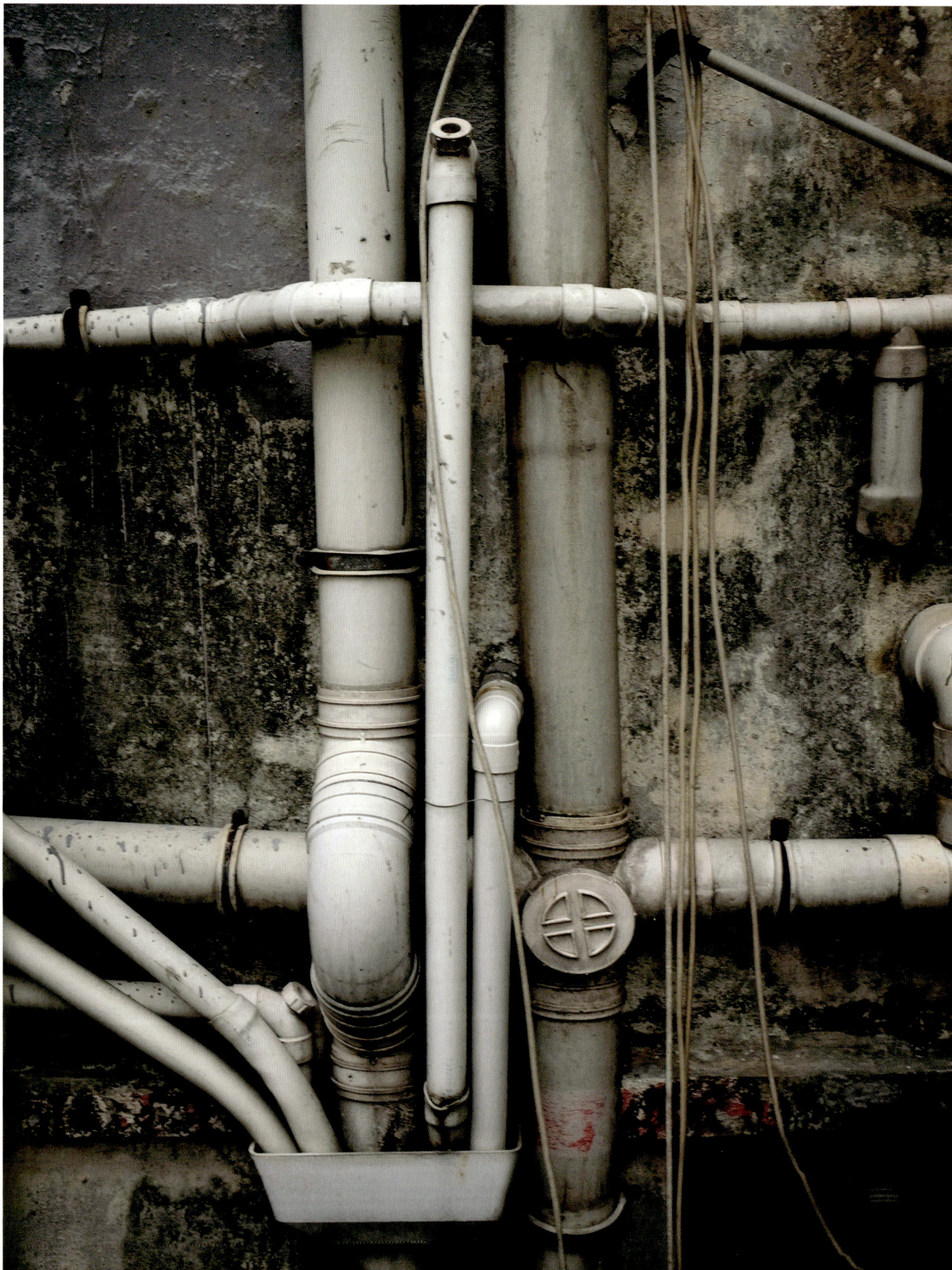

Informal Solutions #106

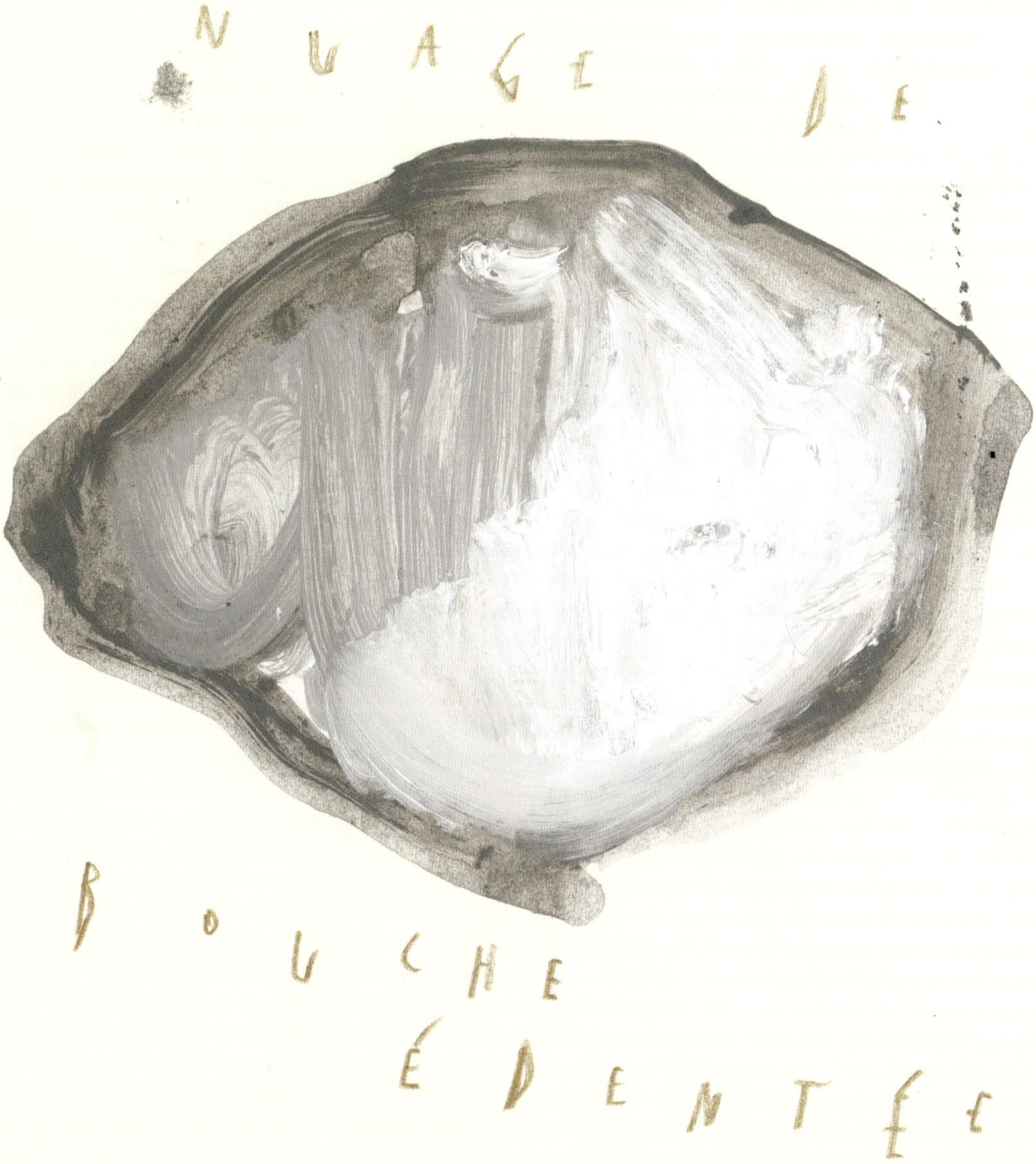

nuage de bouche édentée (cloud of a toothless mouth), 2014, 25 × 19 cm, mixed media on paper

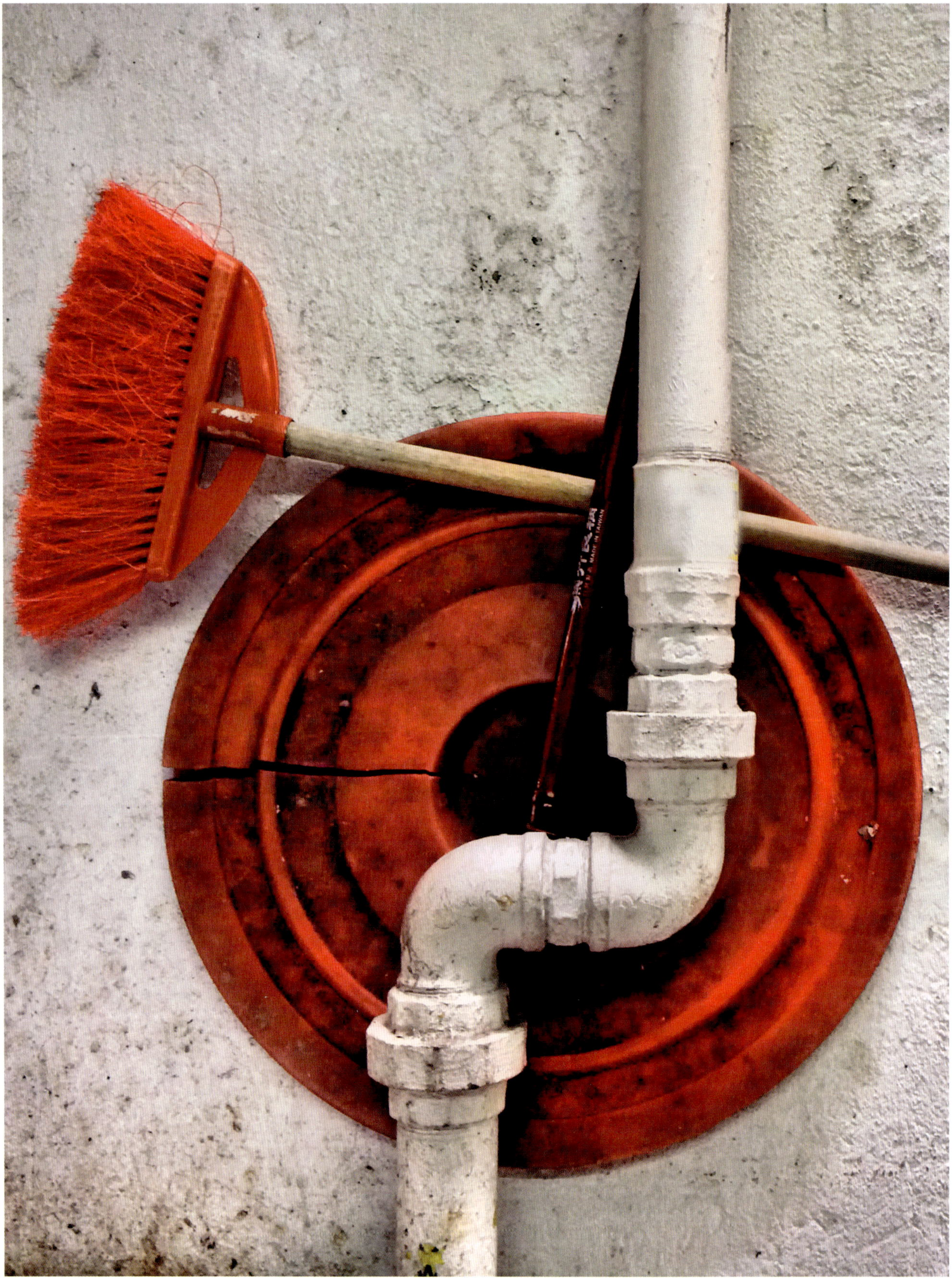

Informal Solutions #108

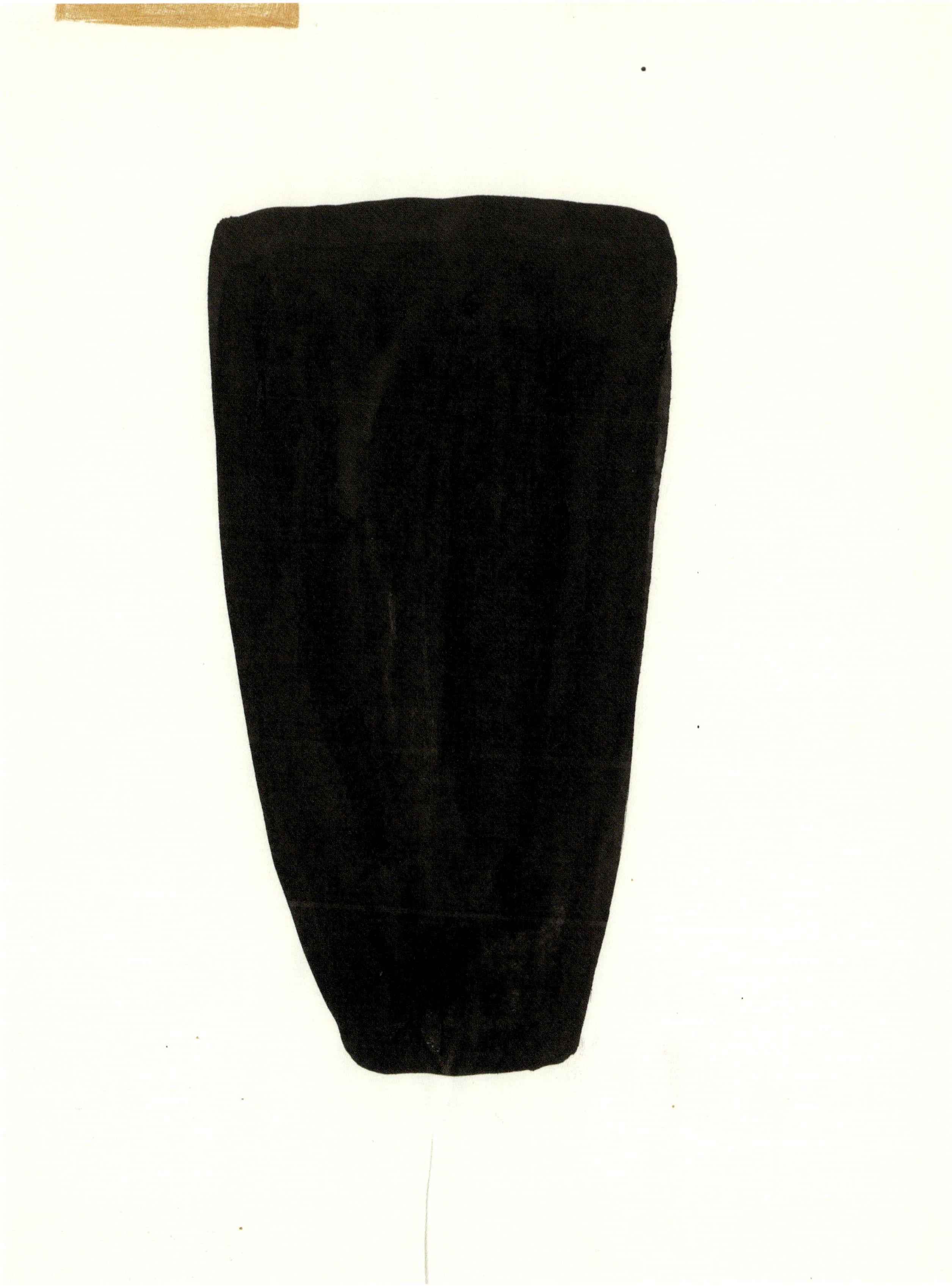

untitled, 2014, 25 × 19 cm, mixed media on paper

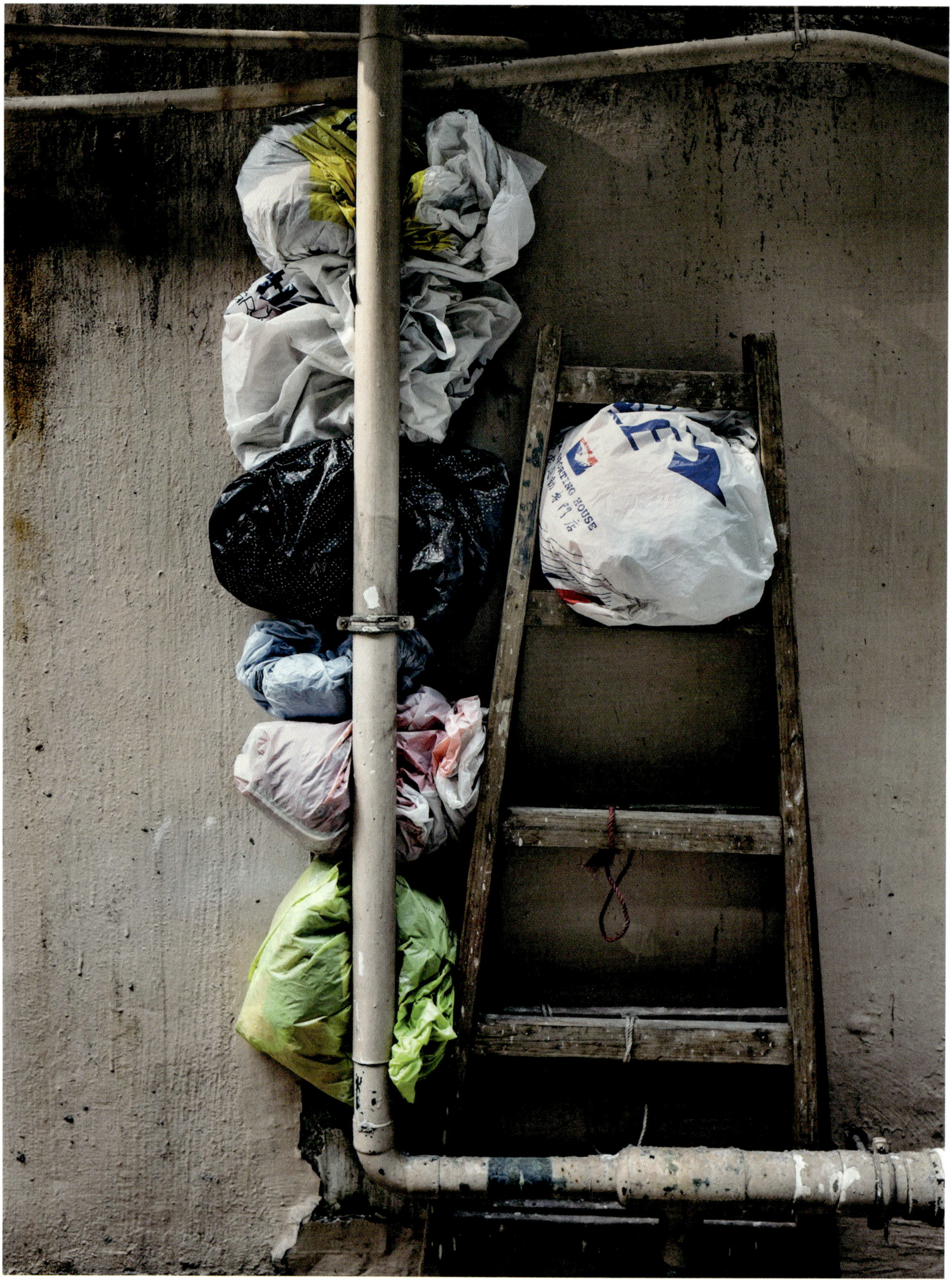

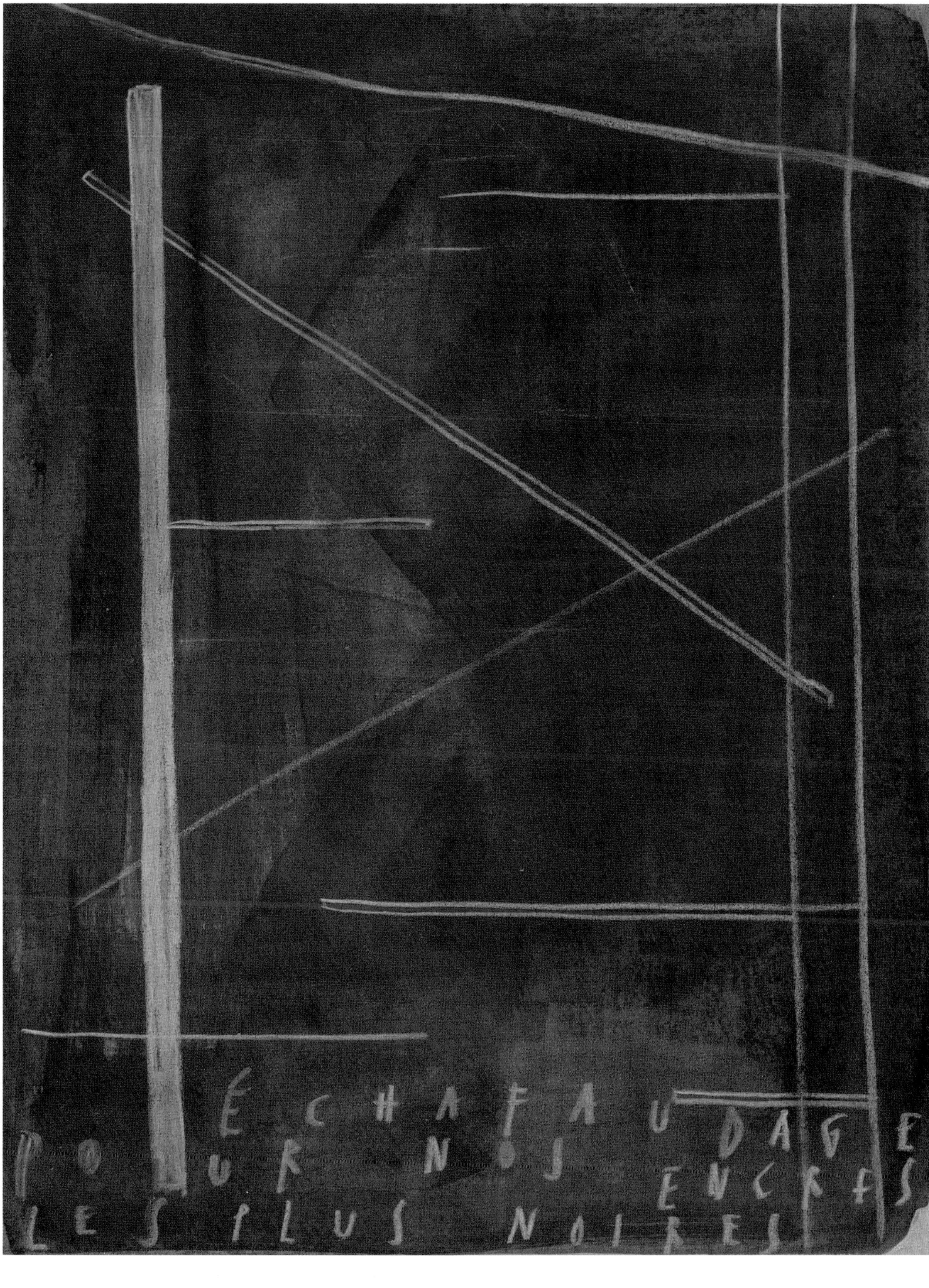

échafaudage pour nos encres les plus noires (scaffolding for our blackest inks), 2014, 25 × 19 cm, mixed media on paper

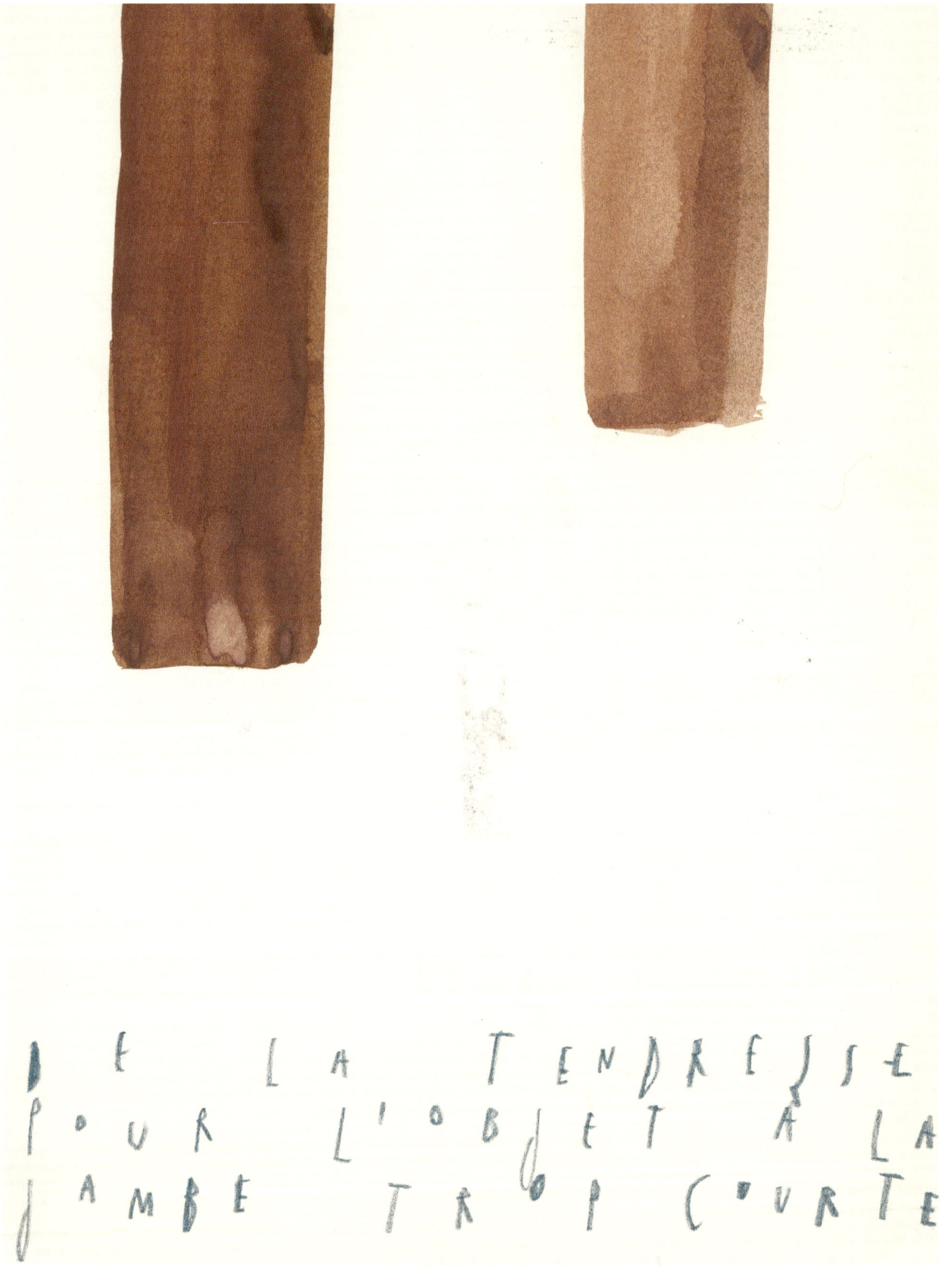

de la tendresse pour l'objet à la jambe trop courte (tenderness for the object with the too short leg), 2014, 25 × 19 cm, mixed media on paper

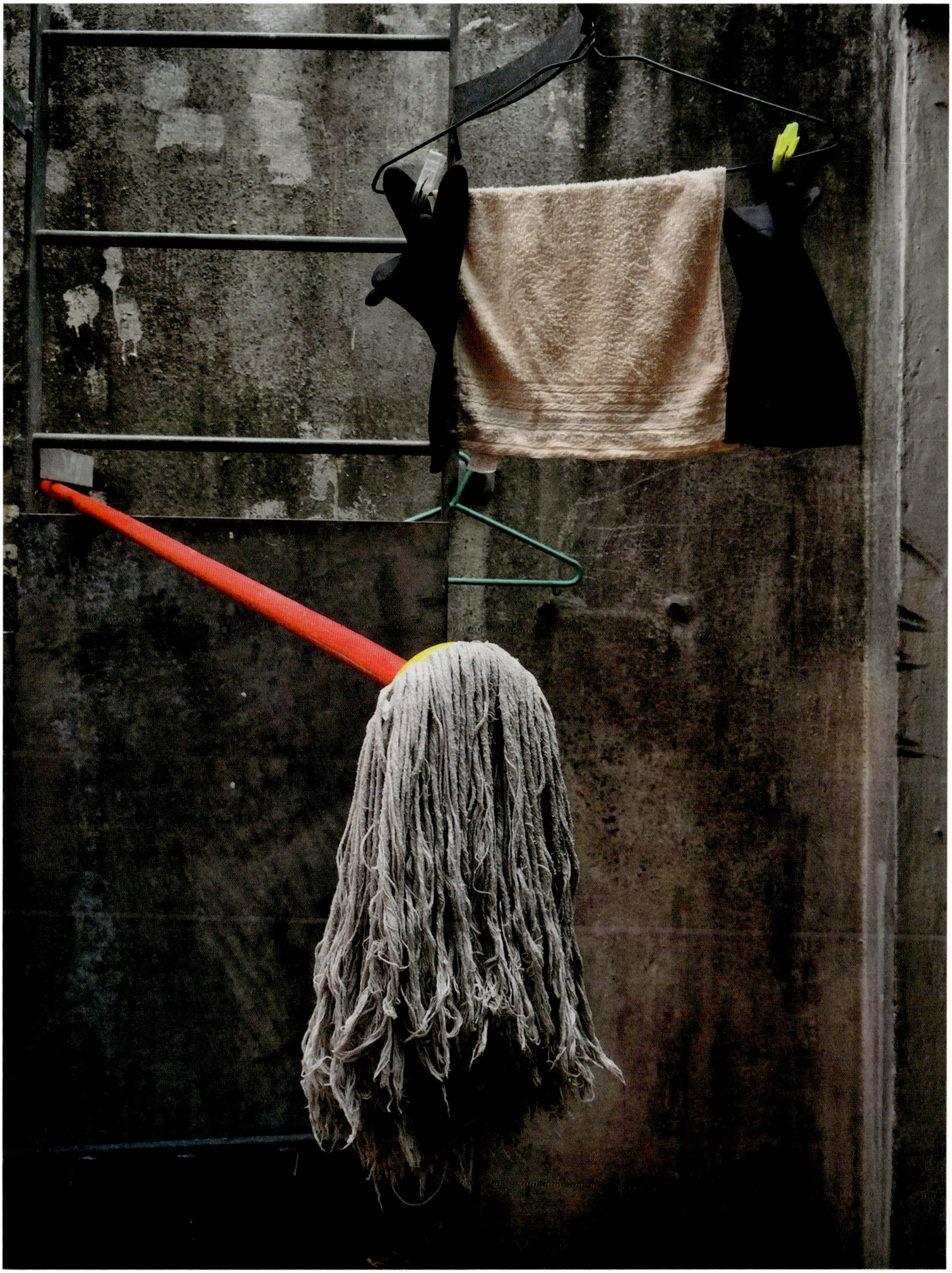

Informal Solutions #110

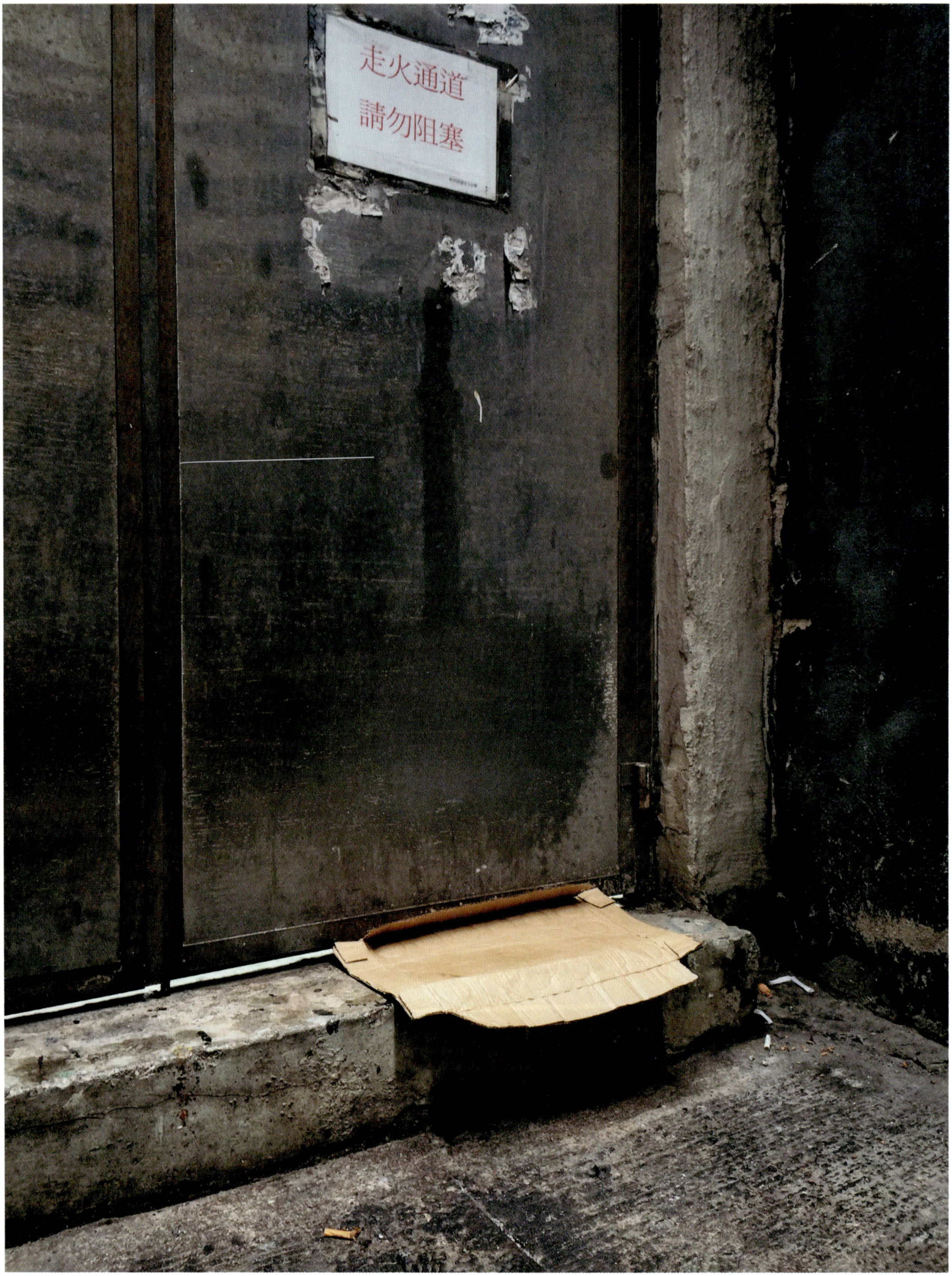
走火通道
請勿阻塞

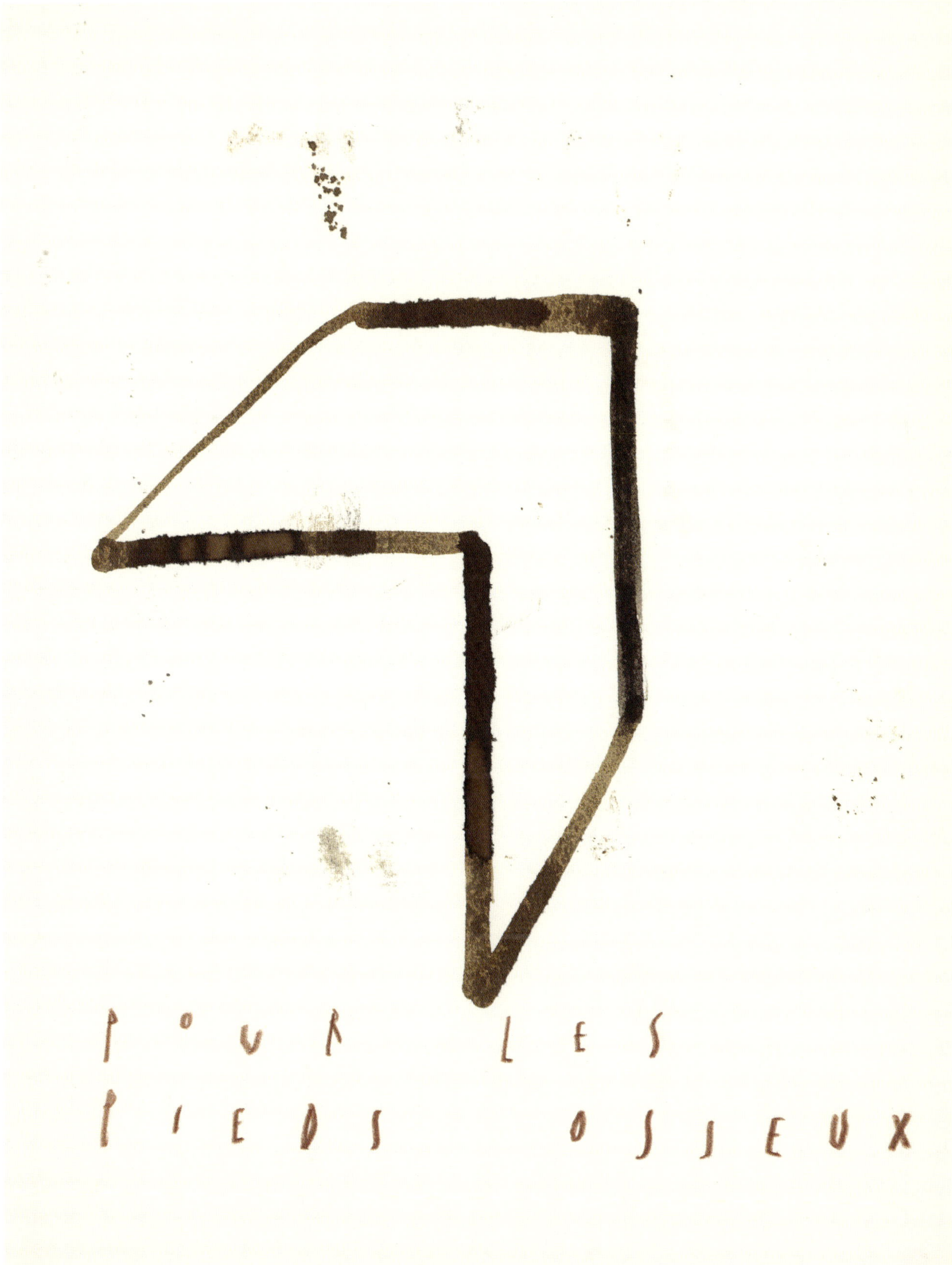

pour les pieds osseux (for the bony feet), 2014, 25 × 19 cm, mixed media on paper

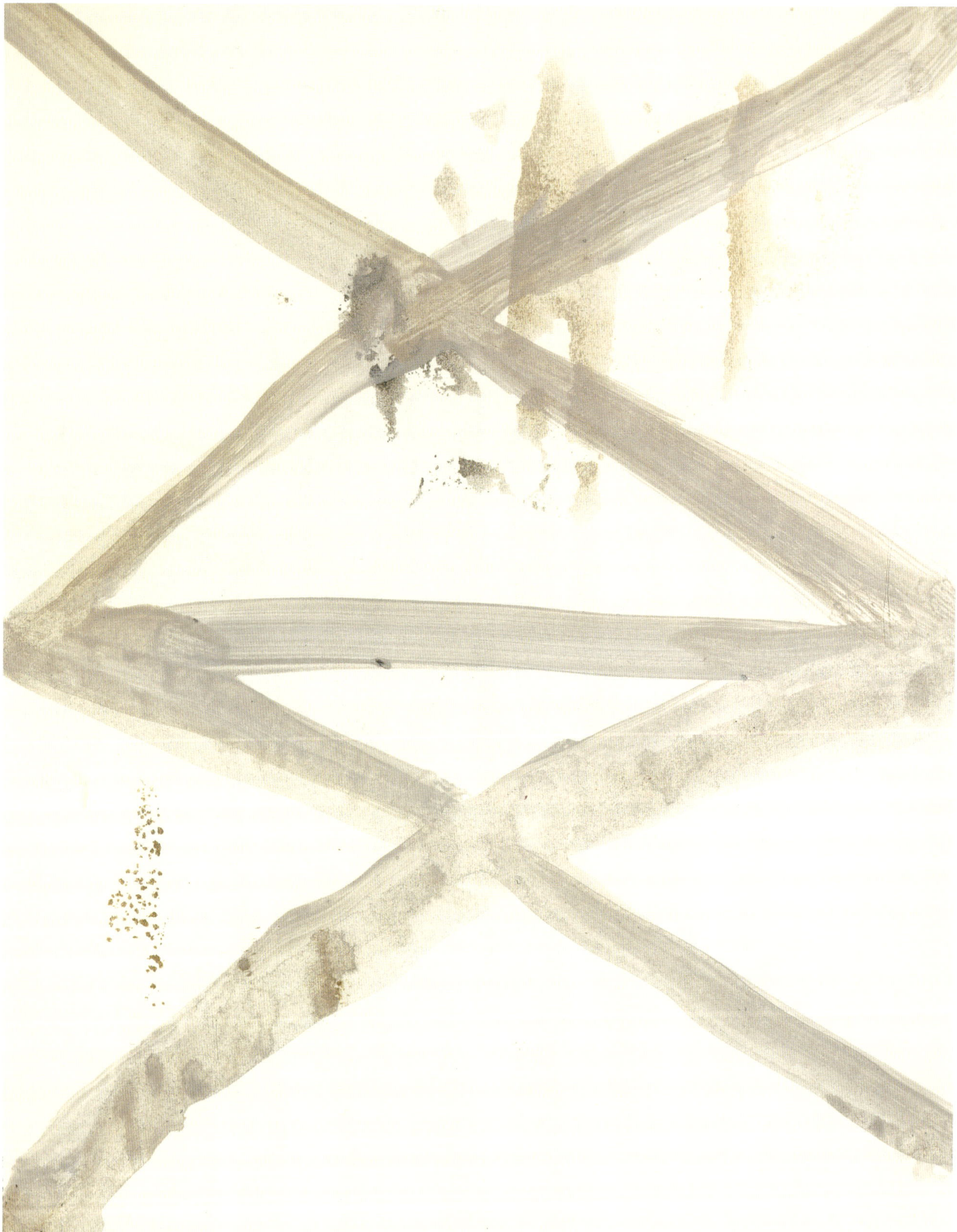

untitled, 2014, 25 × 19 cm, mixed media on paper

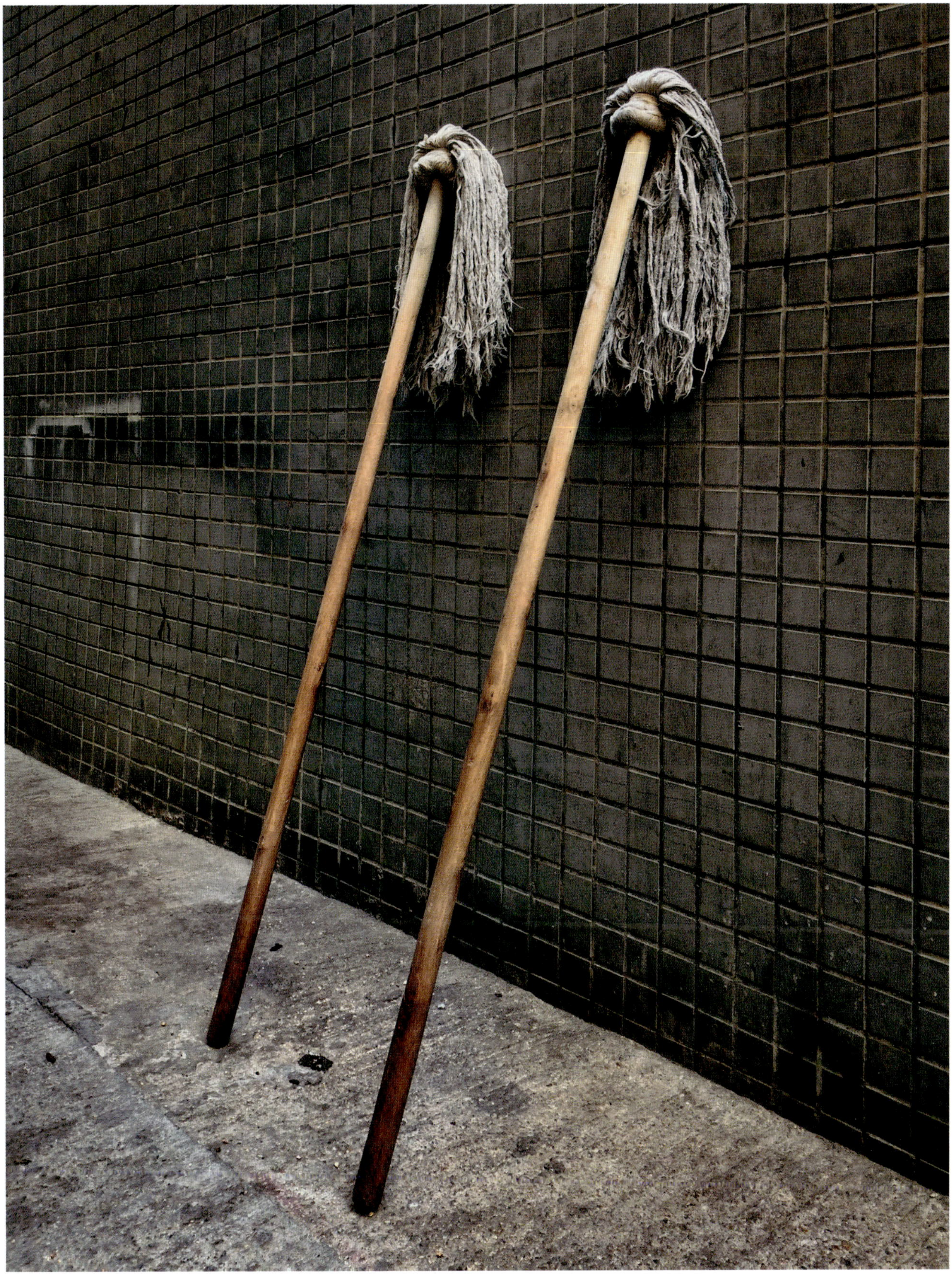

Informal Solutions #112

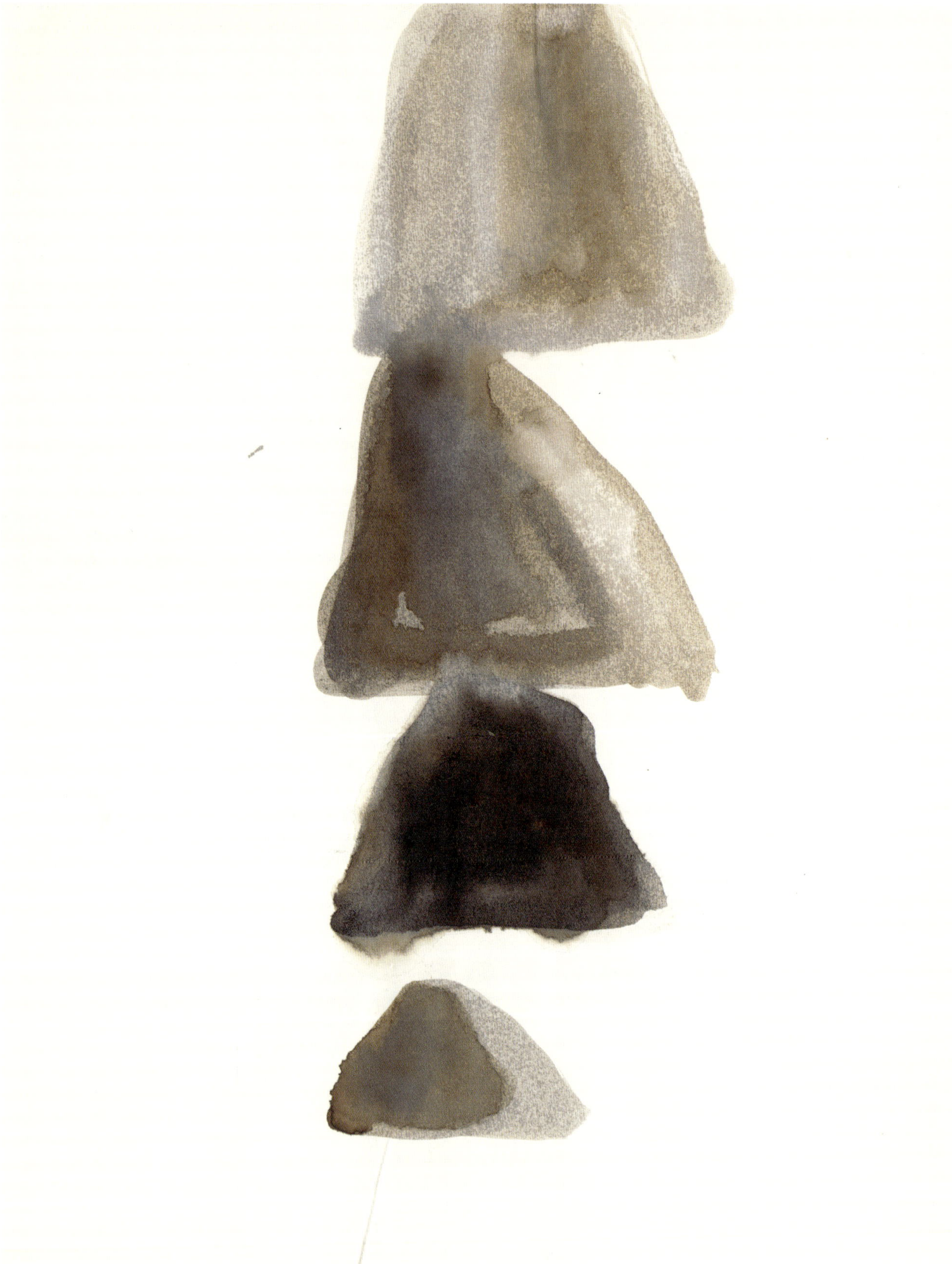

untitled, 2014, 25 × 19 cm, mixed media on paper

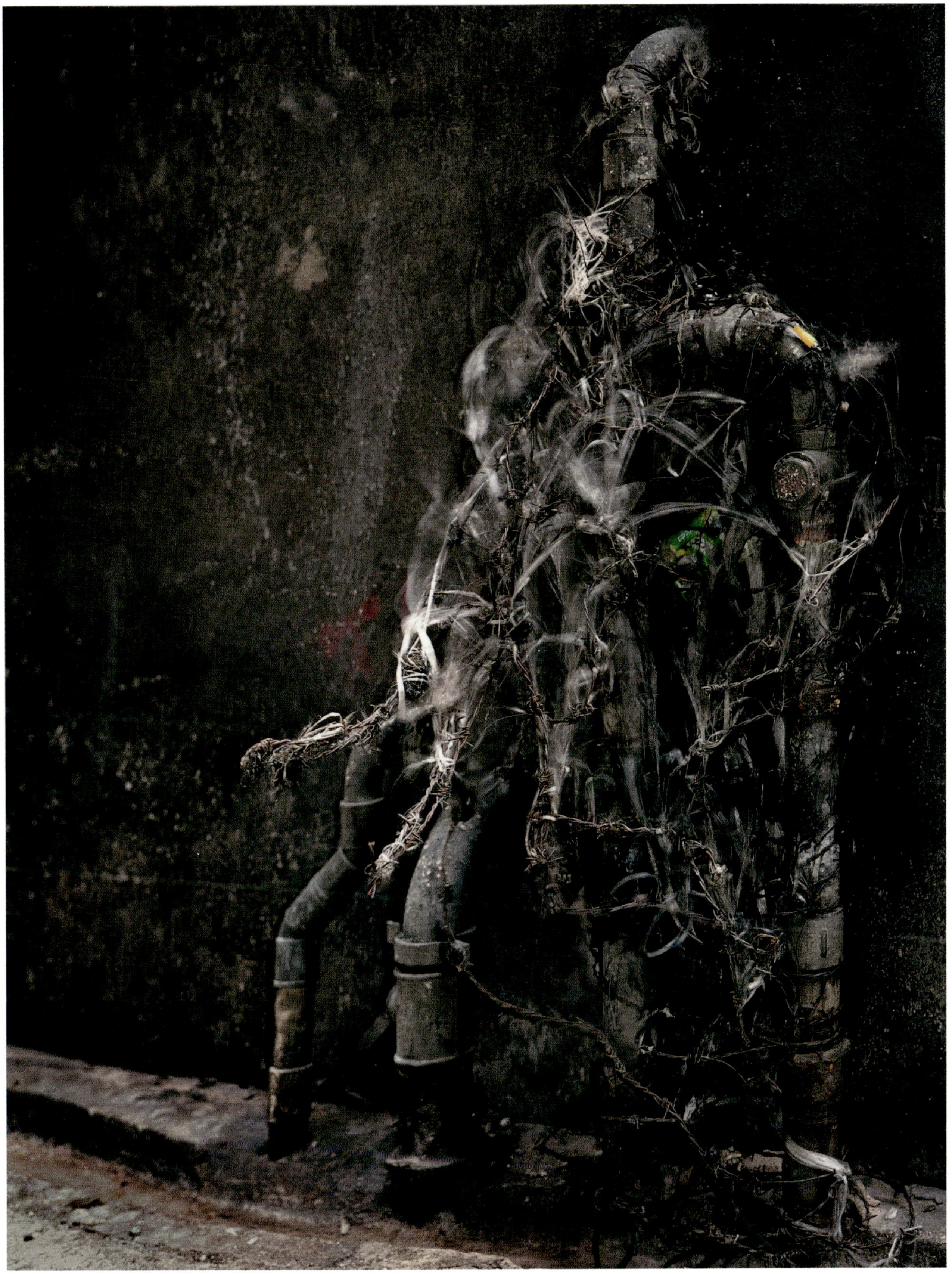

Informal Solutions #113

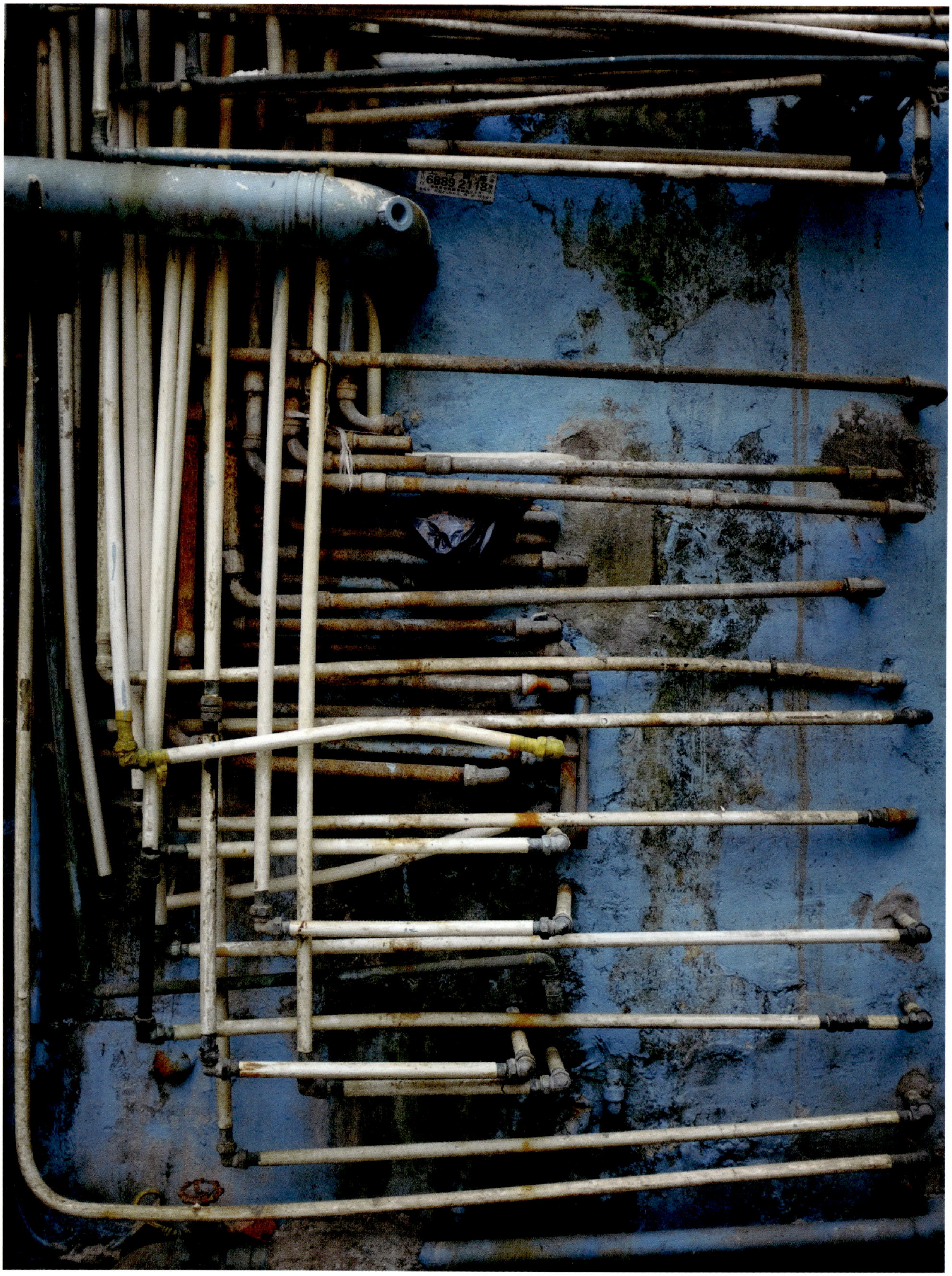

Informal Solutions #114

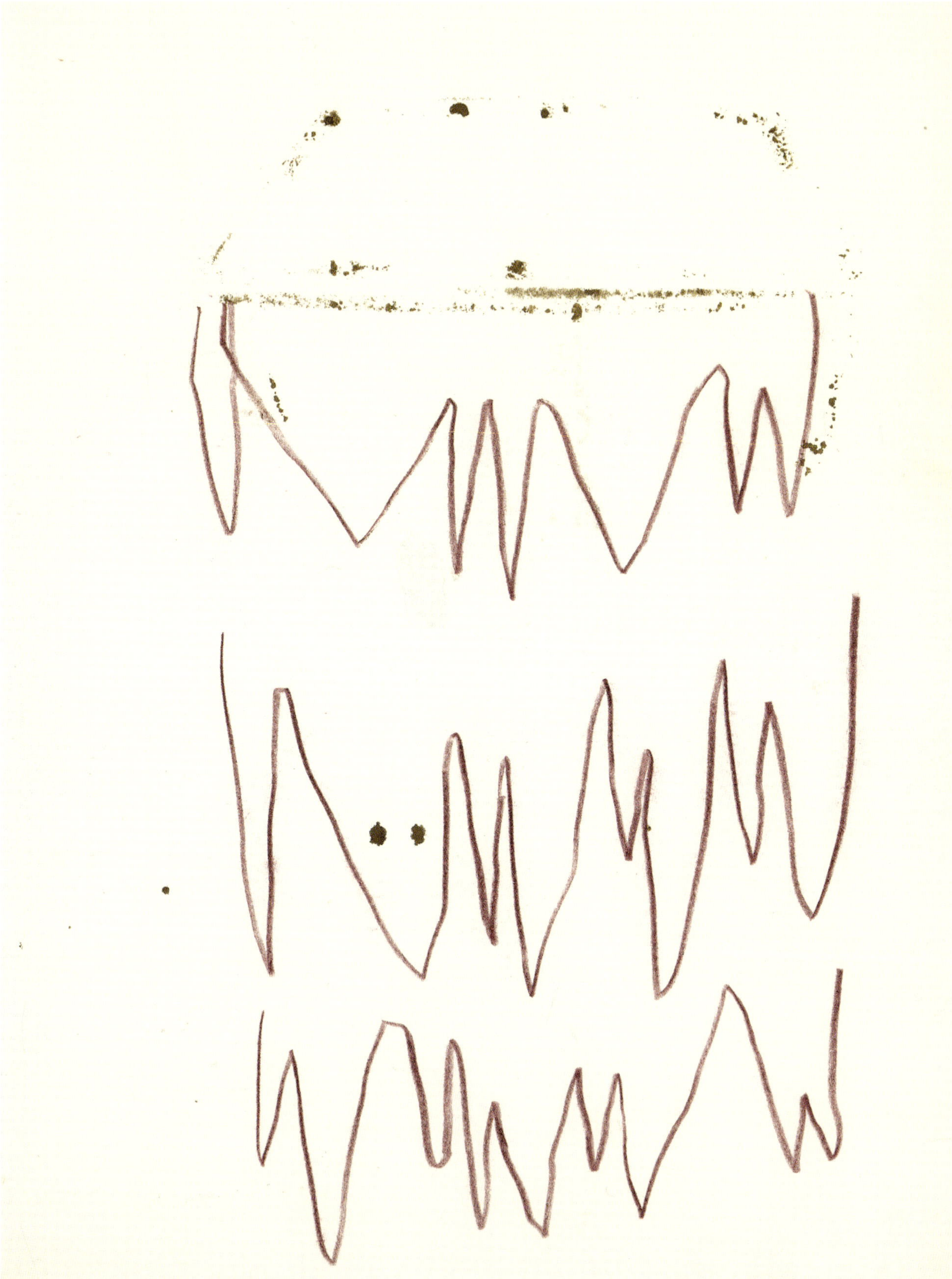

untitled, 2014, 25 × 19 cm, mixed media on paper

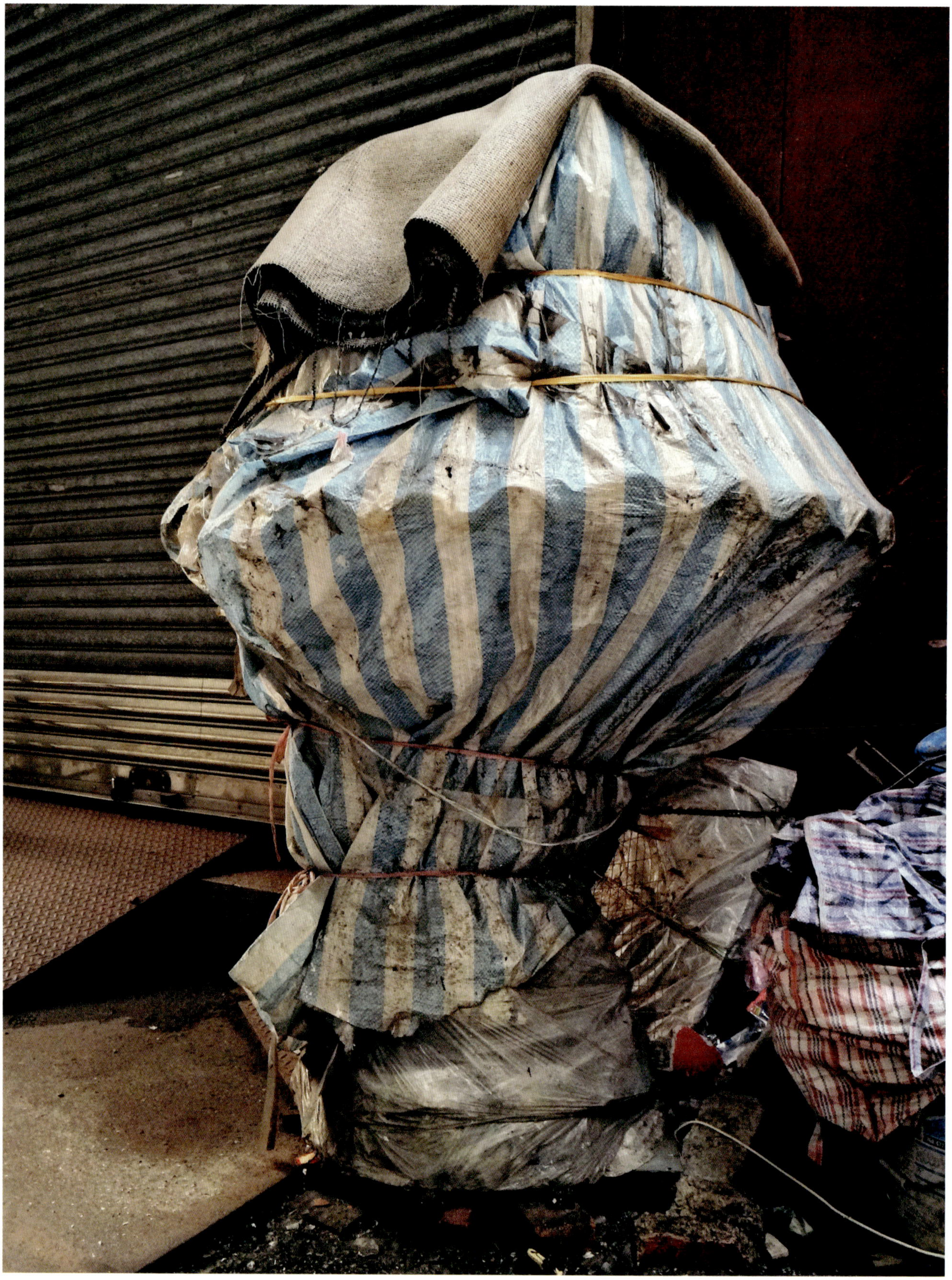

Informal Solutions #115

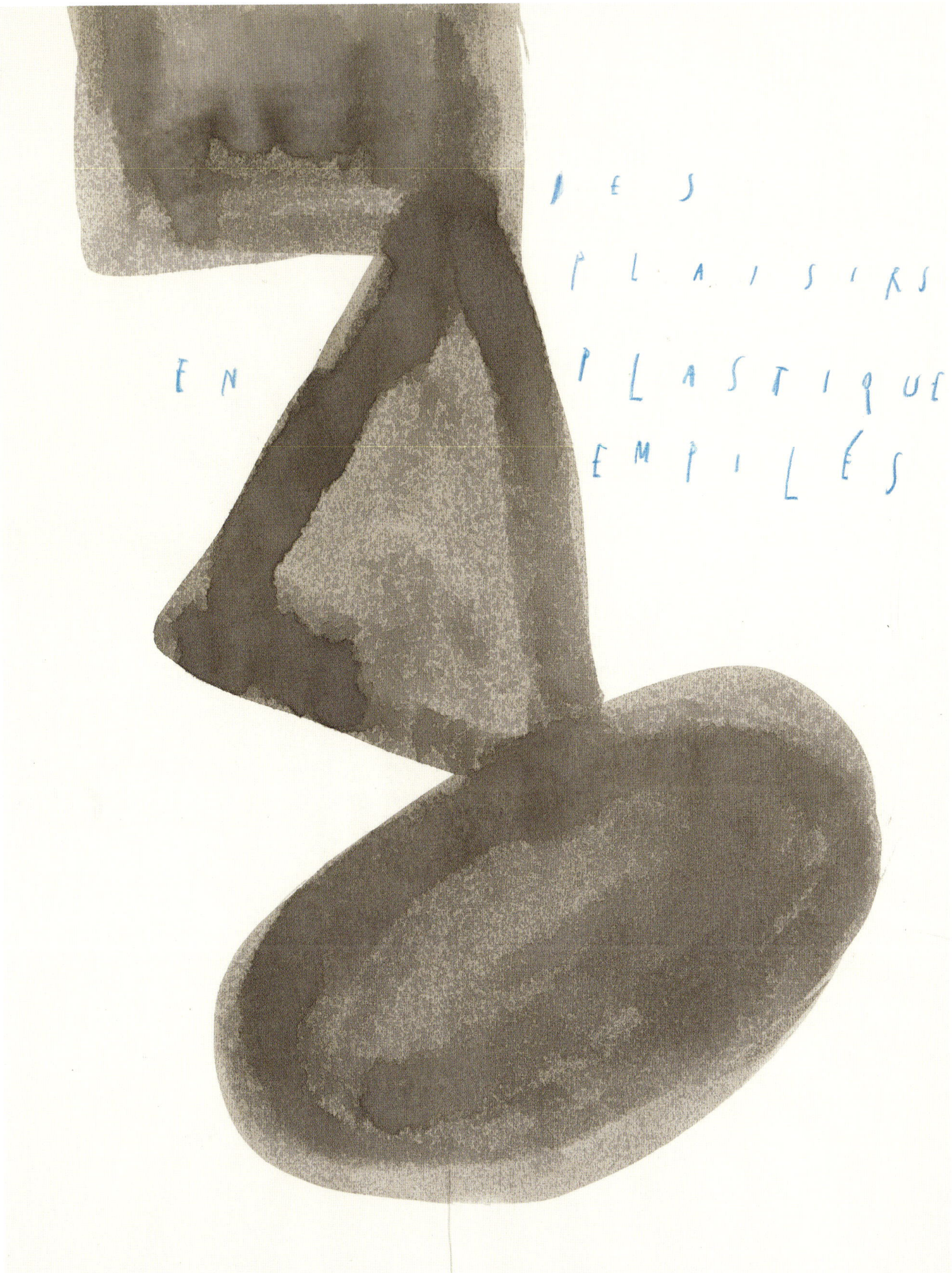

des plaisirs en plastique empilés (stacked plastic pleasures), 2014, 25 × 19 cm, mixed media on paper

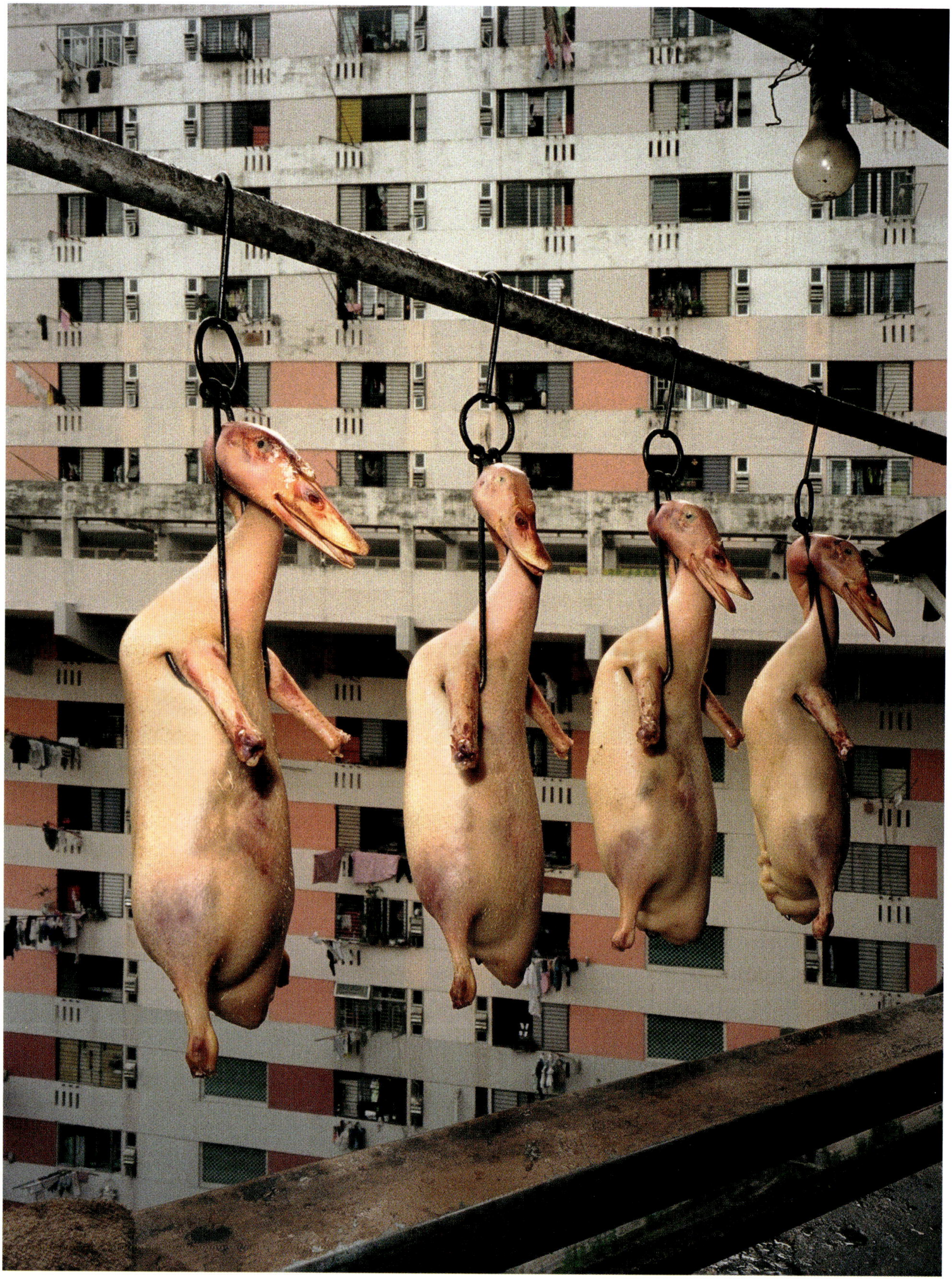

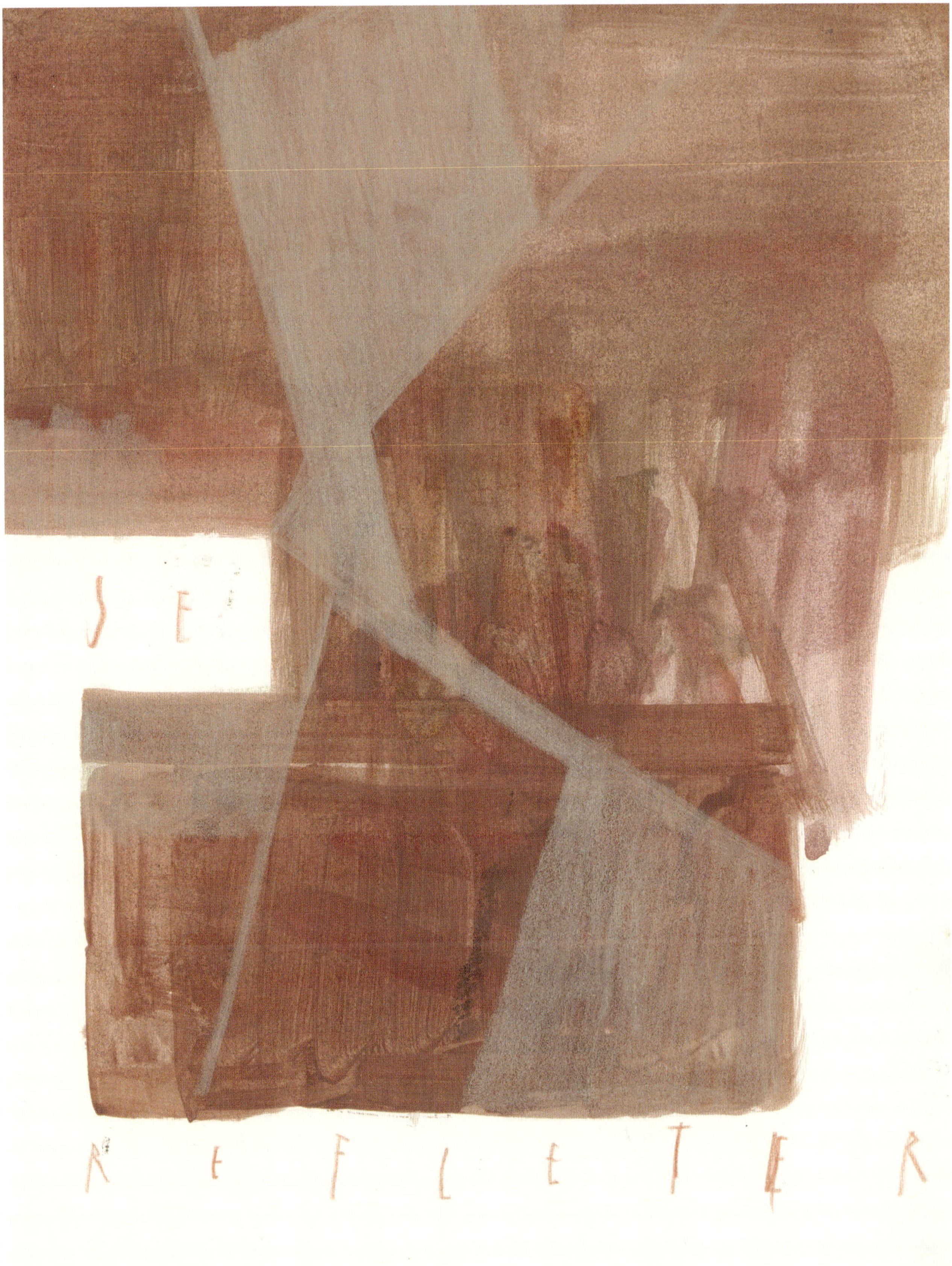

se refléter (reflecting oneself), 2014, 25 × 19 cm, mixed media on paper

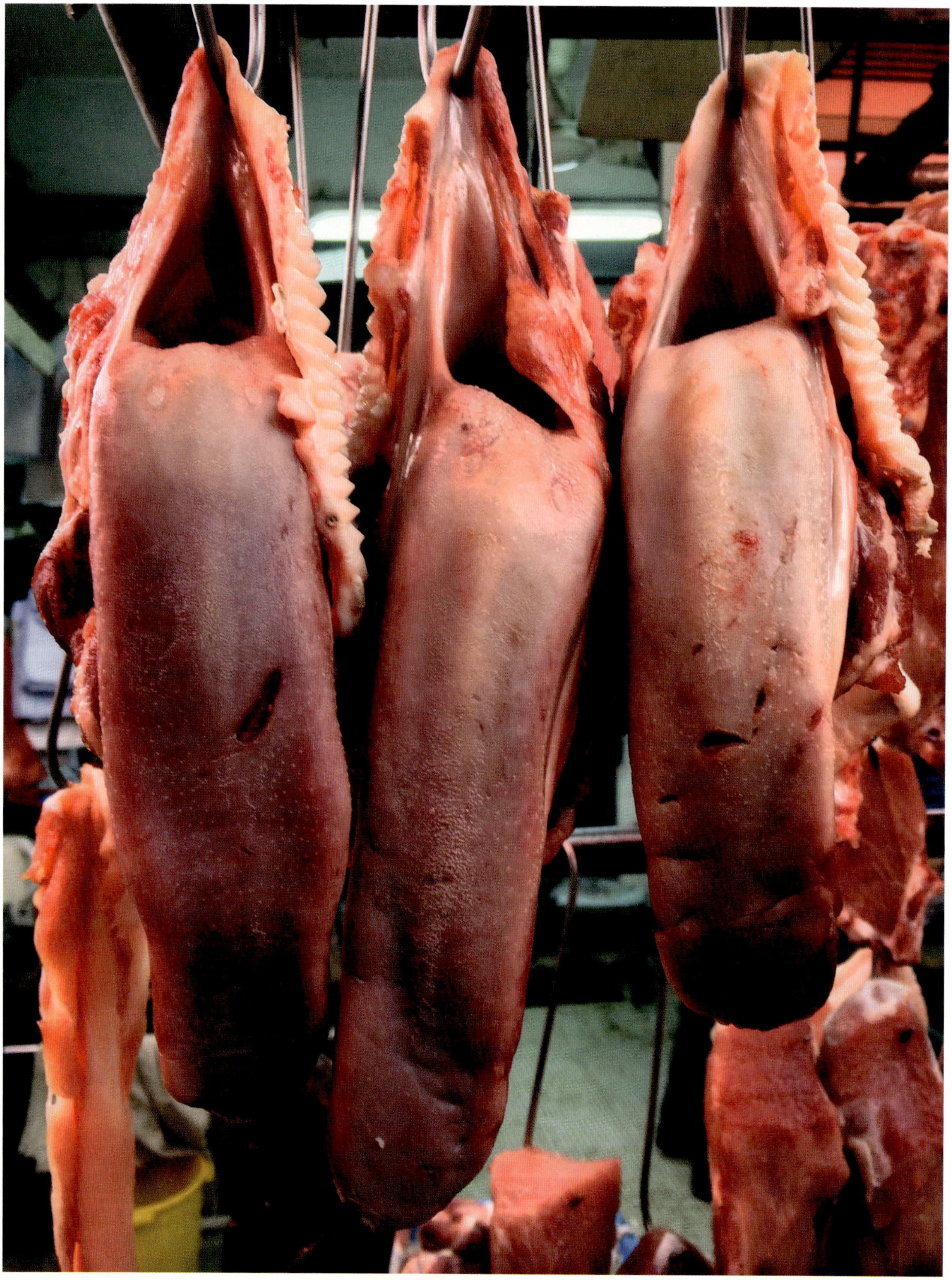

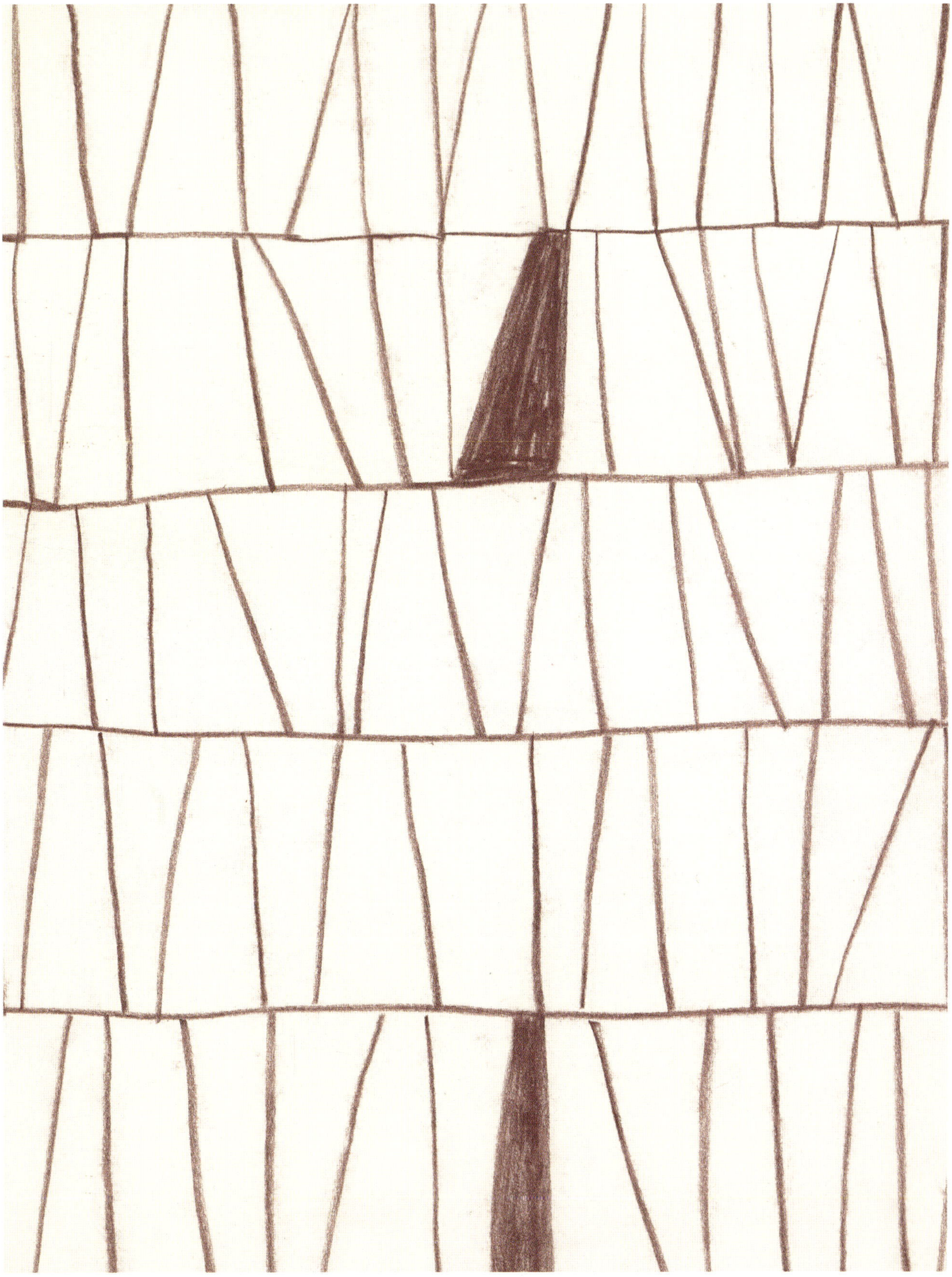

untitled, 2014, 25 × 19 cm, mixed media on paper

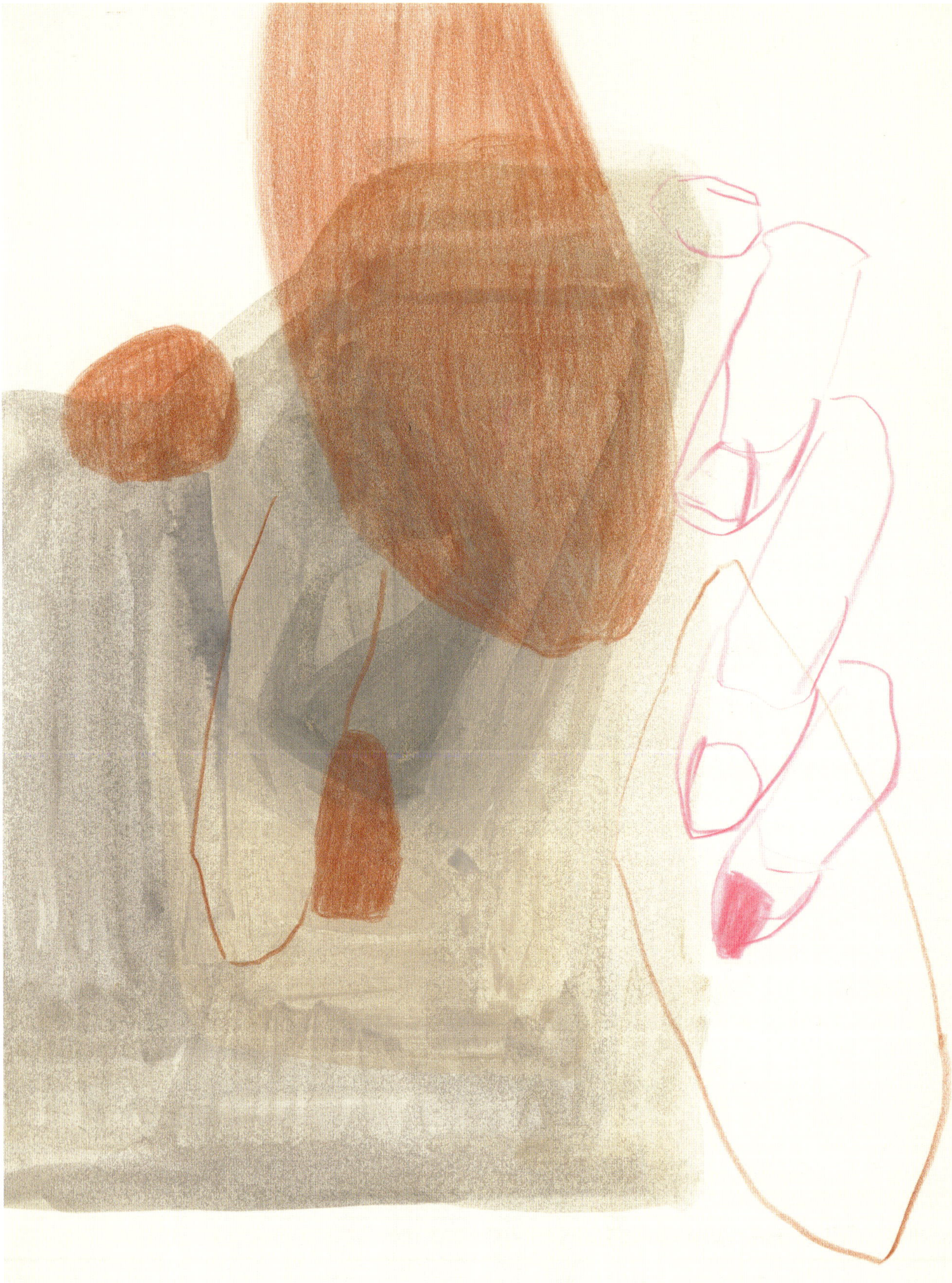

untitled, 2014, 25 × 19 cm, mixed media on paper

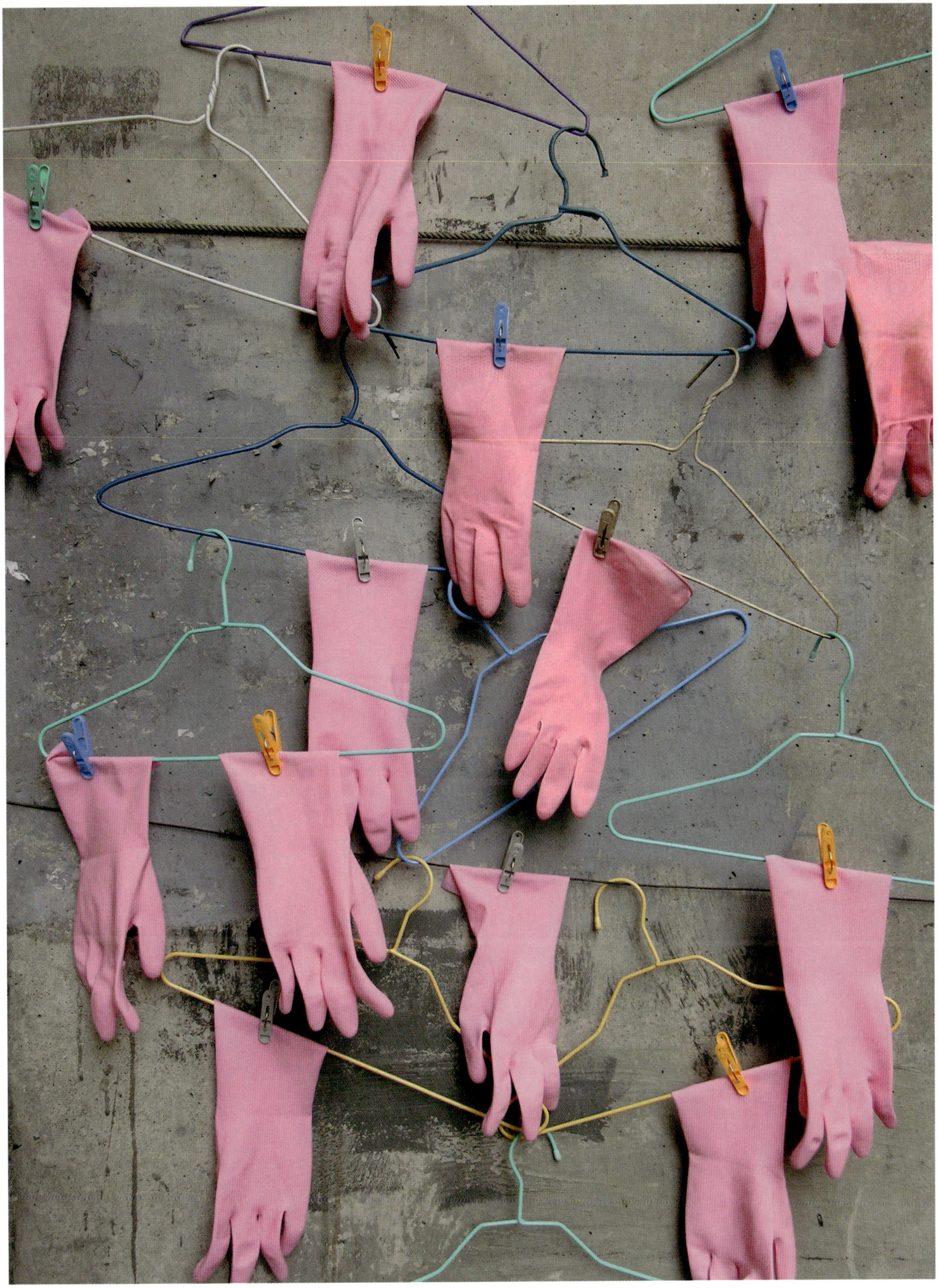

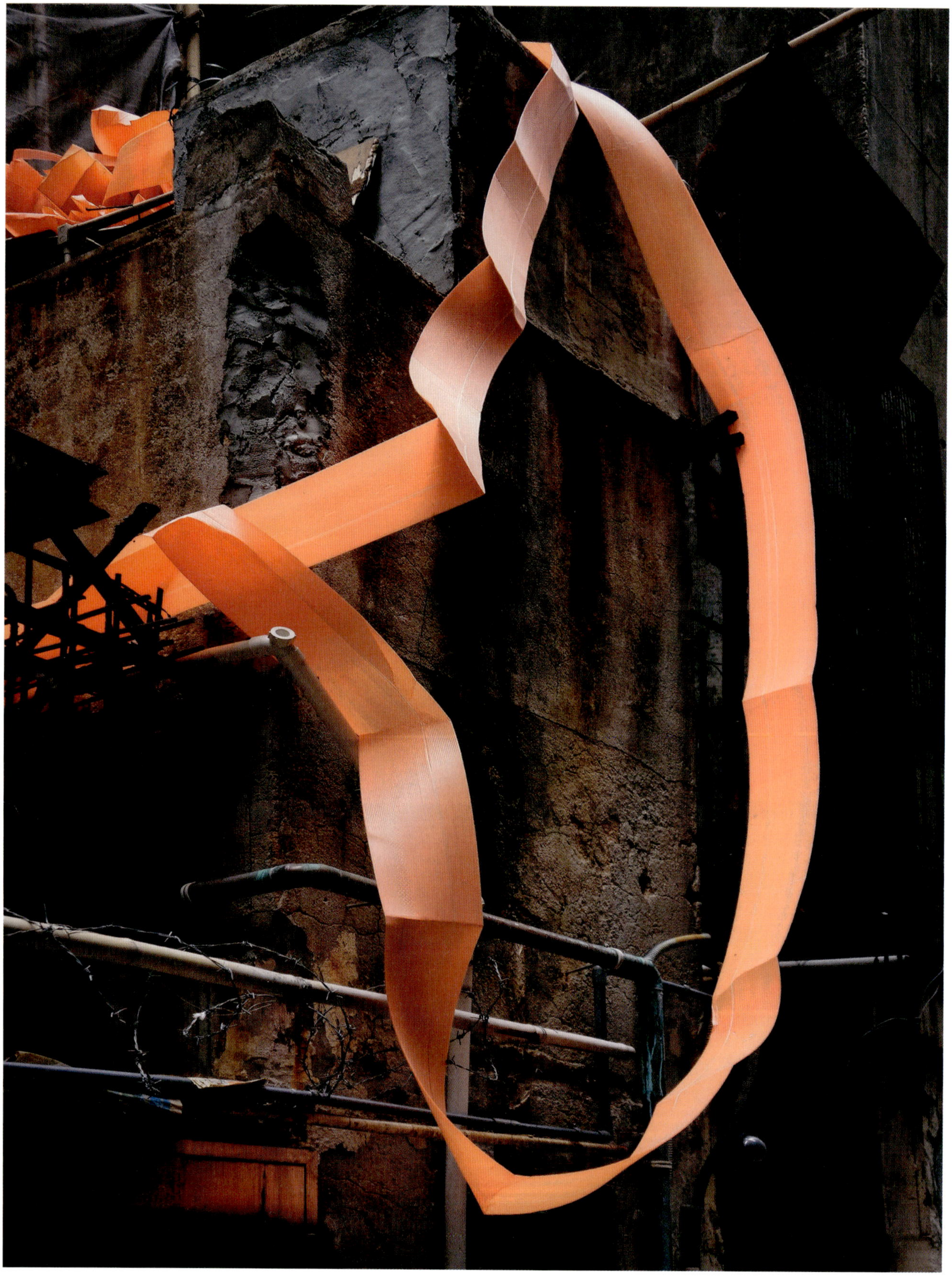

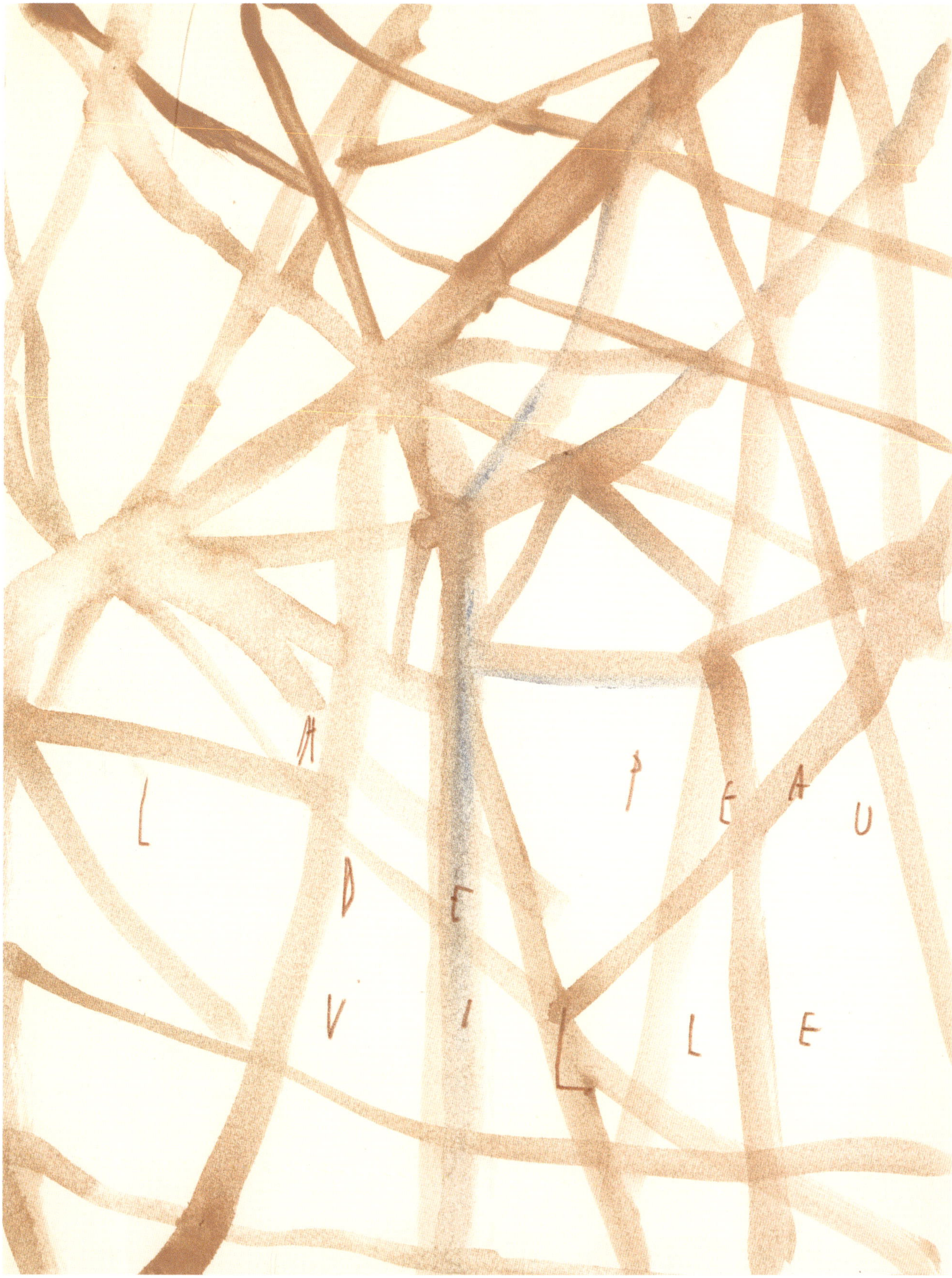

la peau de ville (the city skin), 2014, 25 × 19 cm, mixed media on paper

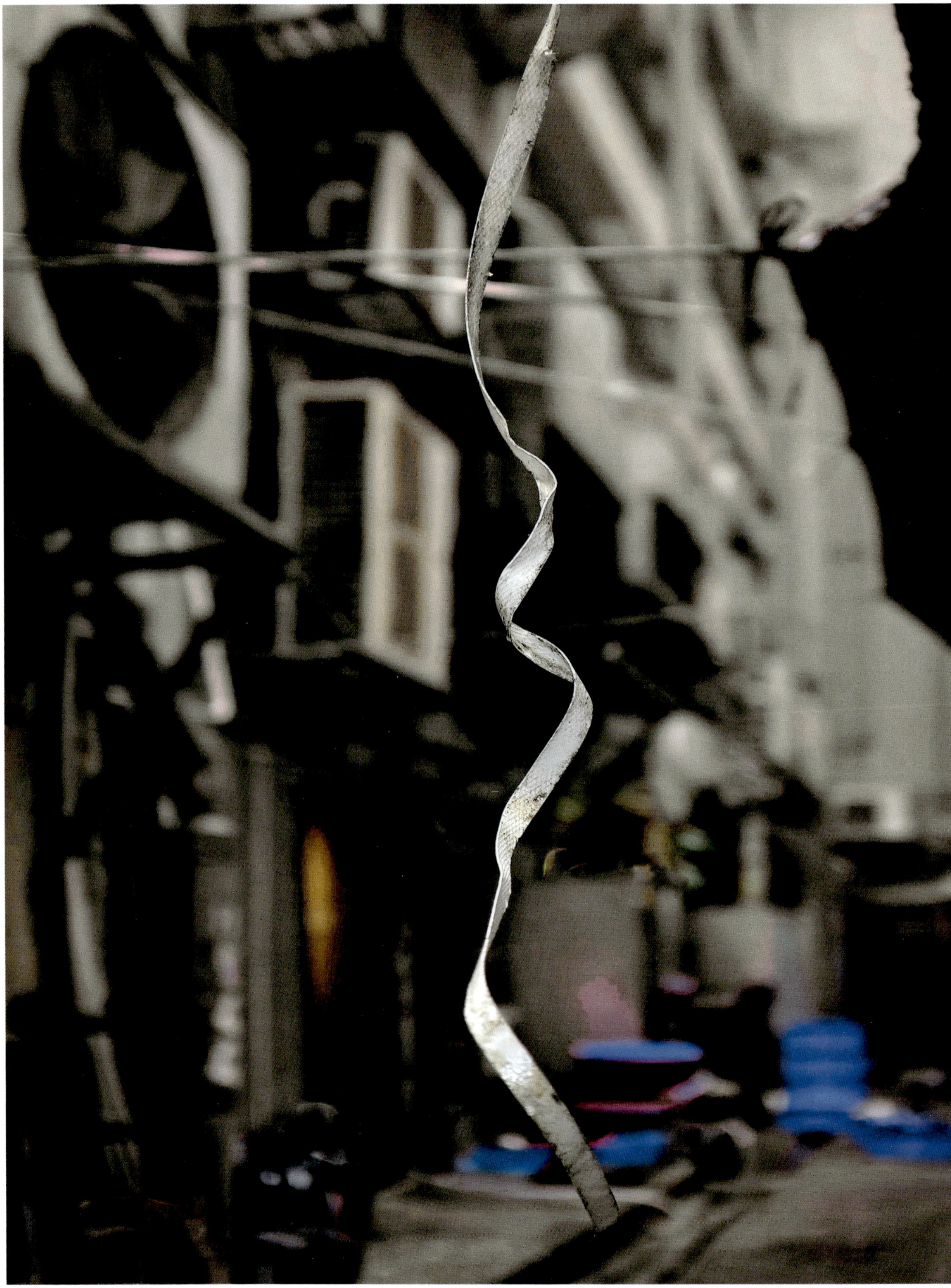

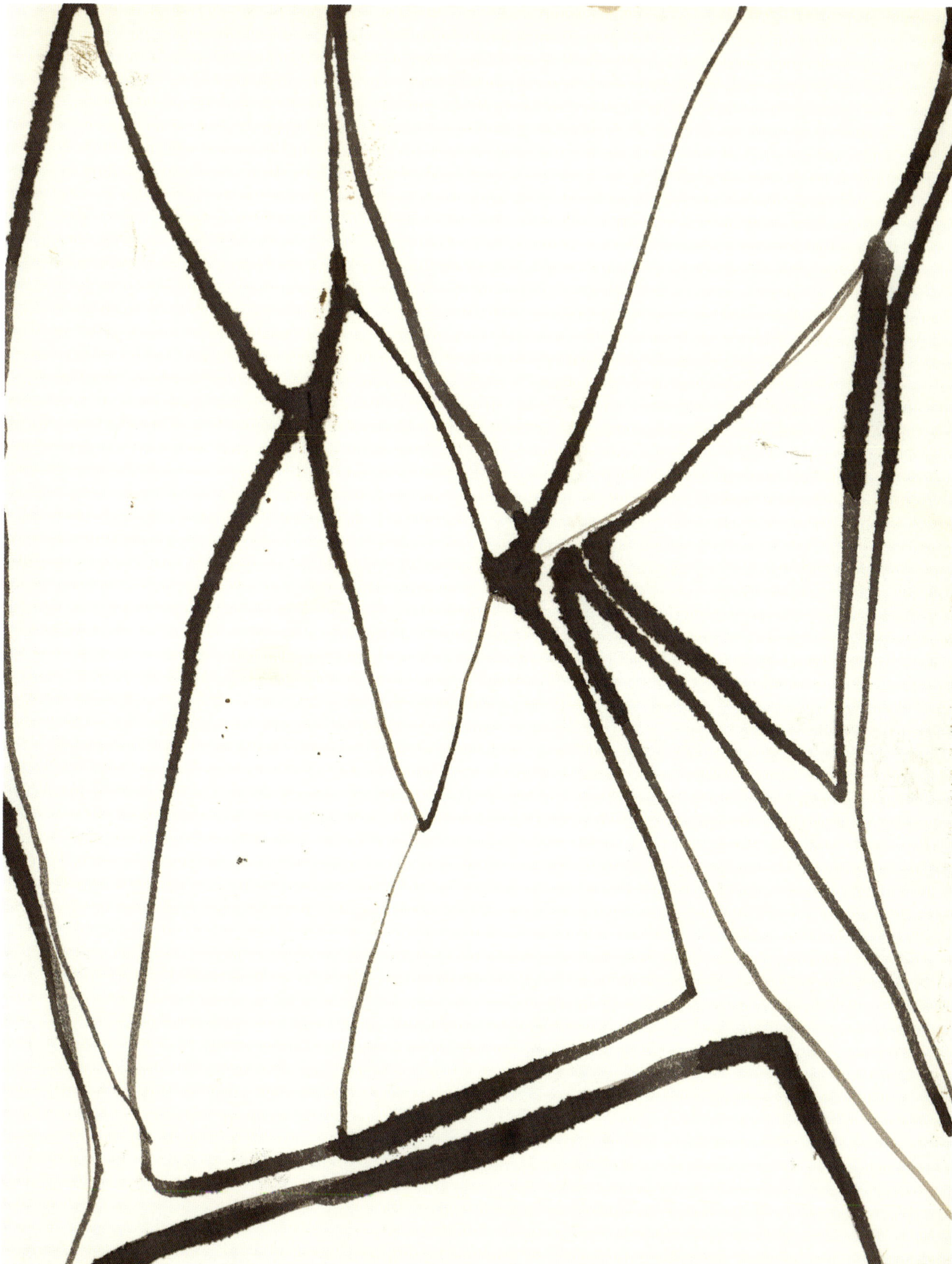

untitled, 2014, 25 × 19 cm, mixed media on paper

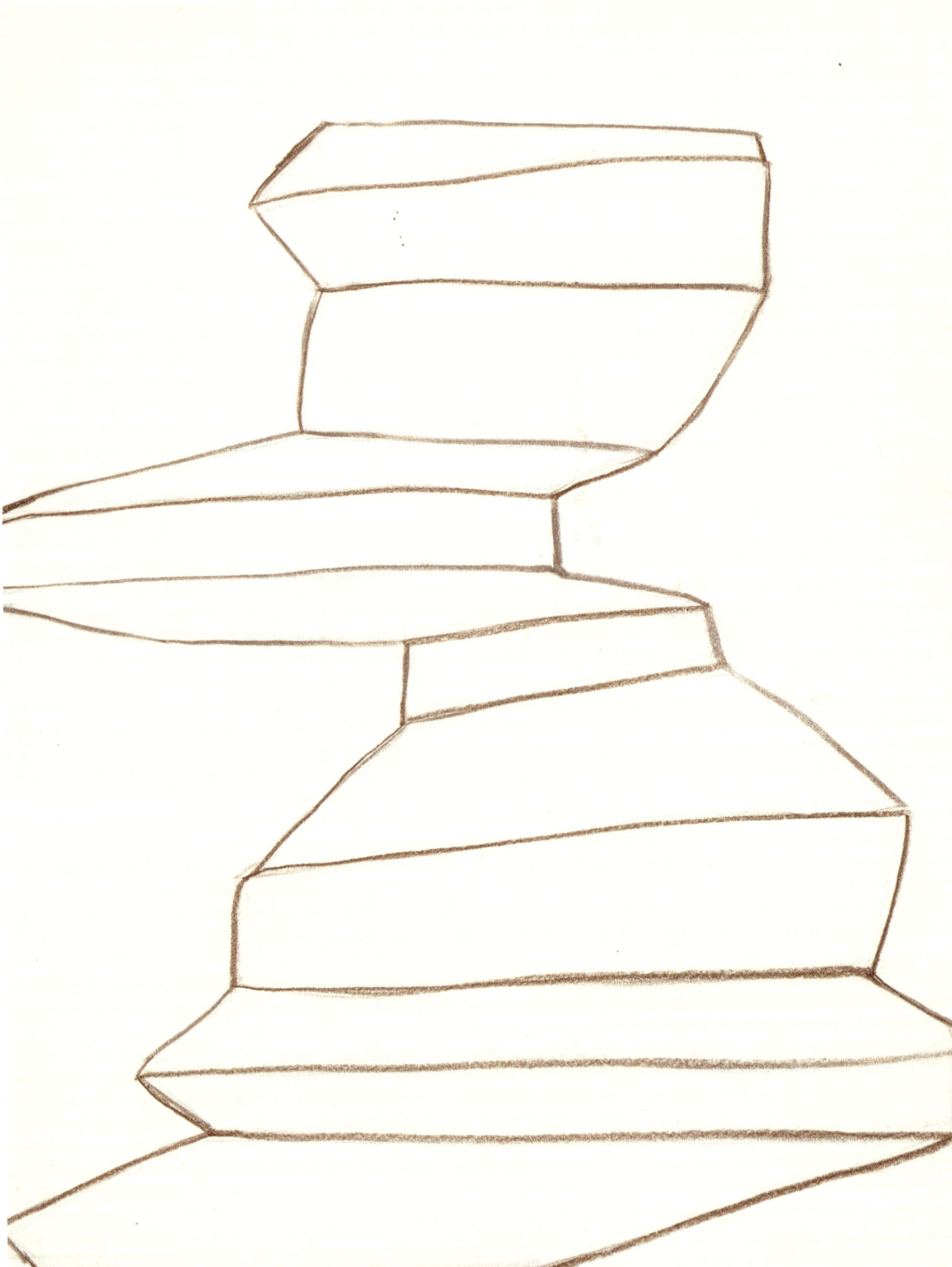

untitled, 2014, 25 × 19 cm, mixed media on paper

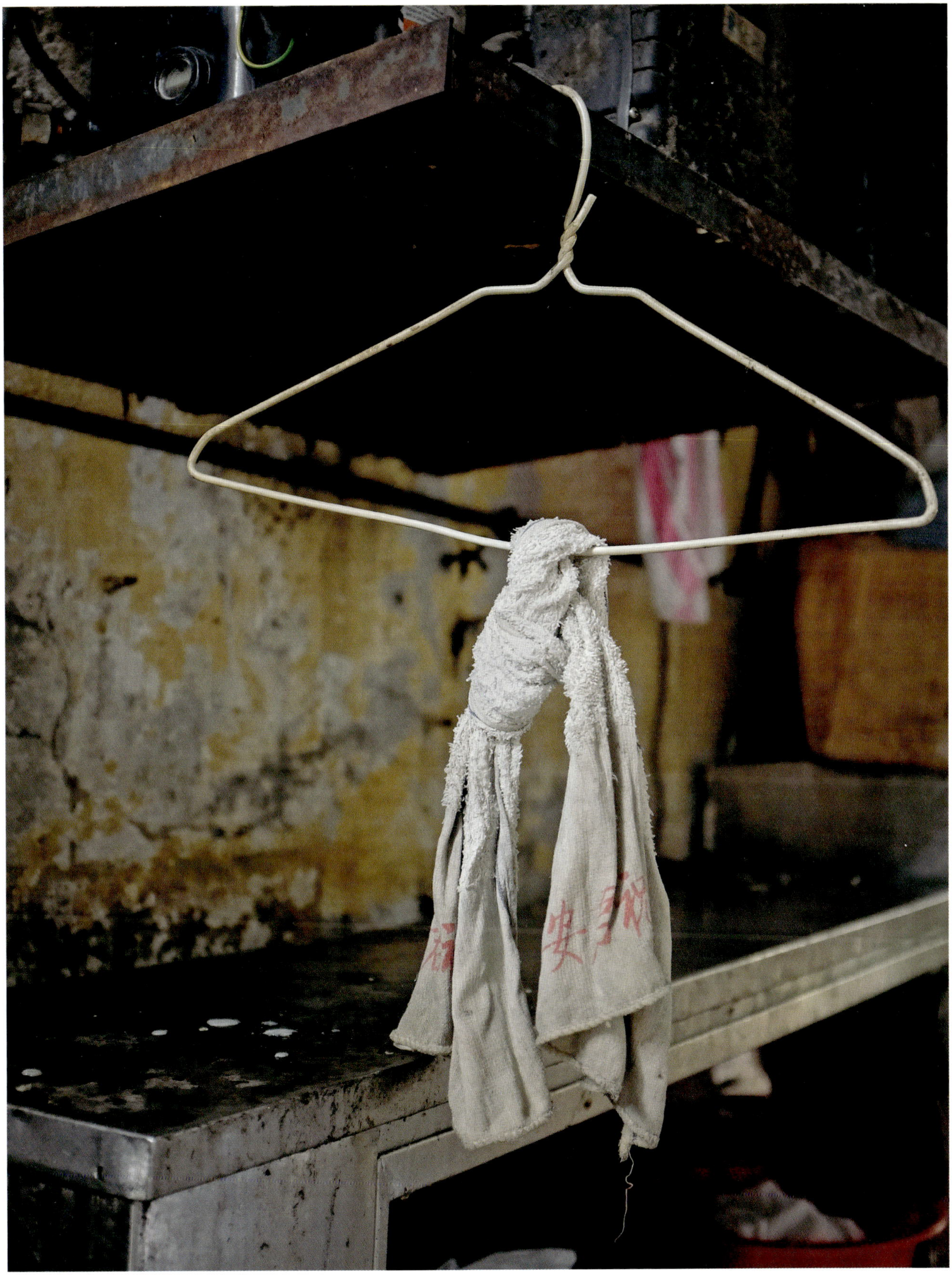

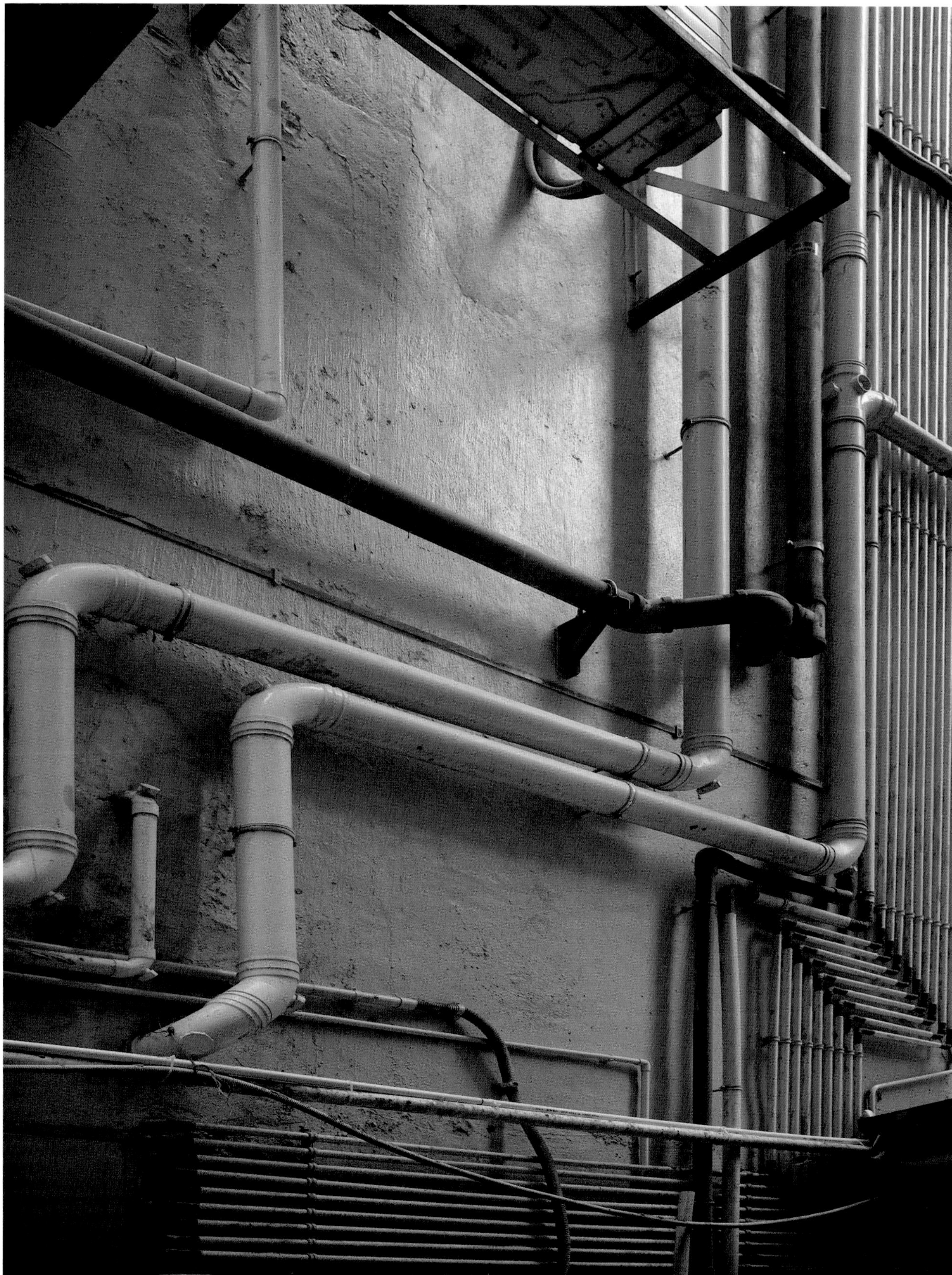

untitled, 2014, 25 × 19 cm, mixed media on paper

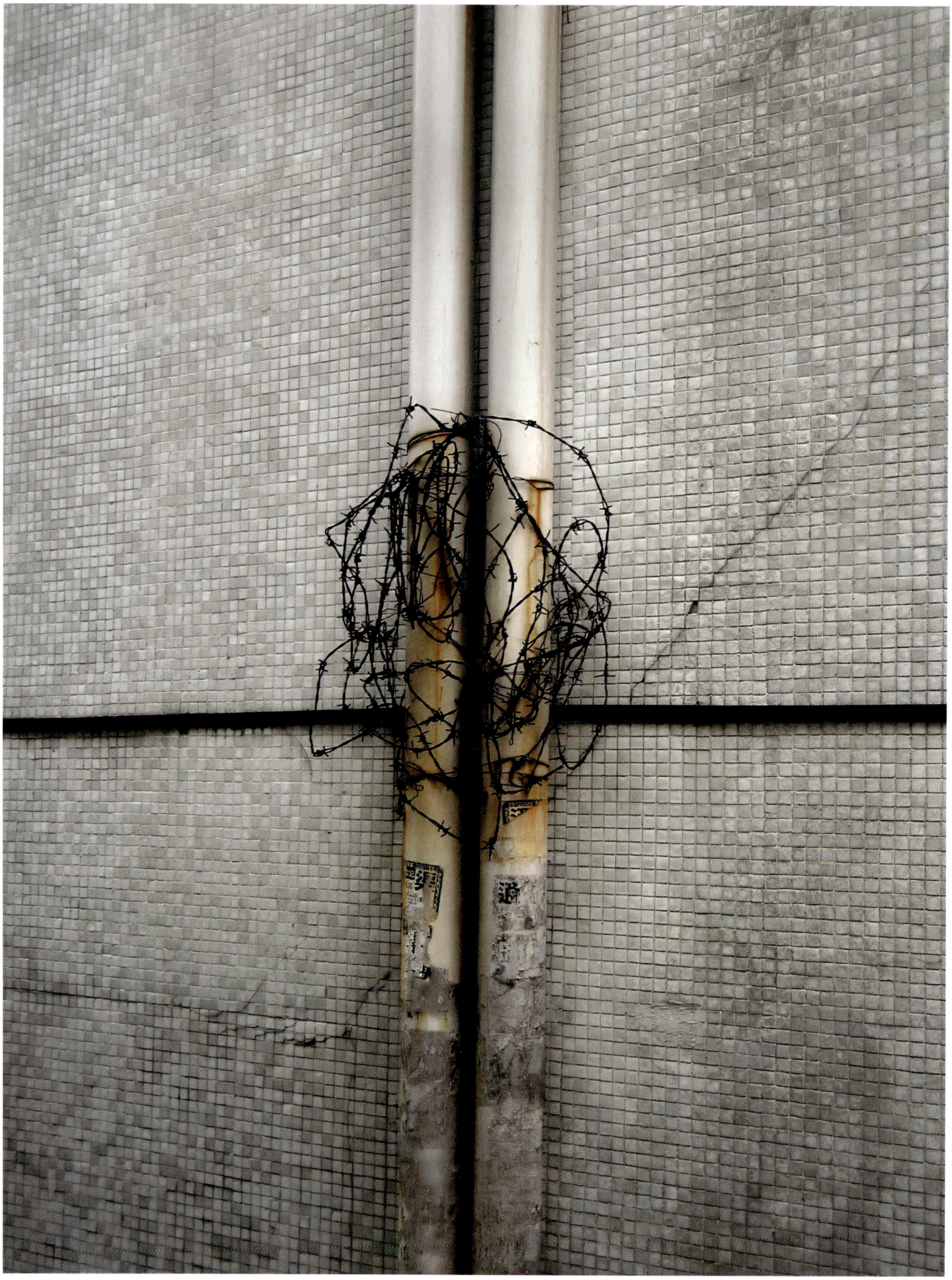

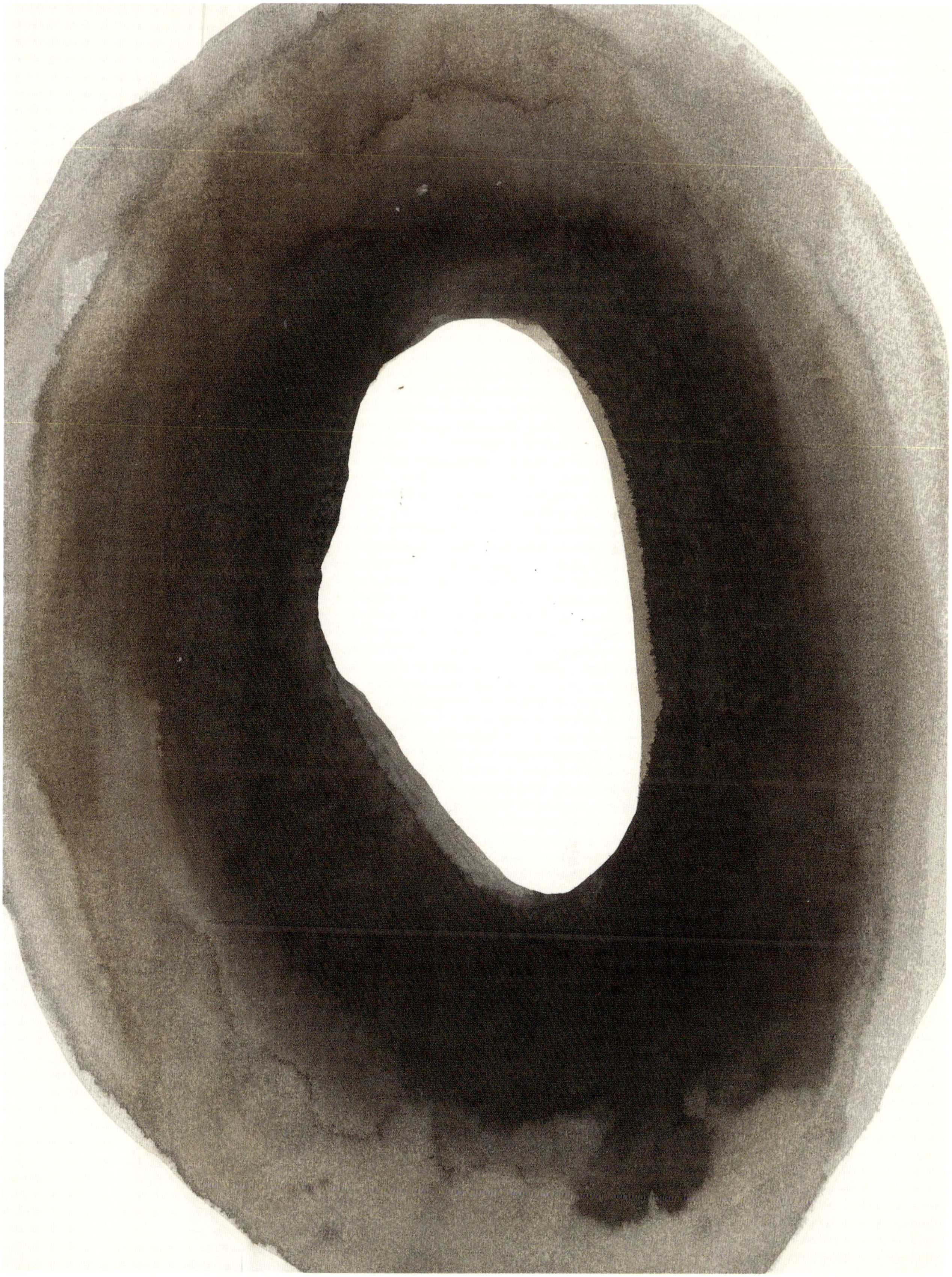

untitled, 2014, 25 × 19 cm, mixed media on paper

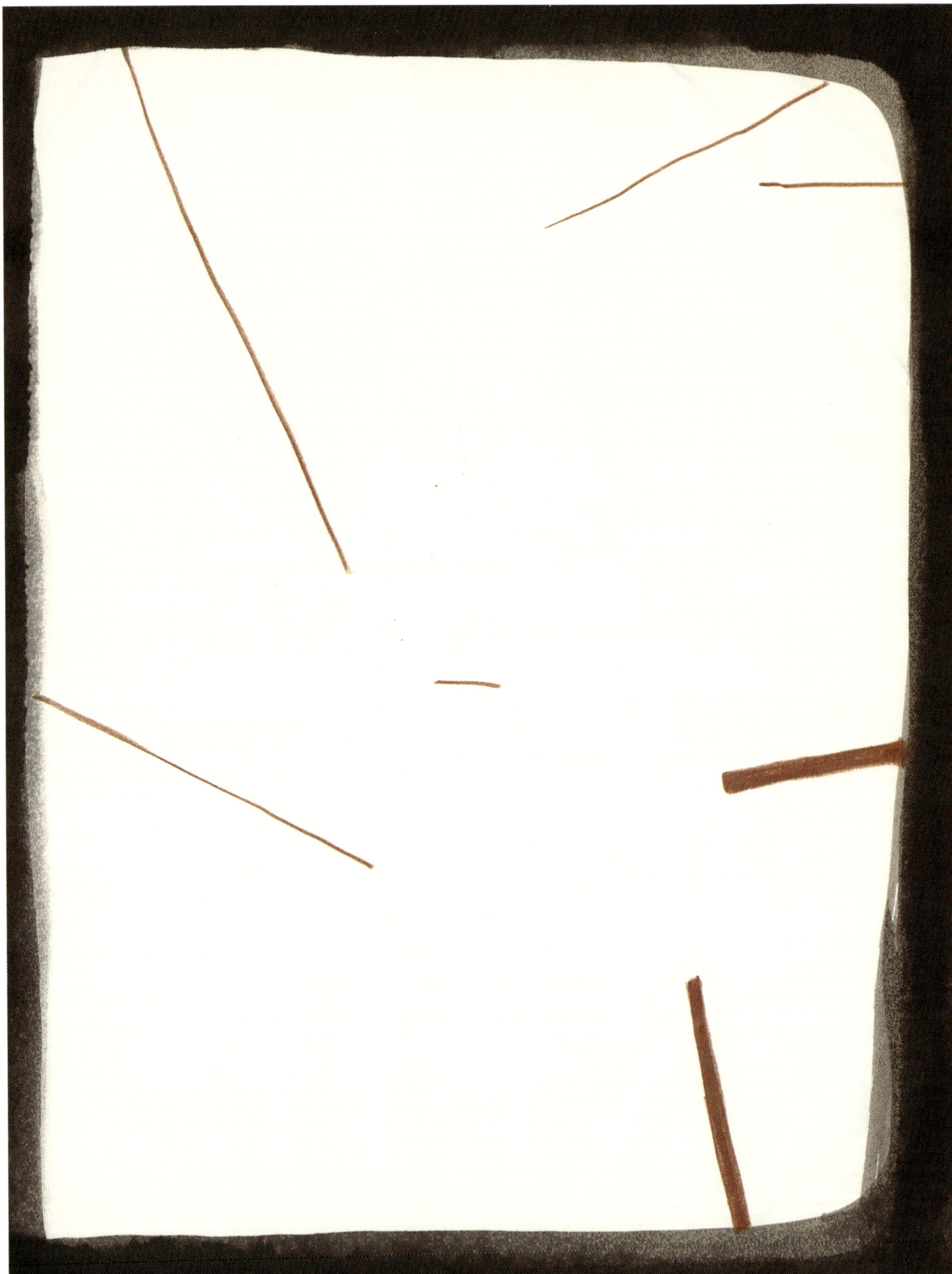

untitled, 2014, 25 × 19 cm, mixed media on paper

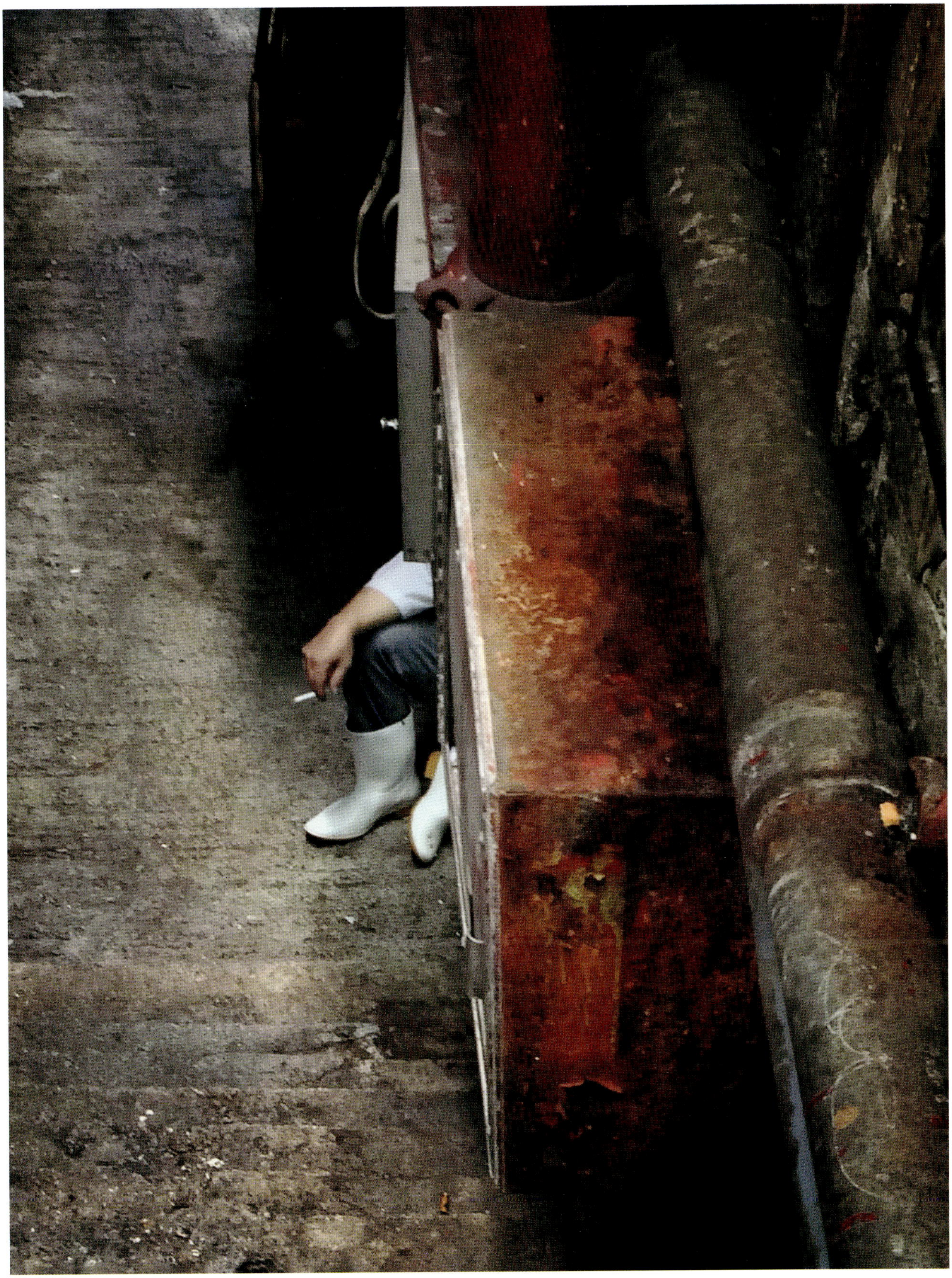

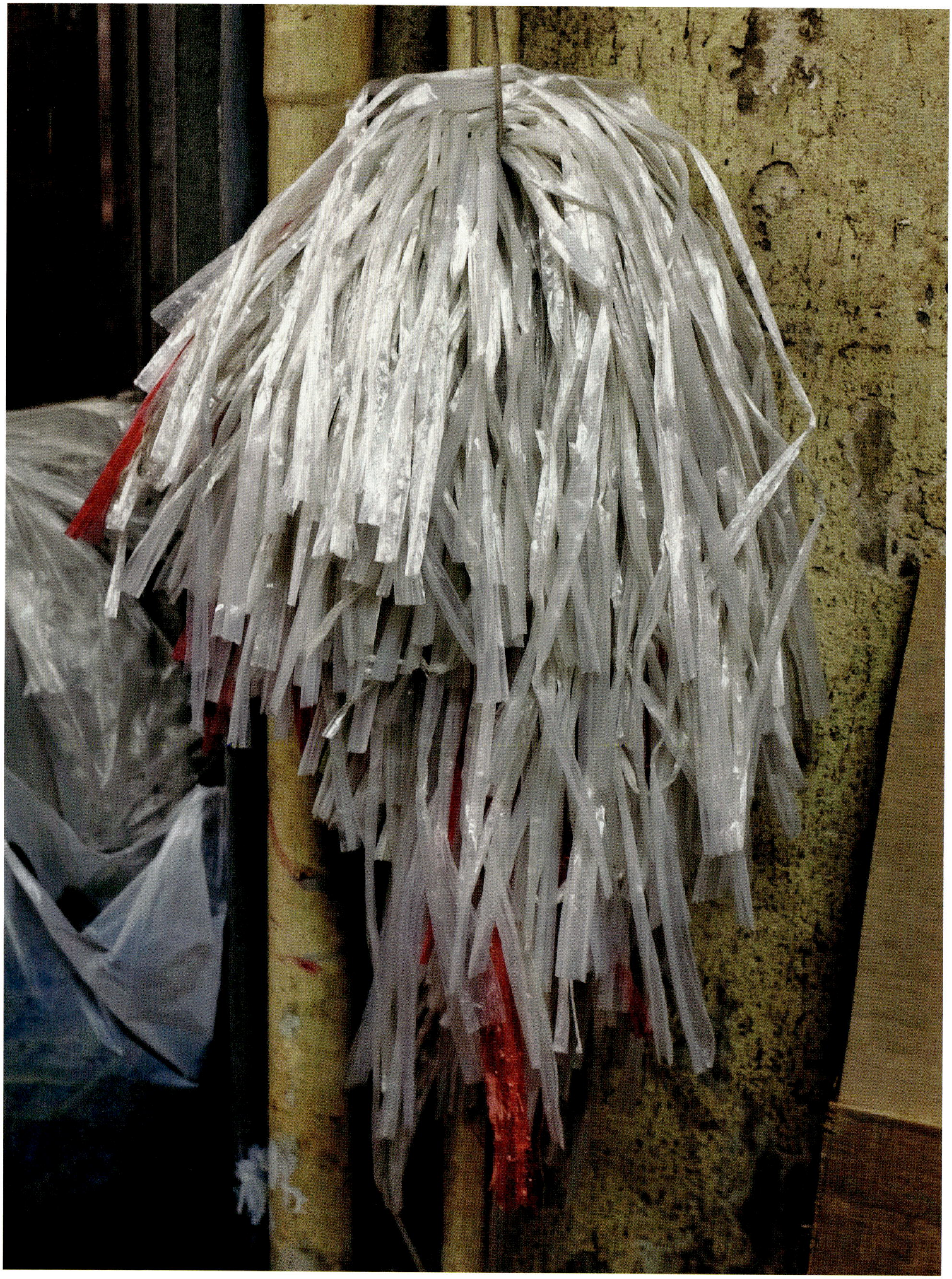

Informal Solutions #123

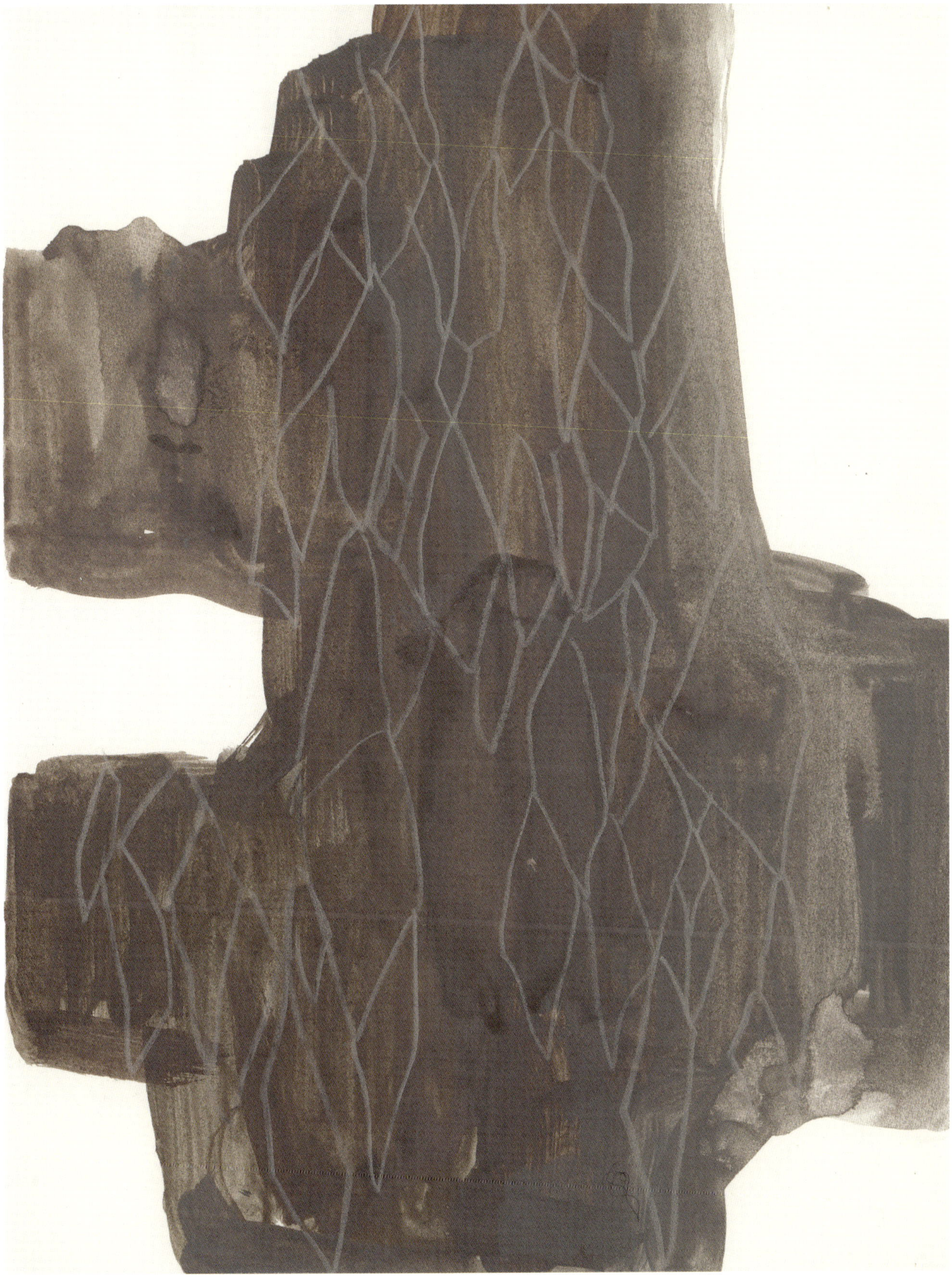

untitled, 2014, 25 × 19 cm, mixed media on paper

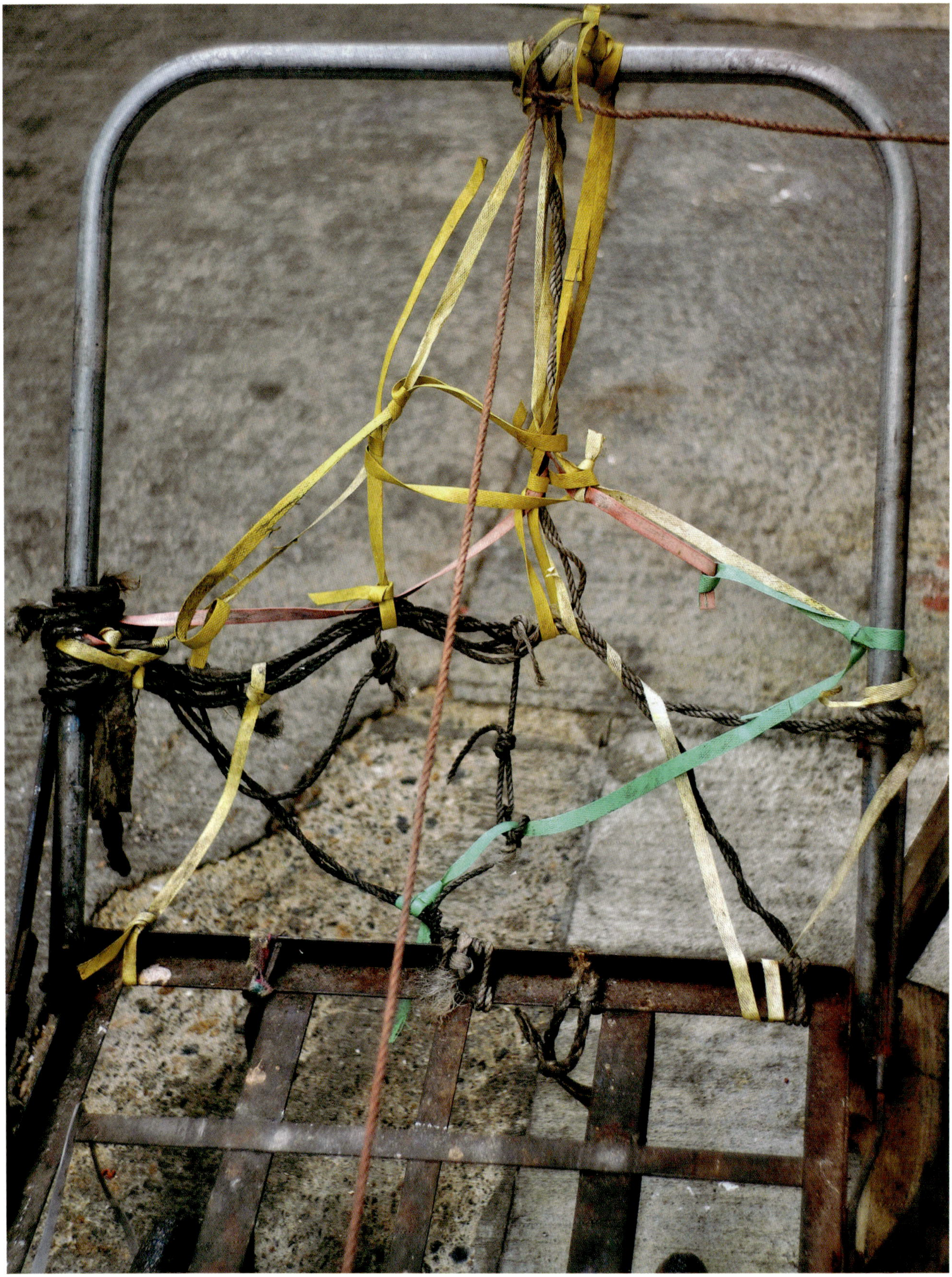

Informal Solutions #124

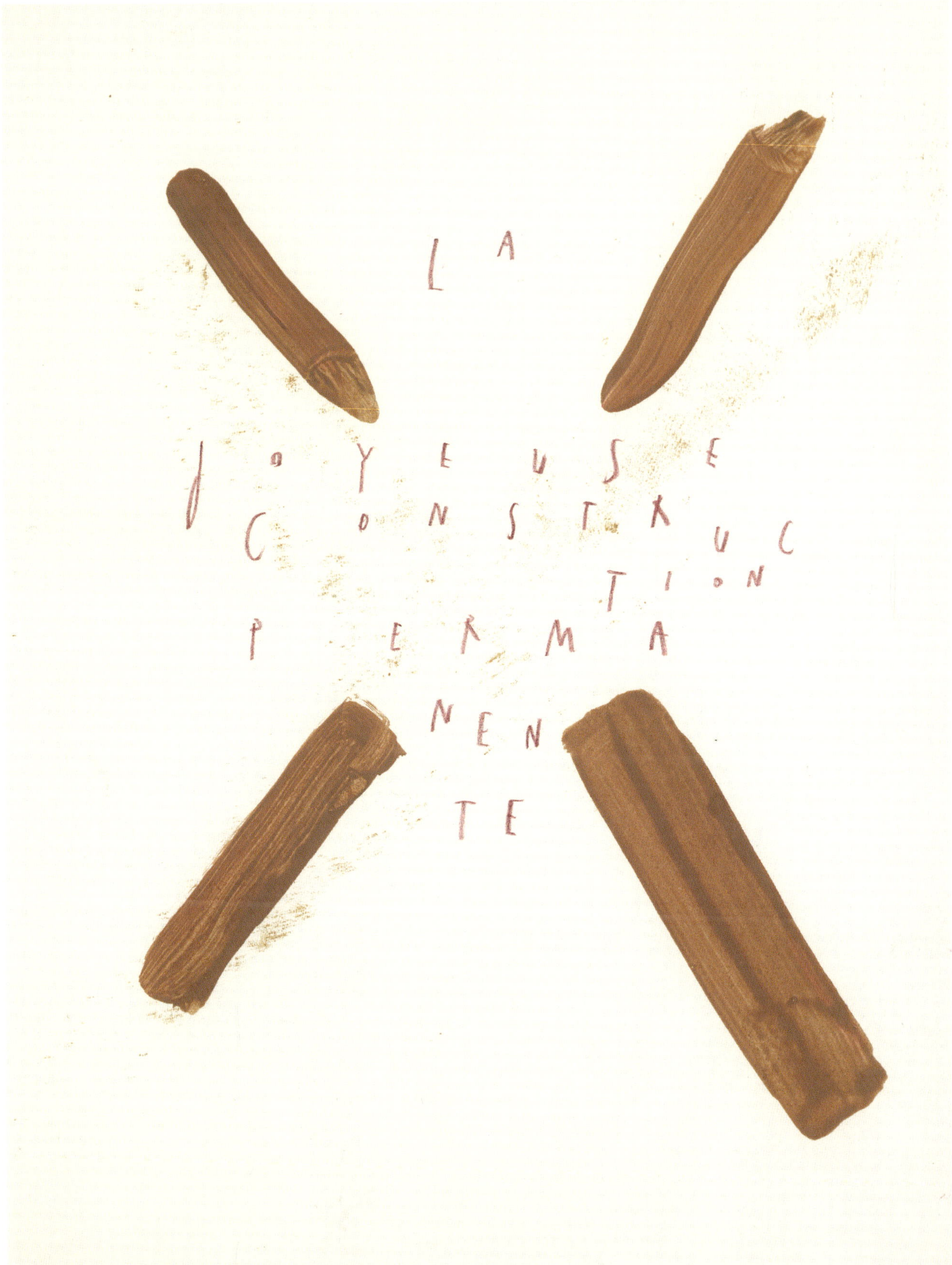

la joyeuse construction permanente (the joyous permanent construction), 2014, 25 × 19 cm, mixed media on paper

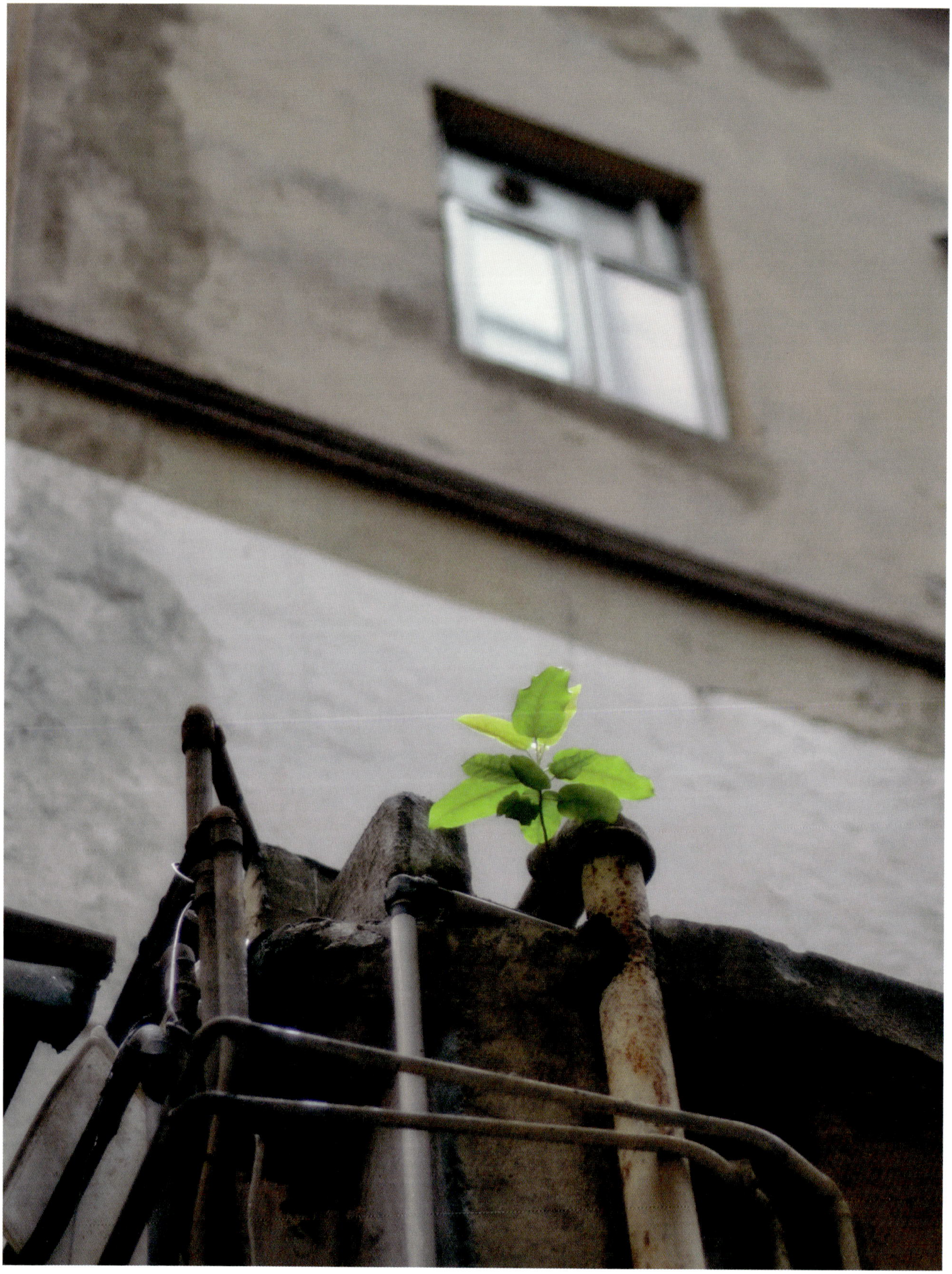

untitled, 2014, 25 × 19 cm, mixed media on paper

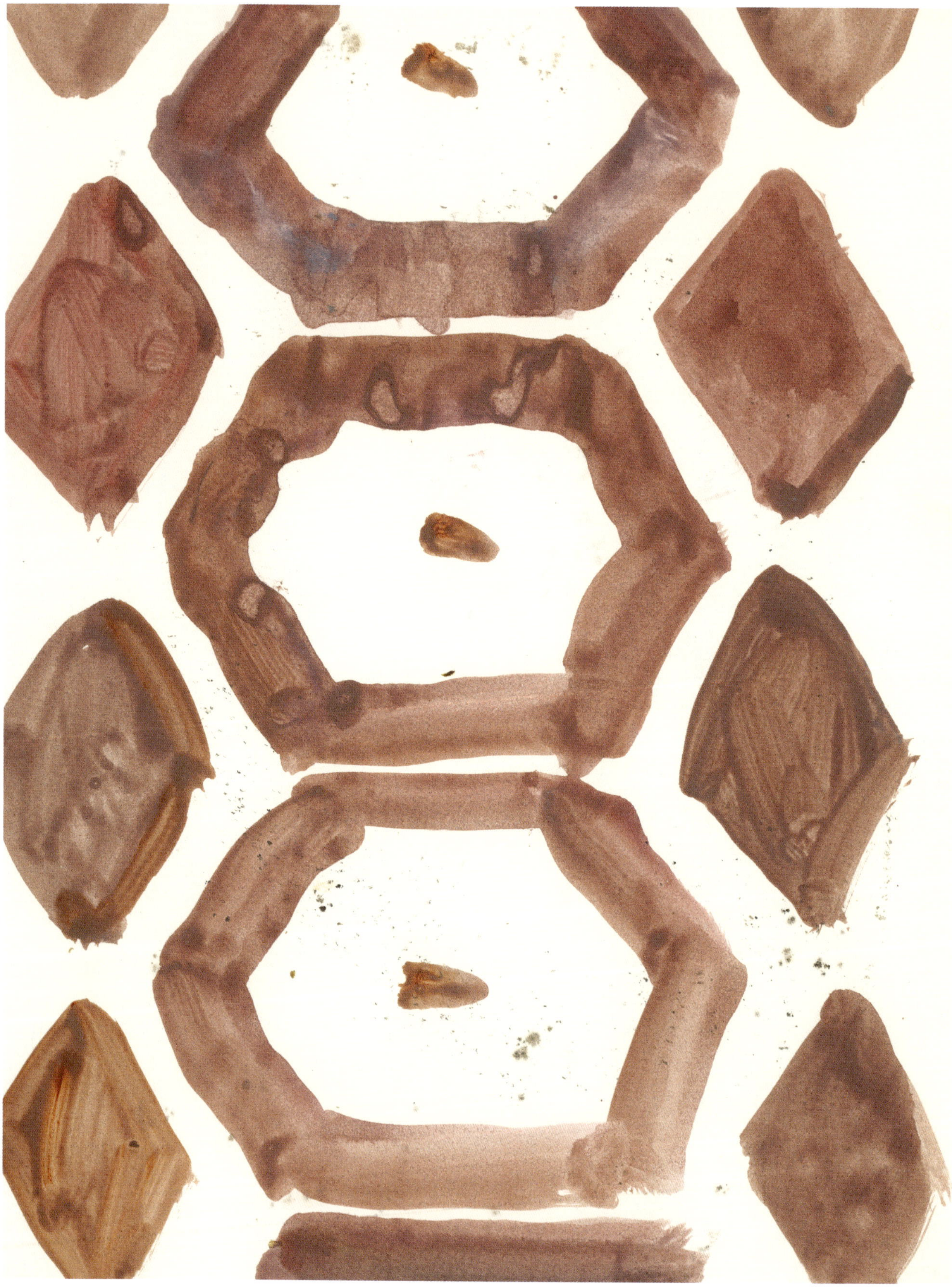

untitled, 2014, 25 × 19 cm, mixed media on paper

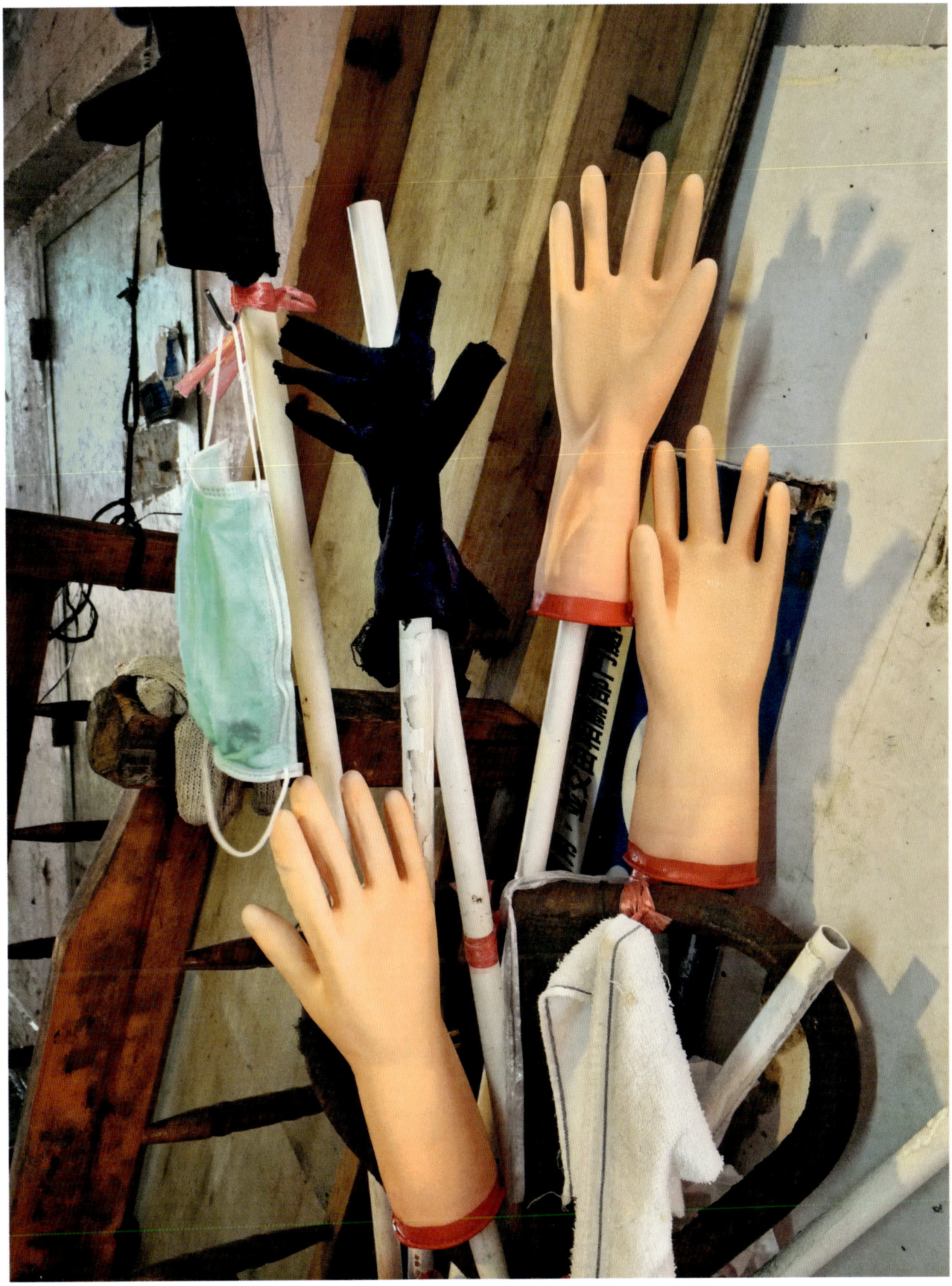

Informal Solutions #126

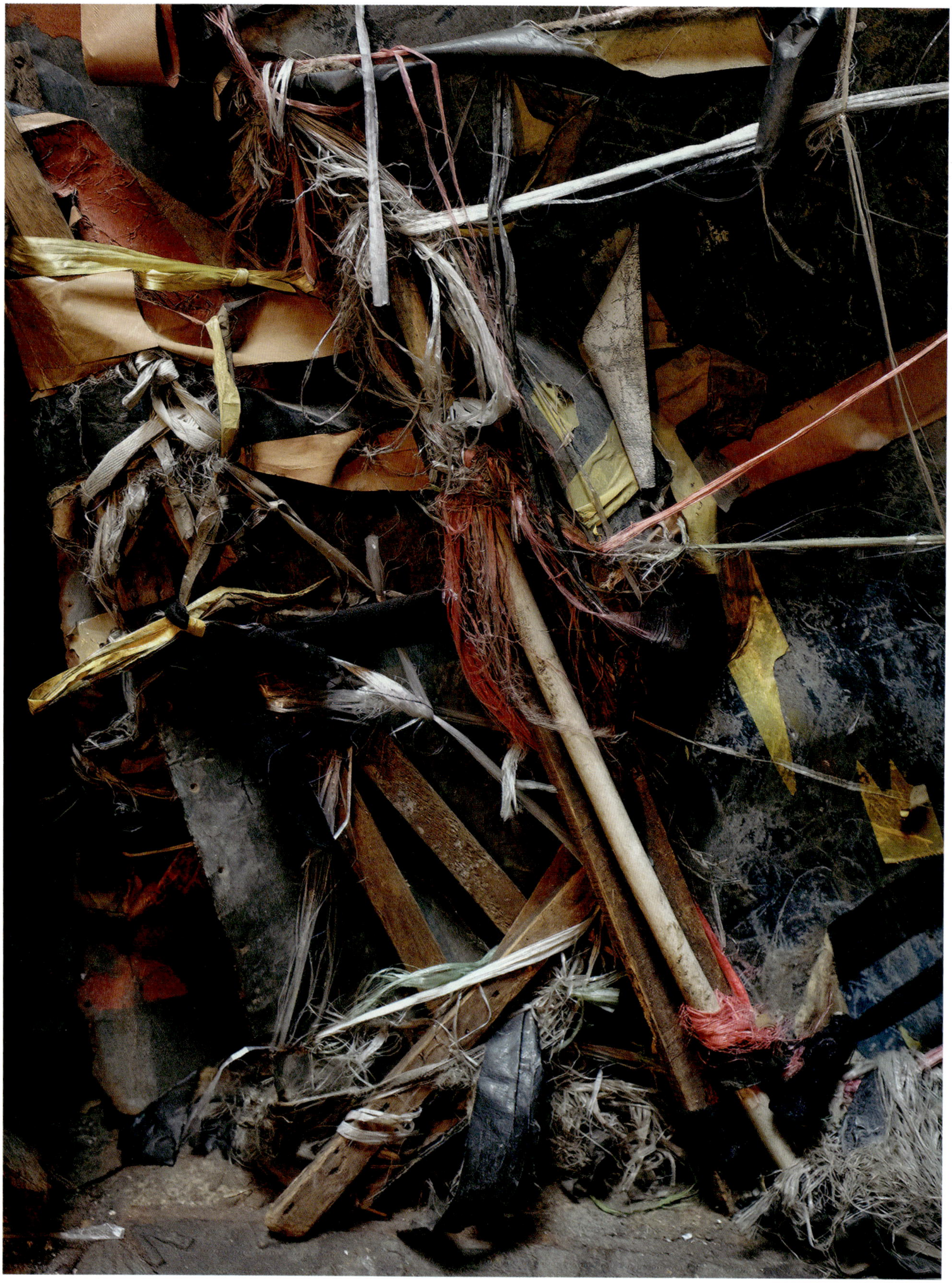

Informal Solutions #127

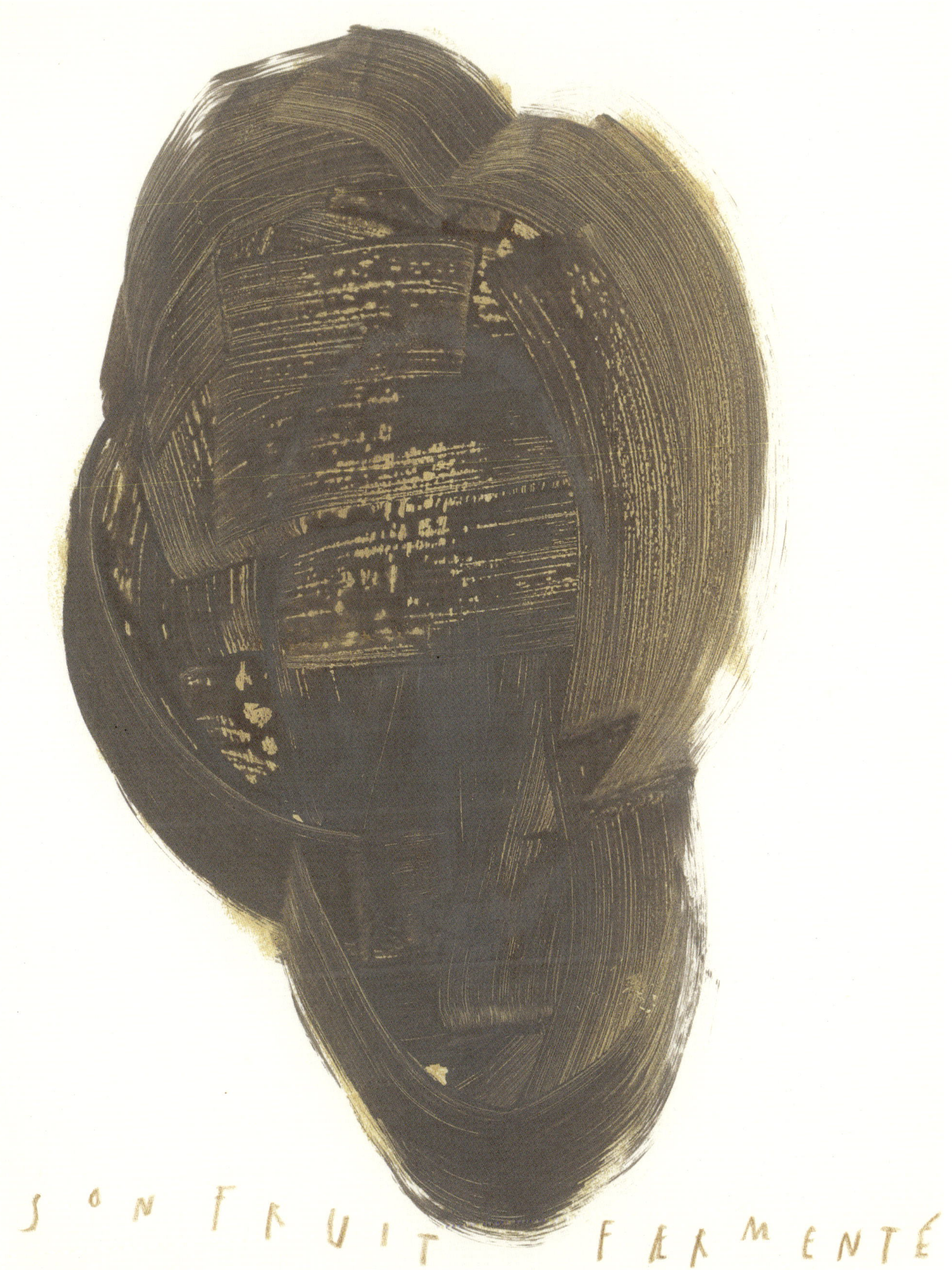

son fruit fermenté (his fermented fruit), 2014, 25 × 19 cm, mixed media on paper

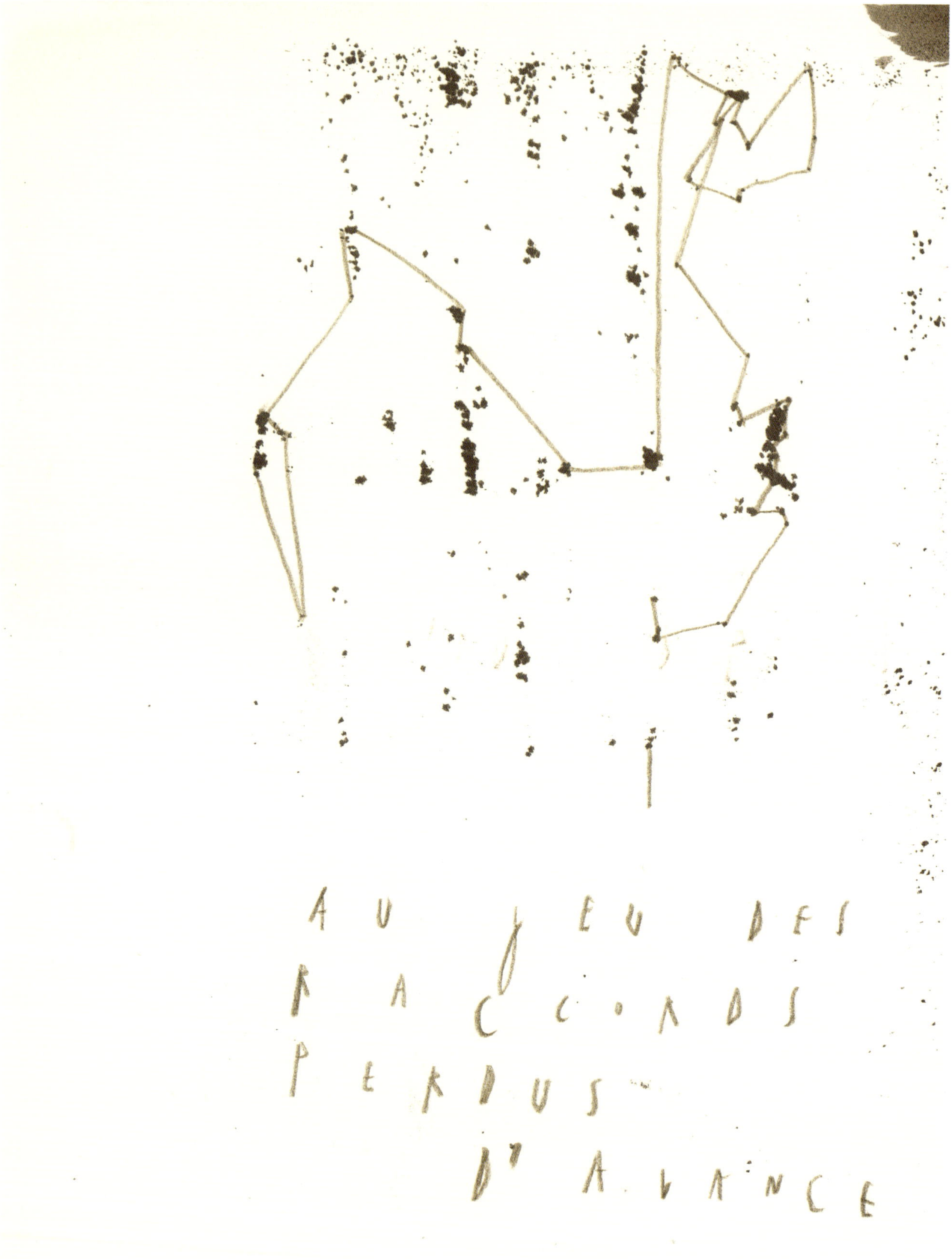

au jeu des raccords perdus d'avance (at the game of connections lost in advance), 2014, 25 × 19 cm, mixed media on paper

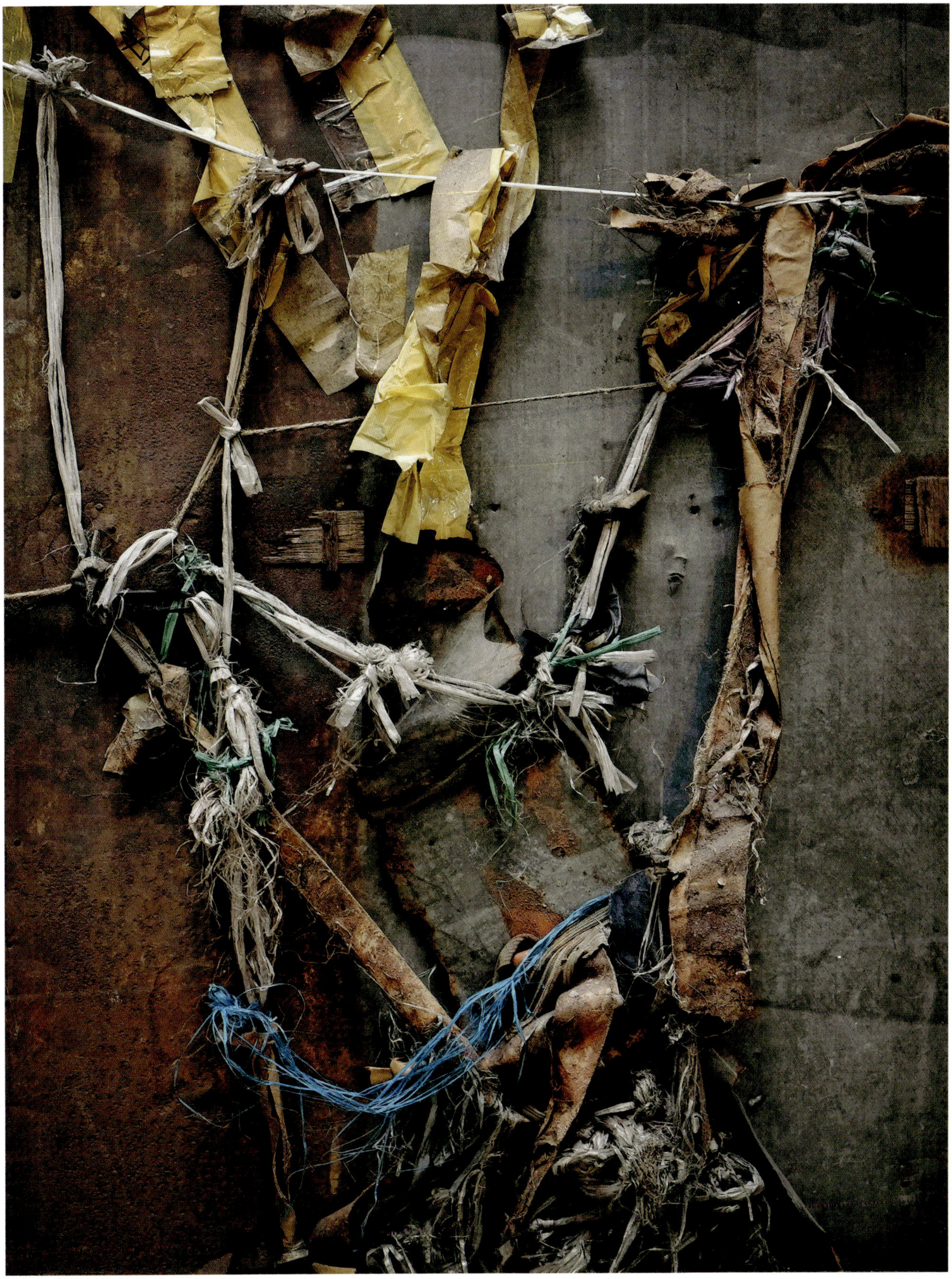

Informal Solutions #128

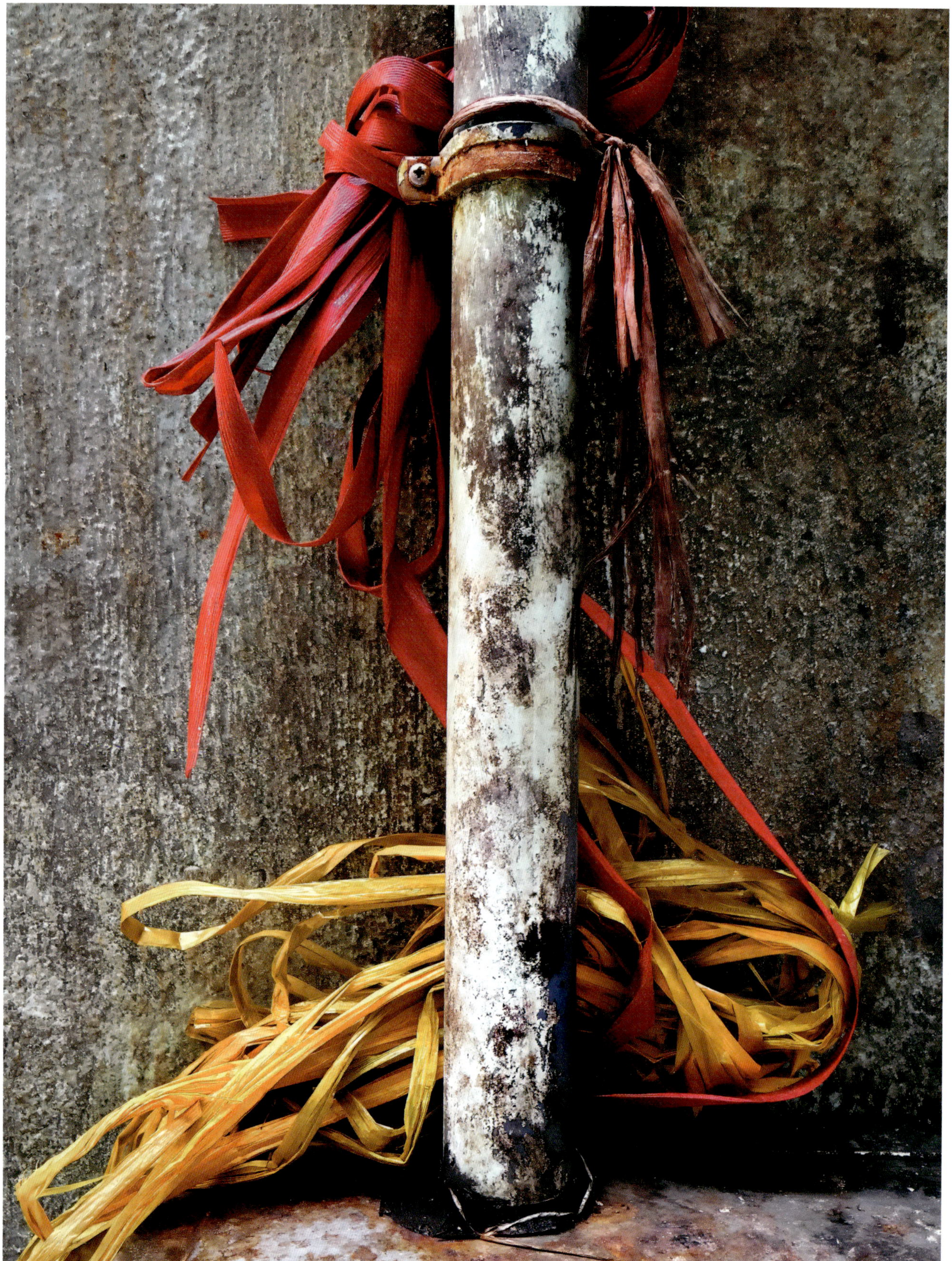

Informal Solutions #129

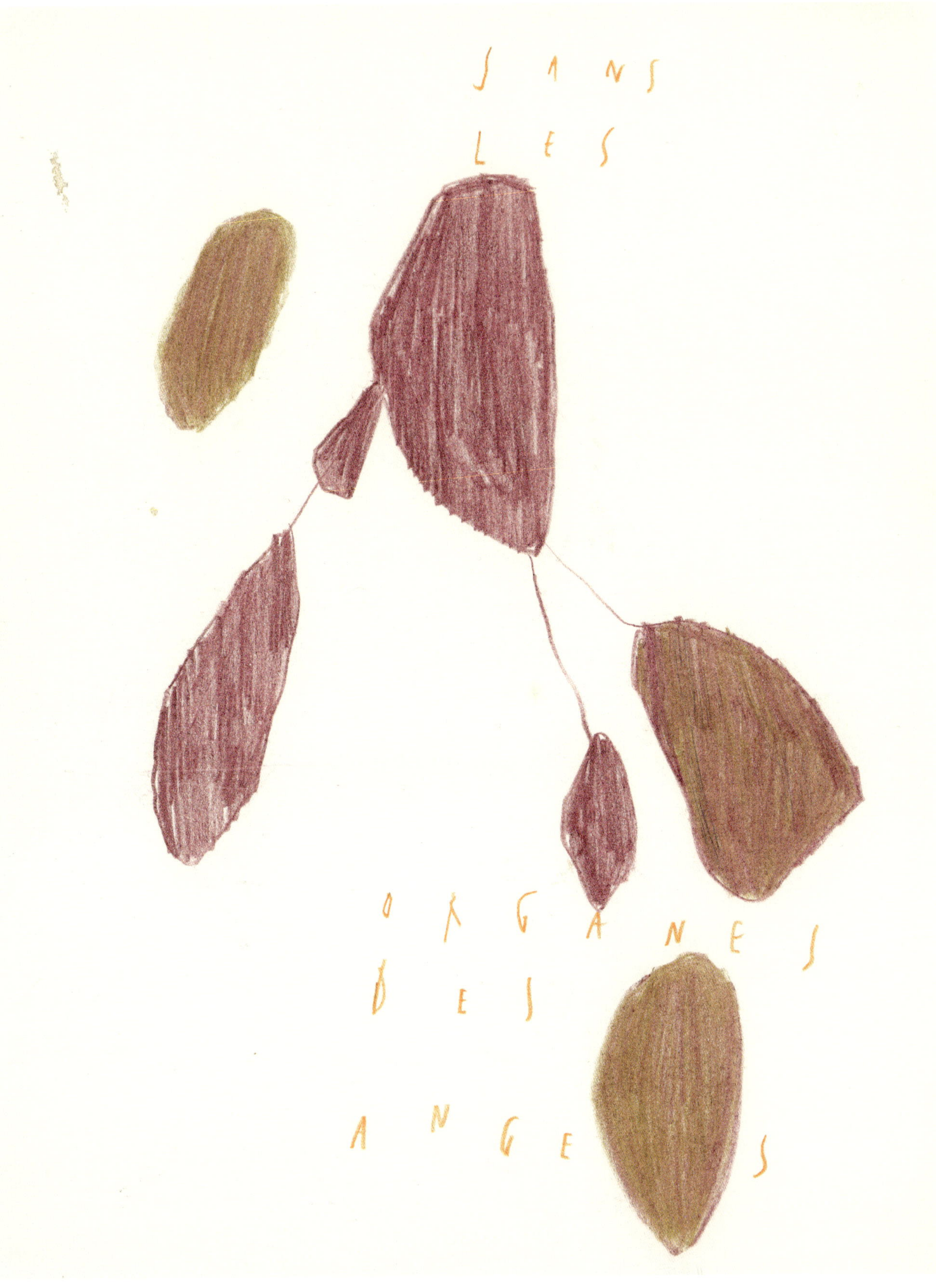

sans les organes des anges (without the angels' organs), 2014, 25 × 19 cm, mixed media on paper

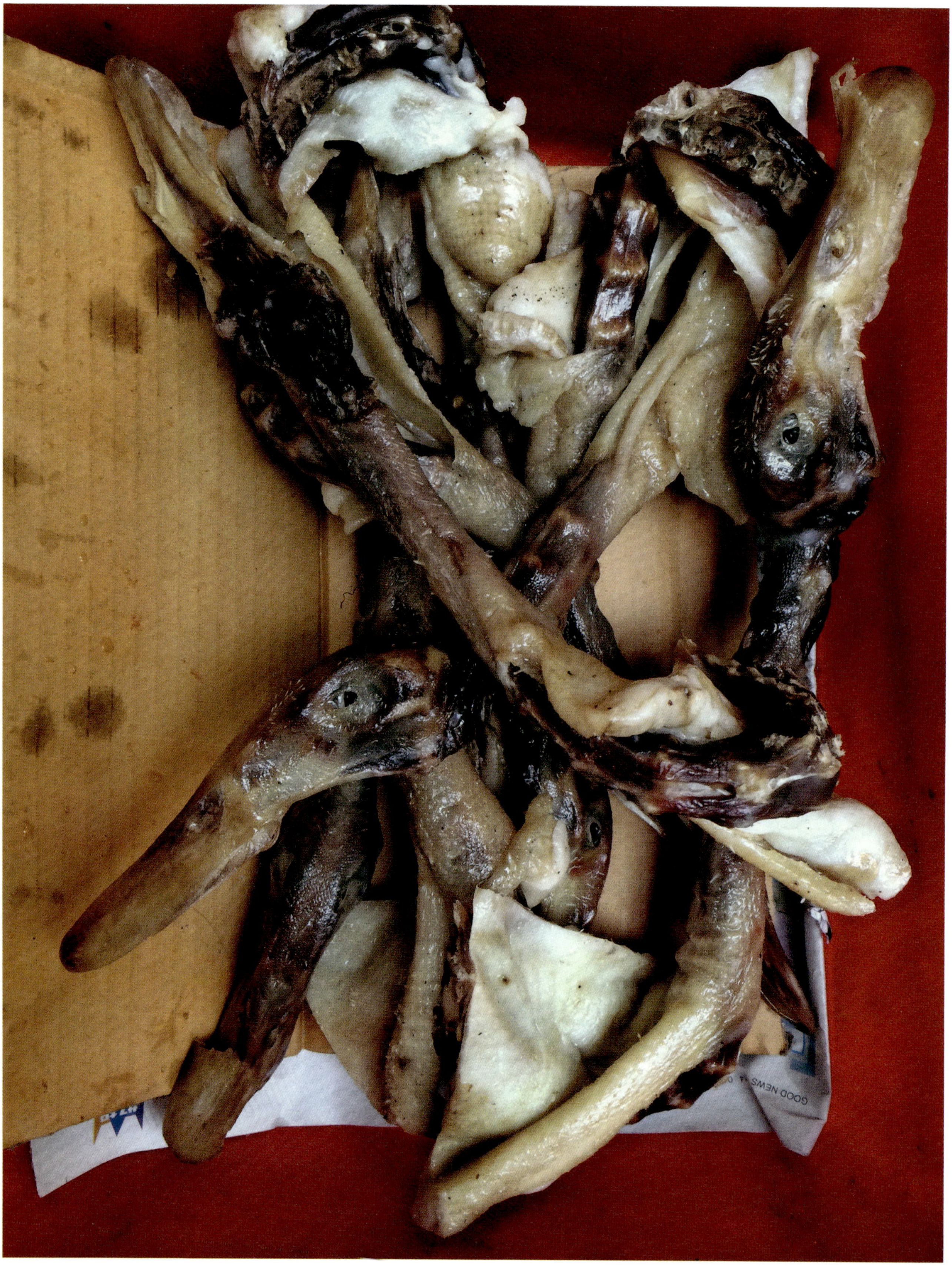

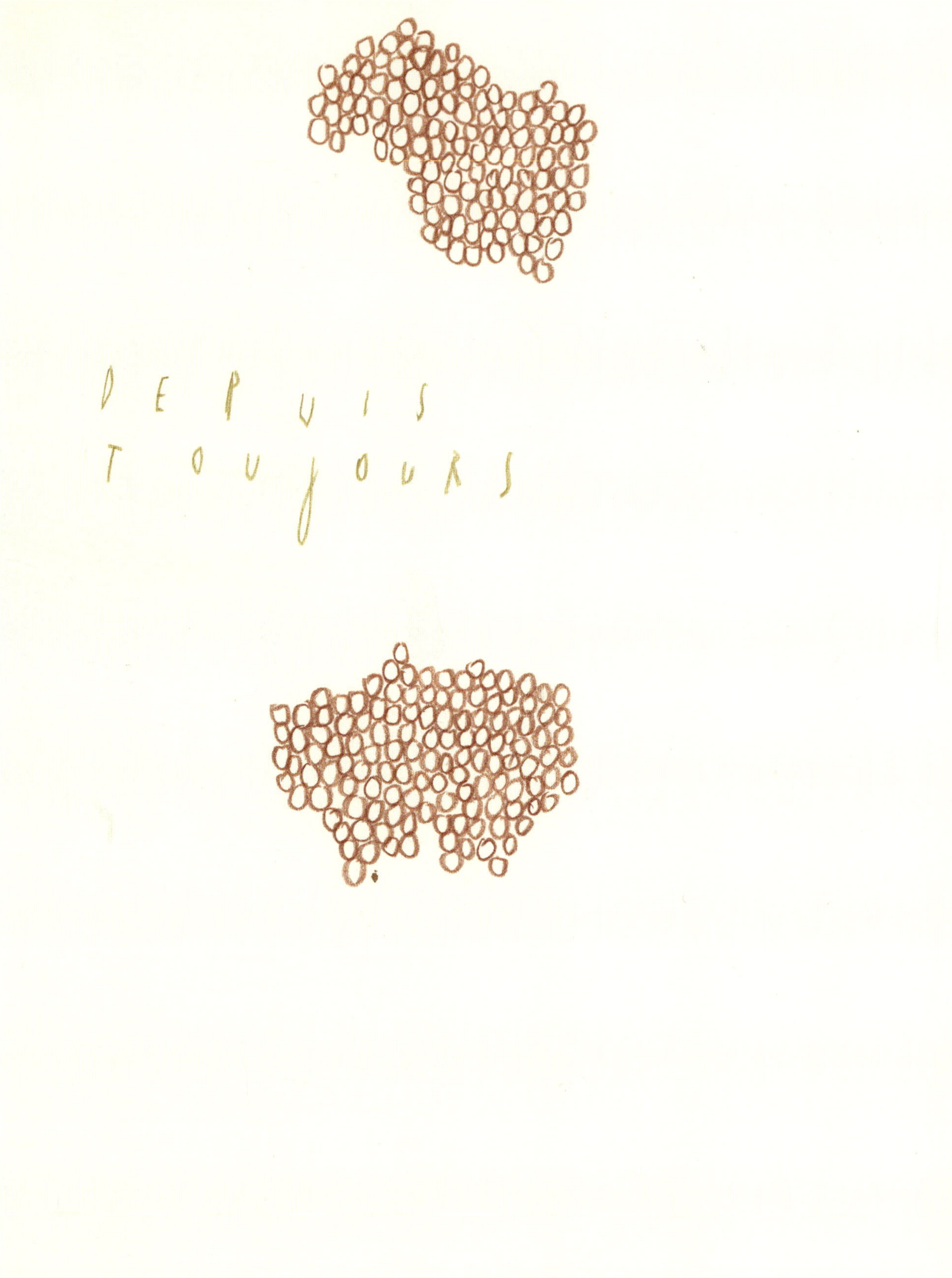

depuis toujours (since forever), 2014, 25 × 19 cm, mixed media on paper

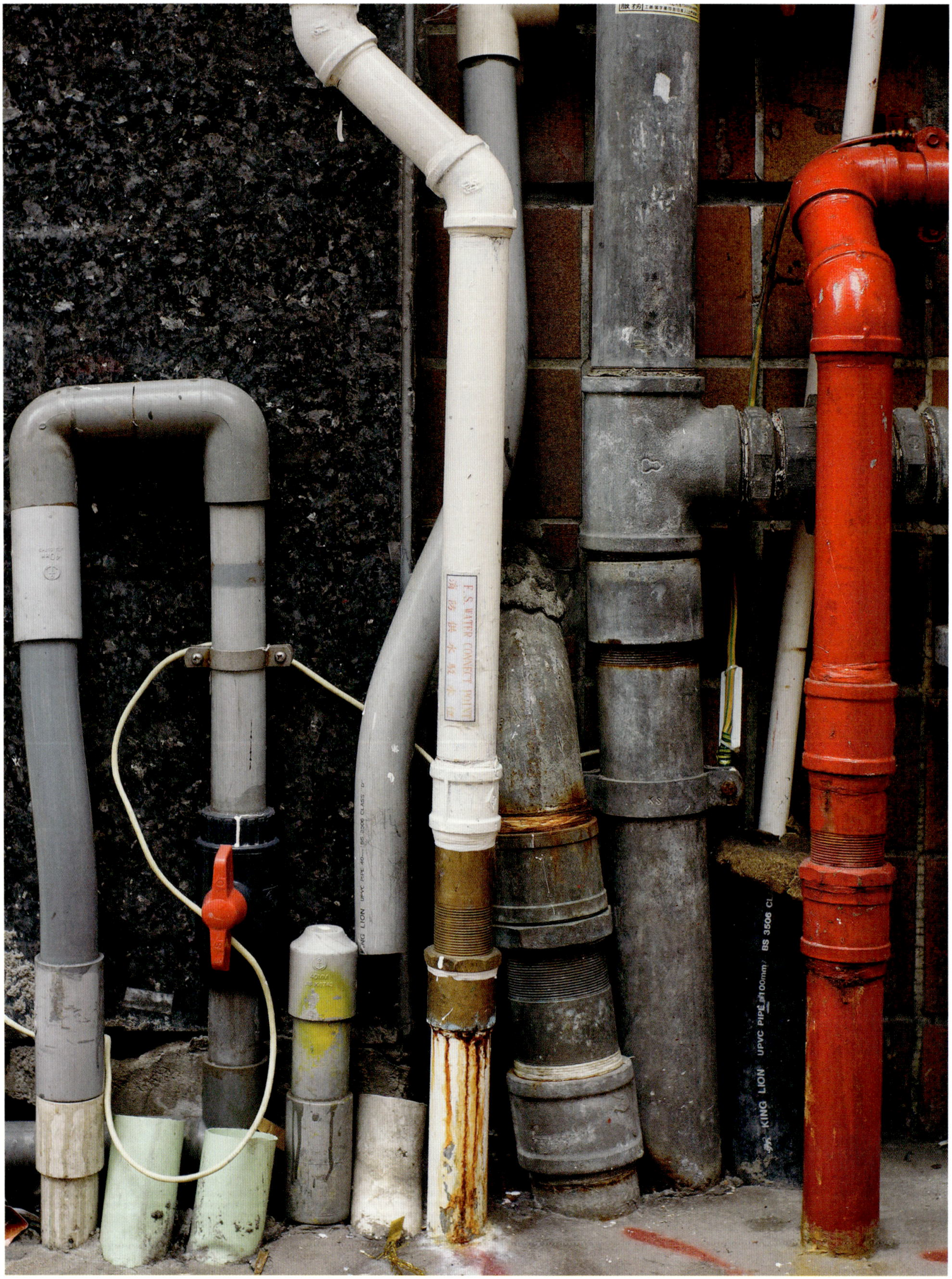
F.S. WATER CONNECT POINT

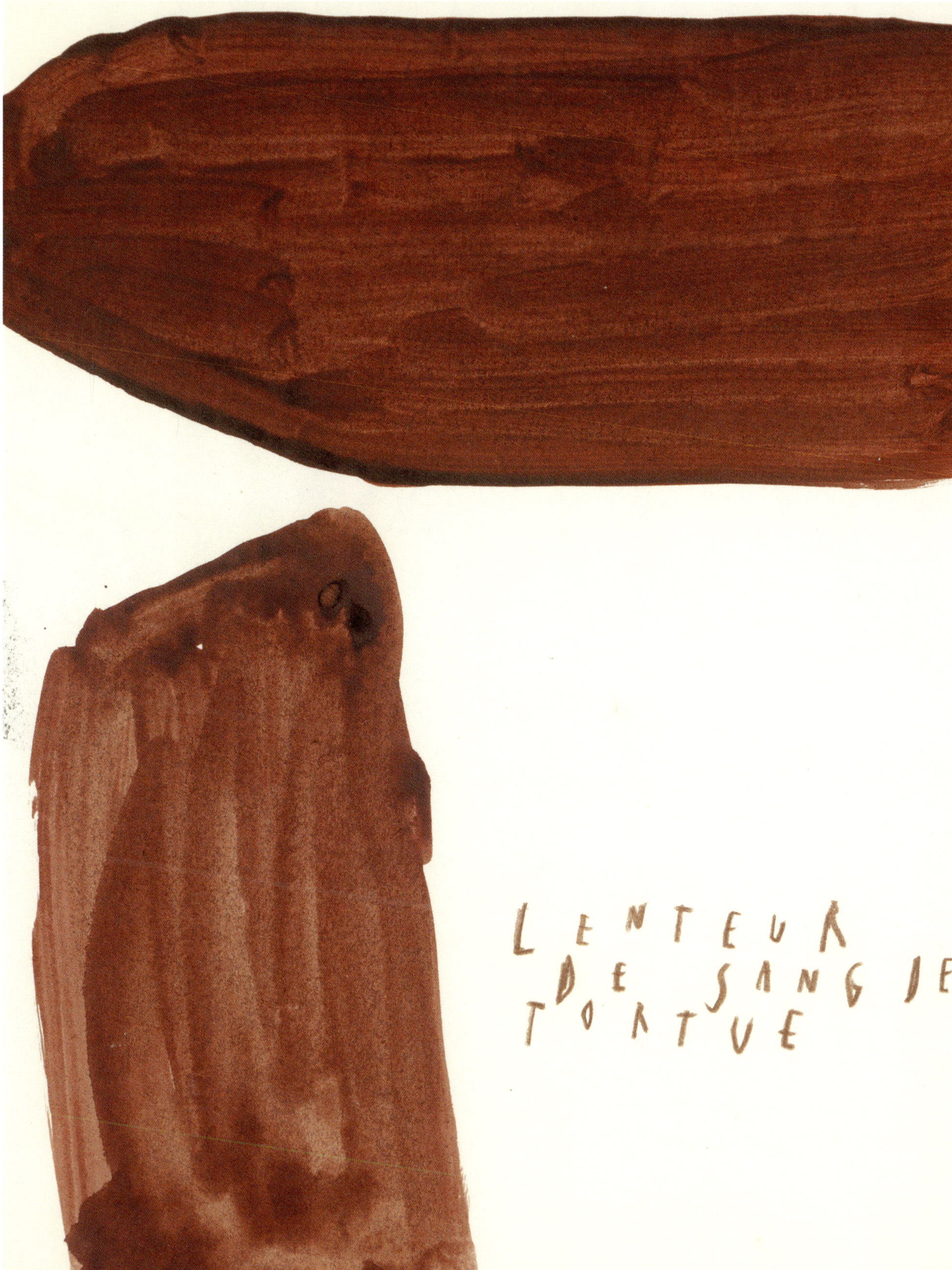

lenteur de sang de tortue (slowness of turtle blood), 2014, 25 × 19 cm, mixed media on paper

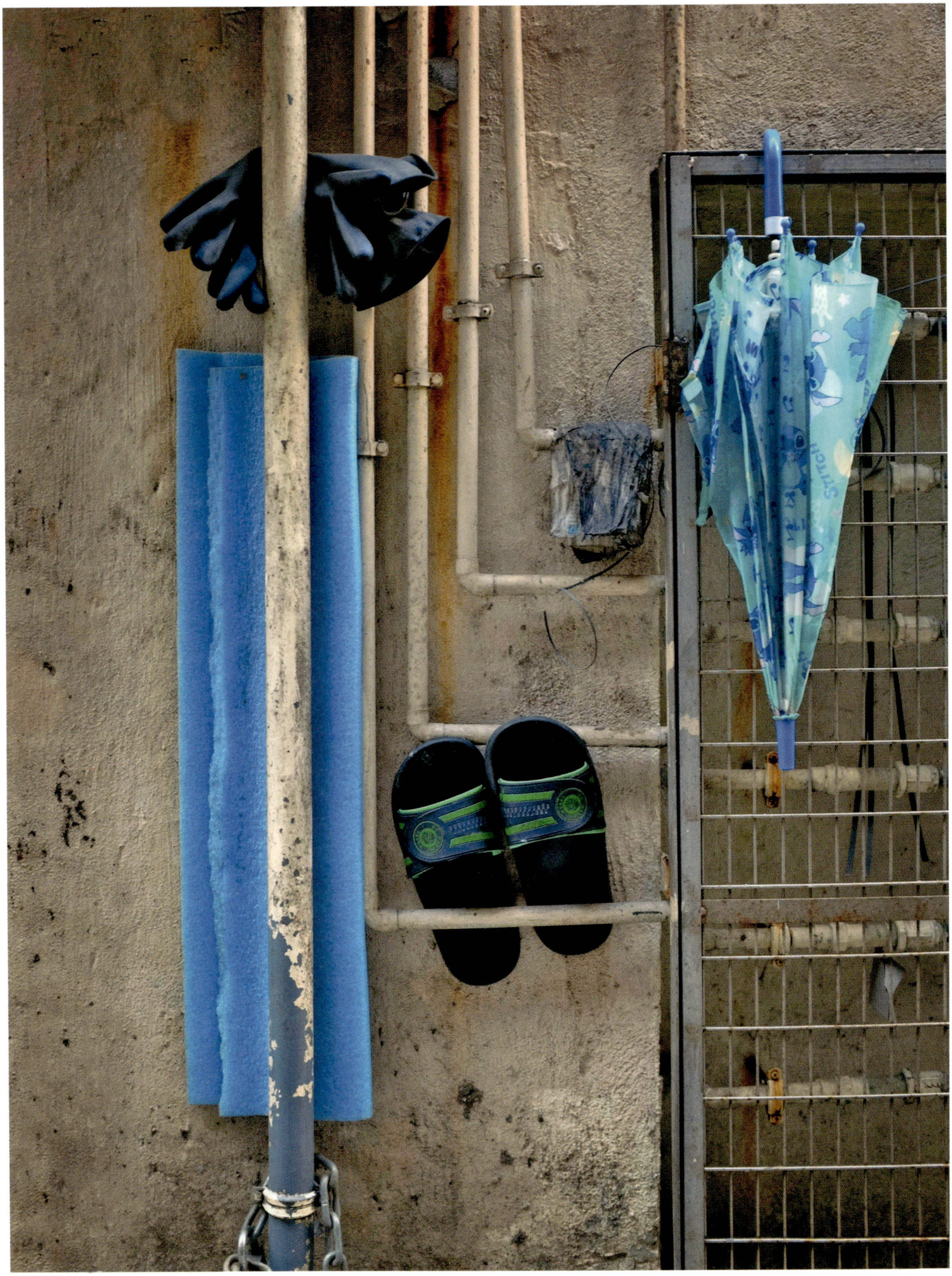

Informal Solutions #132

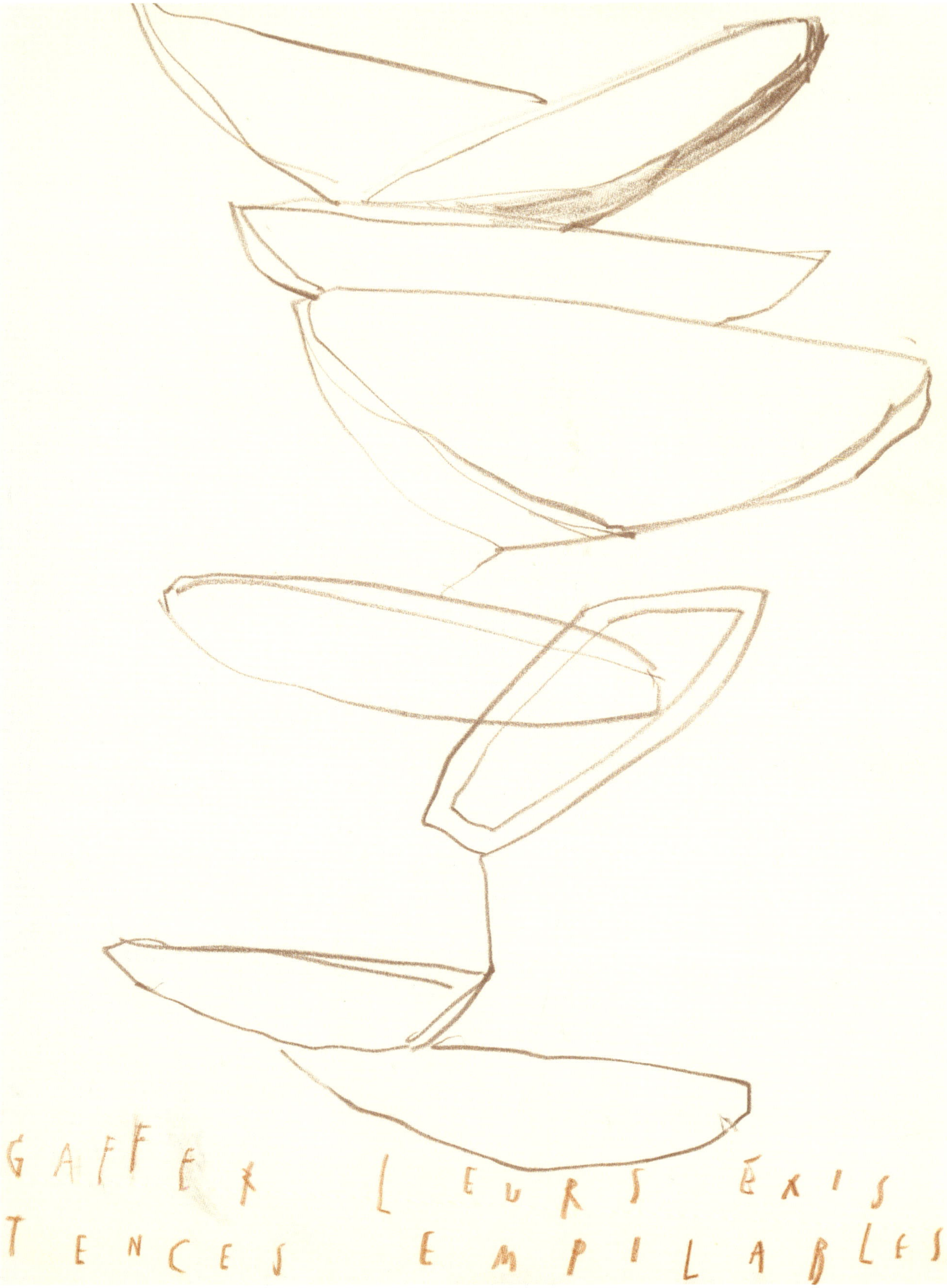

gaffer leurs existences empilables (espying their stackable existences), 2014, 25 × 19 cm, mixed media on paper

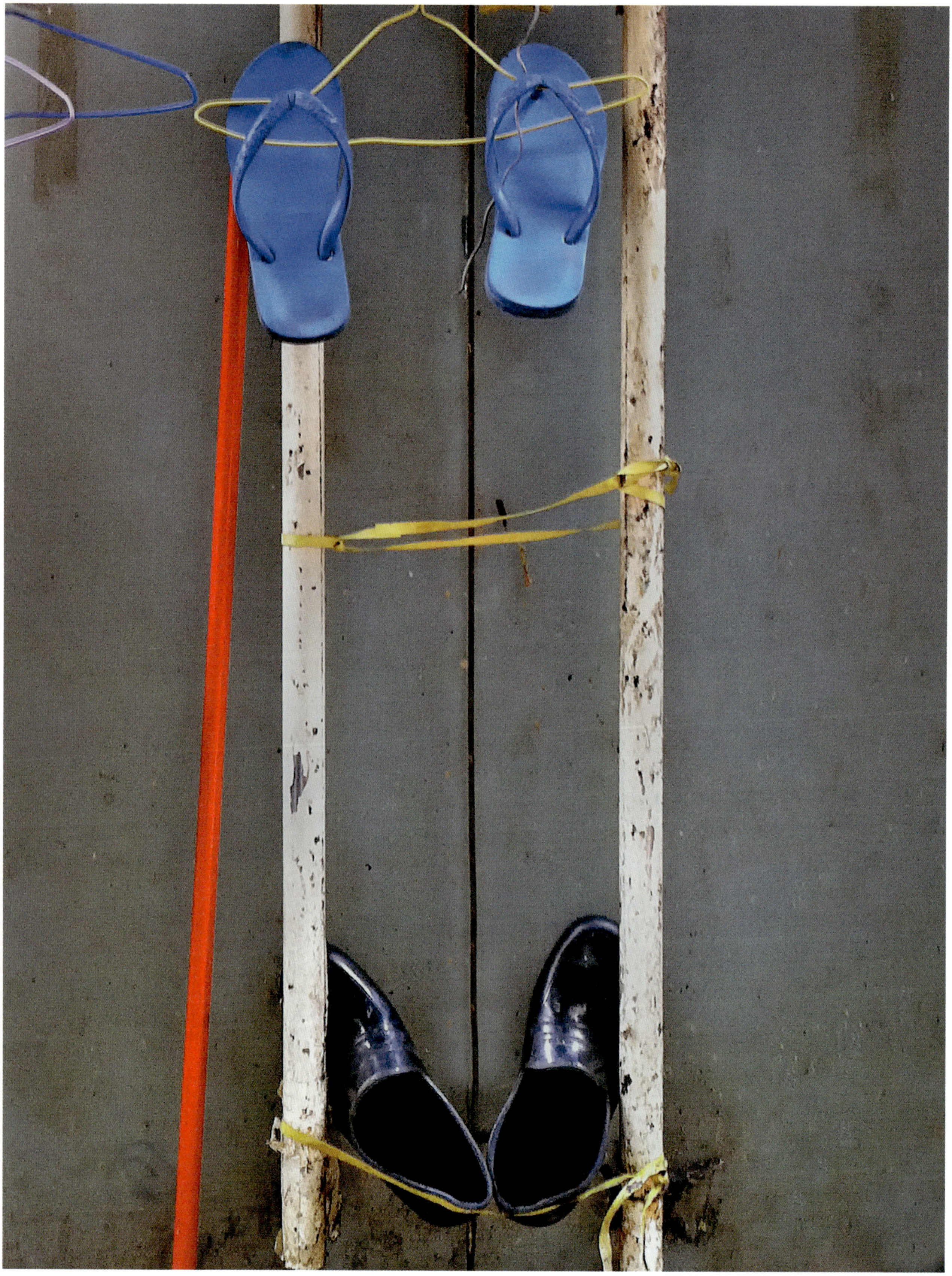

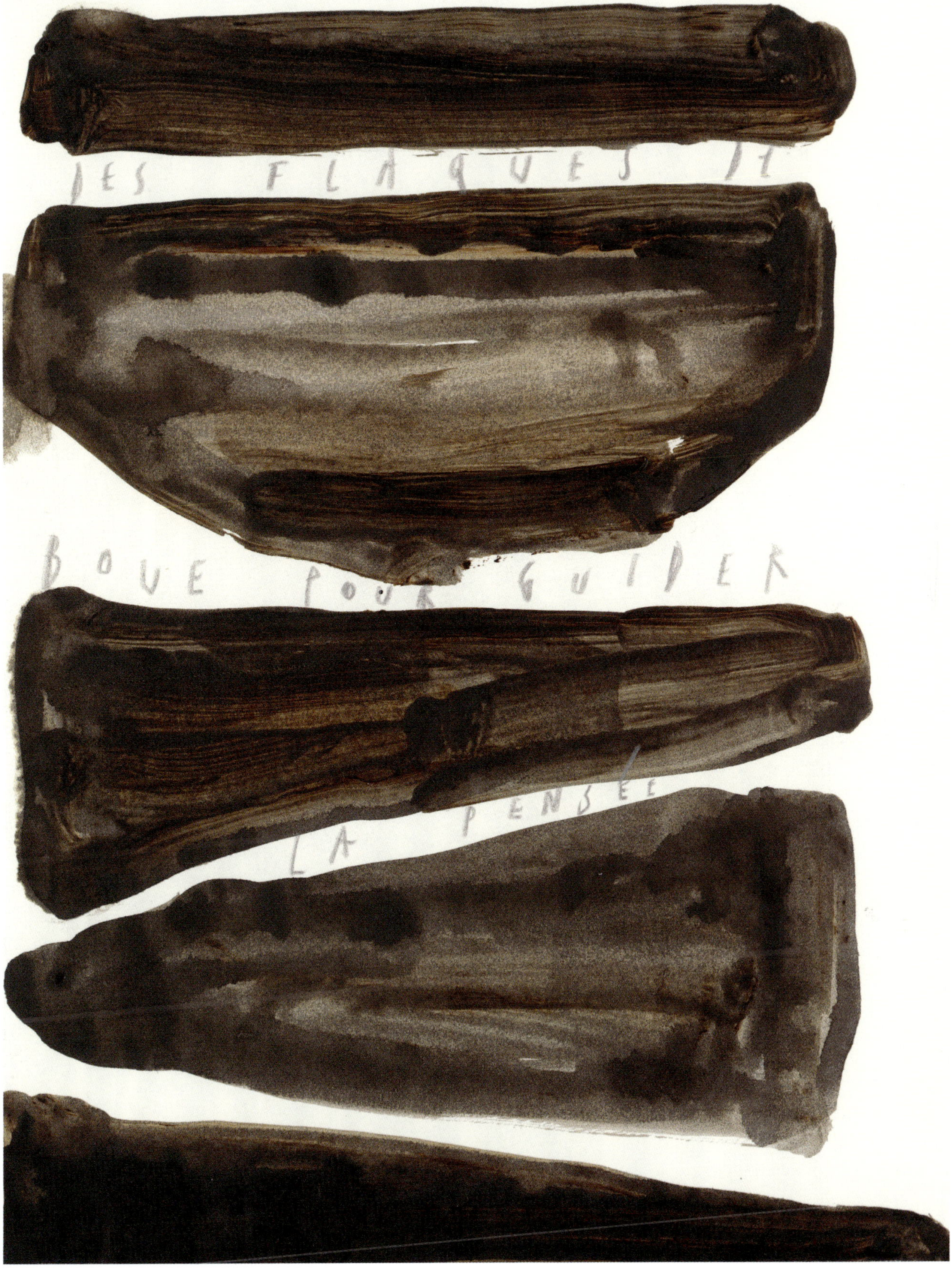

des flaques de boue pour guider la pensée (puddles of mud to guide your thoughts), 2014, 25 × 19 cm, mixed media on paper

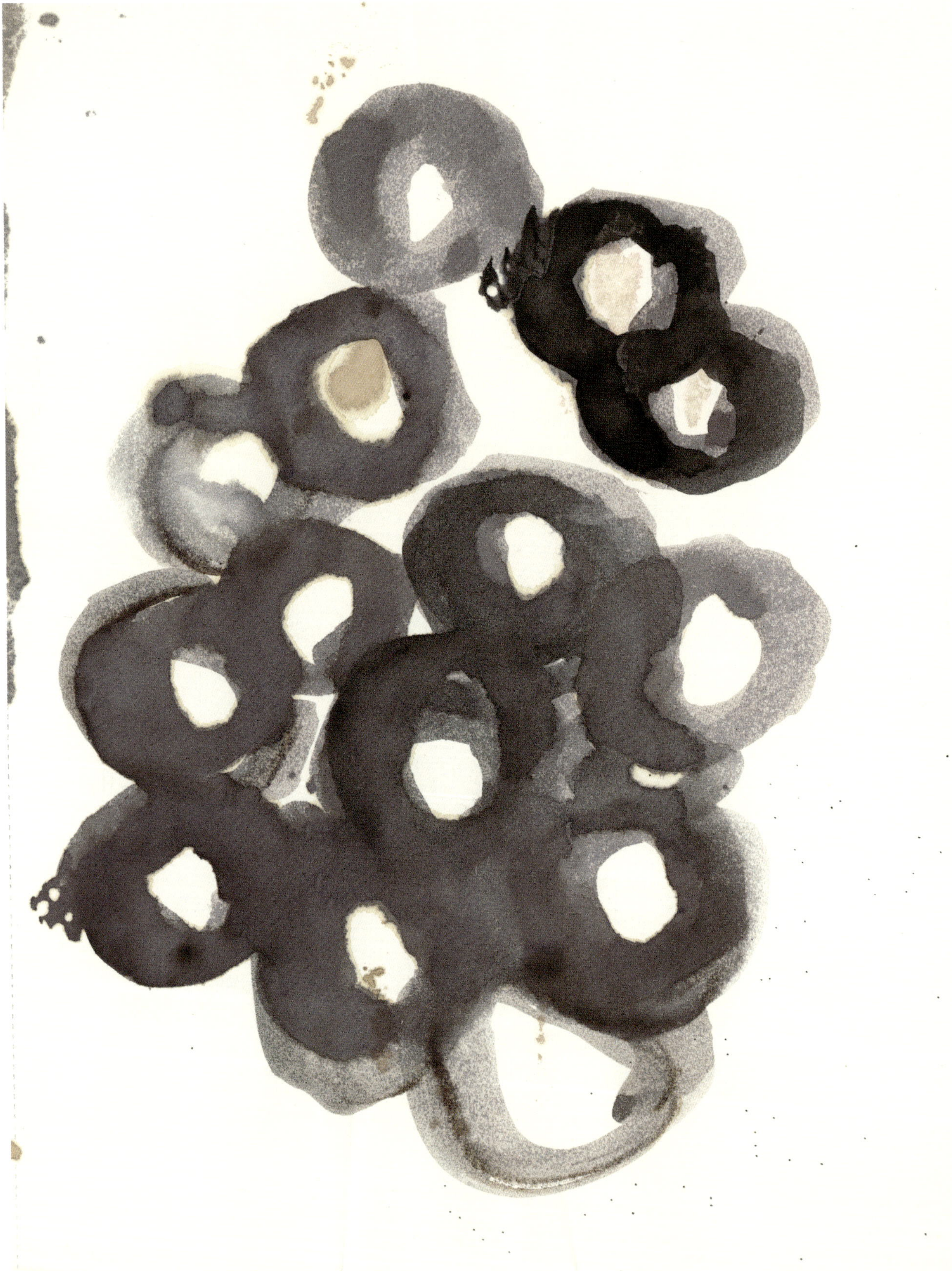

untitled, 2014, 25 × 19 cm, mixed media on paper

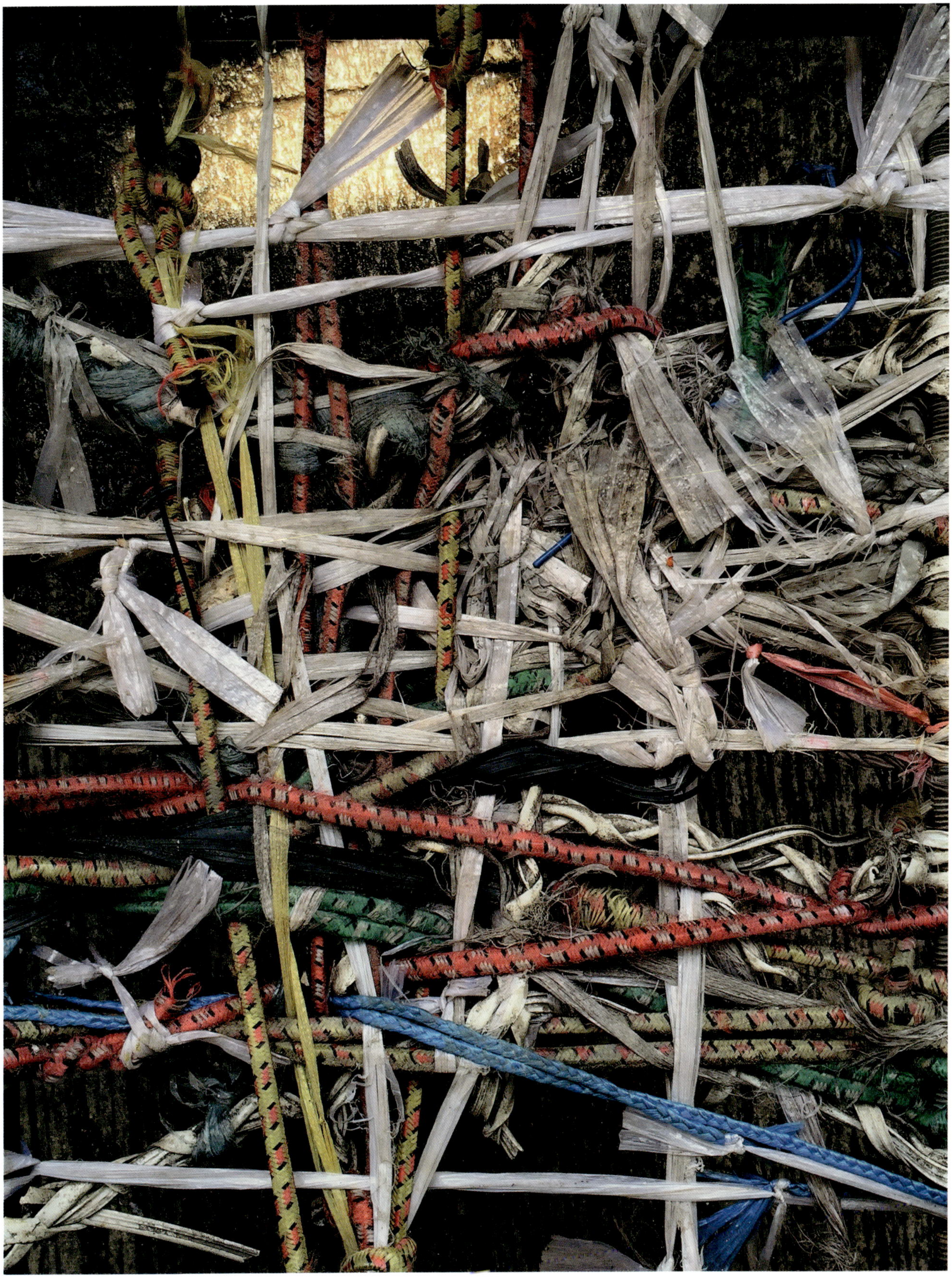

Informal Solutions #133

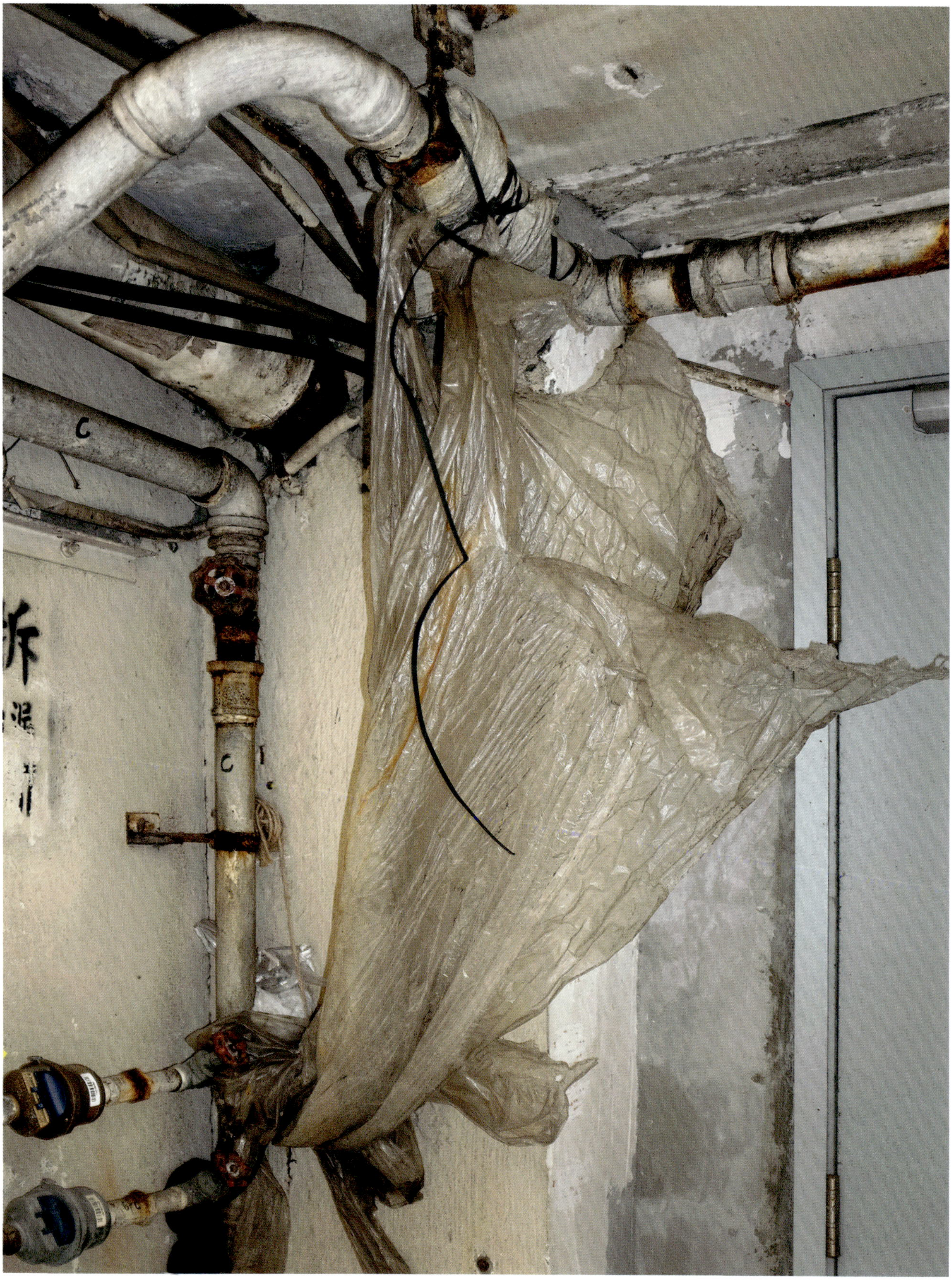

Informal Solutions #134

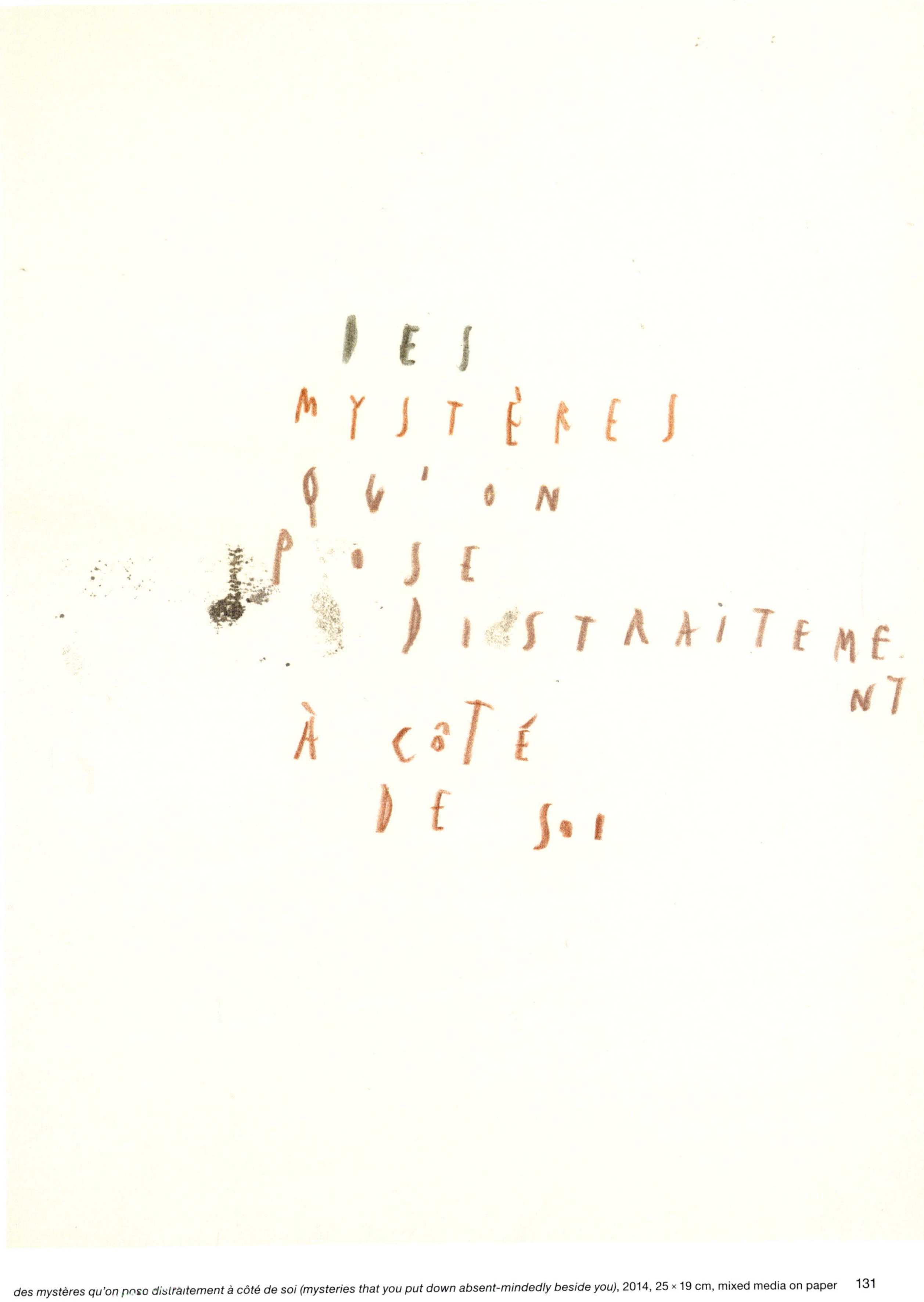

des mystères qu'on pose distraitement à côté de soi (mysteries that you put down absent-mindedly beside you), 2014, 25 × 19 cm, mixed media on paper

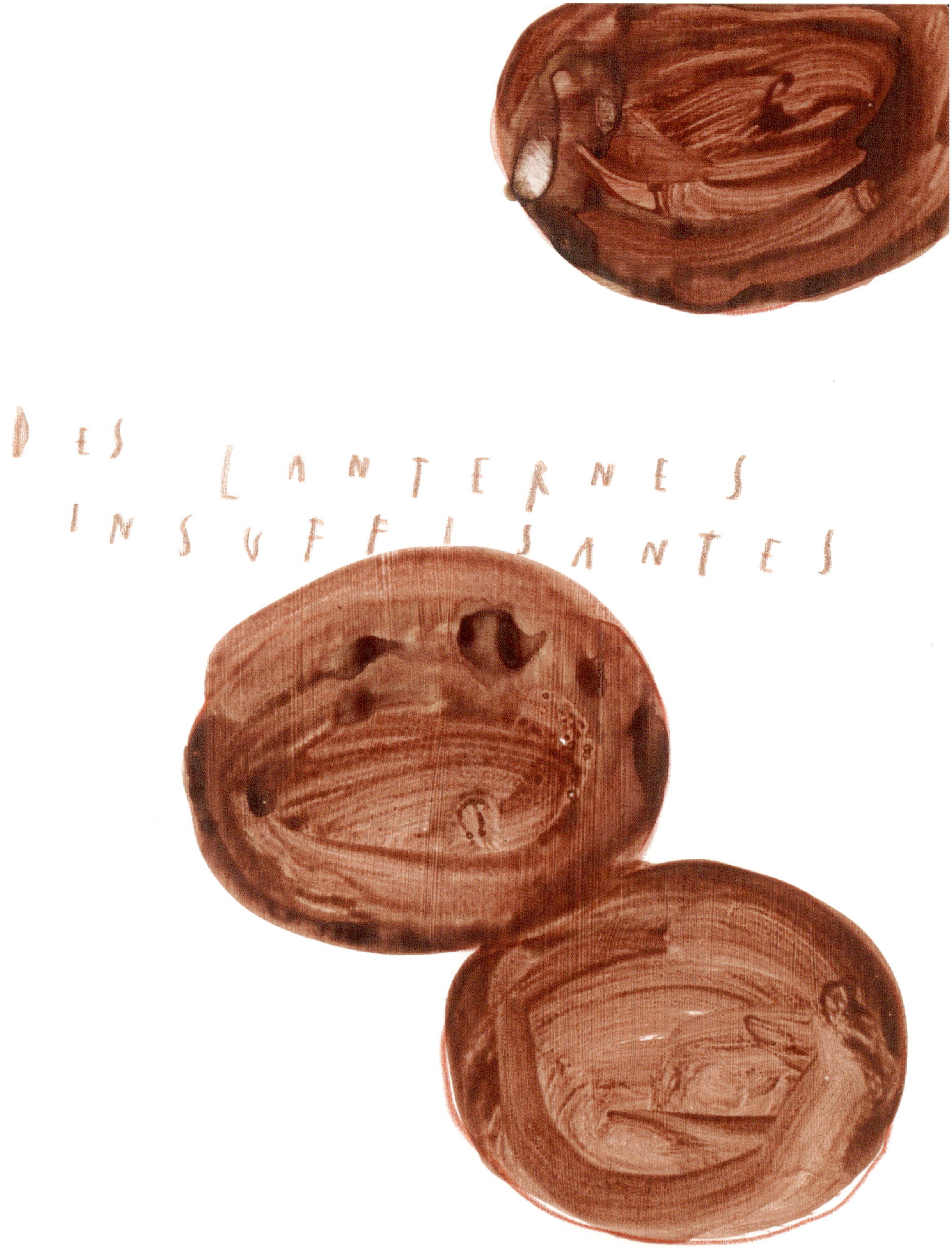

des lanternes insuffisantes (insufficient lanterns), 2014, 25 × 19 cm, mixed media on paper

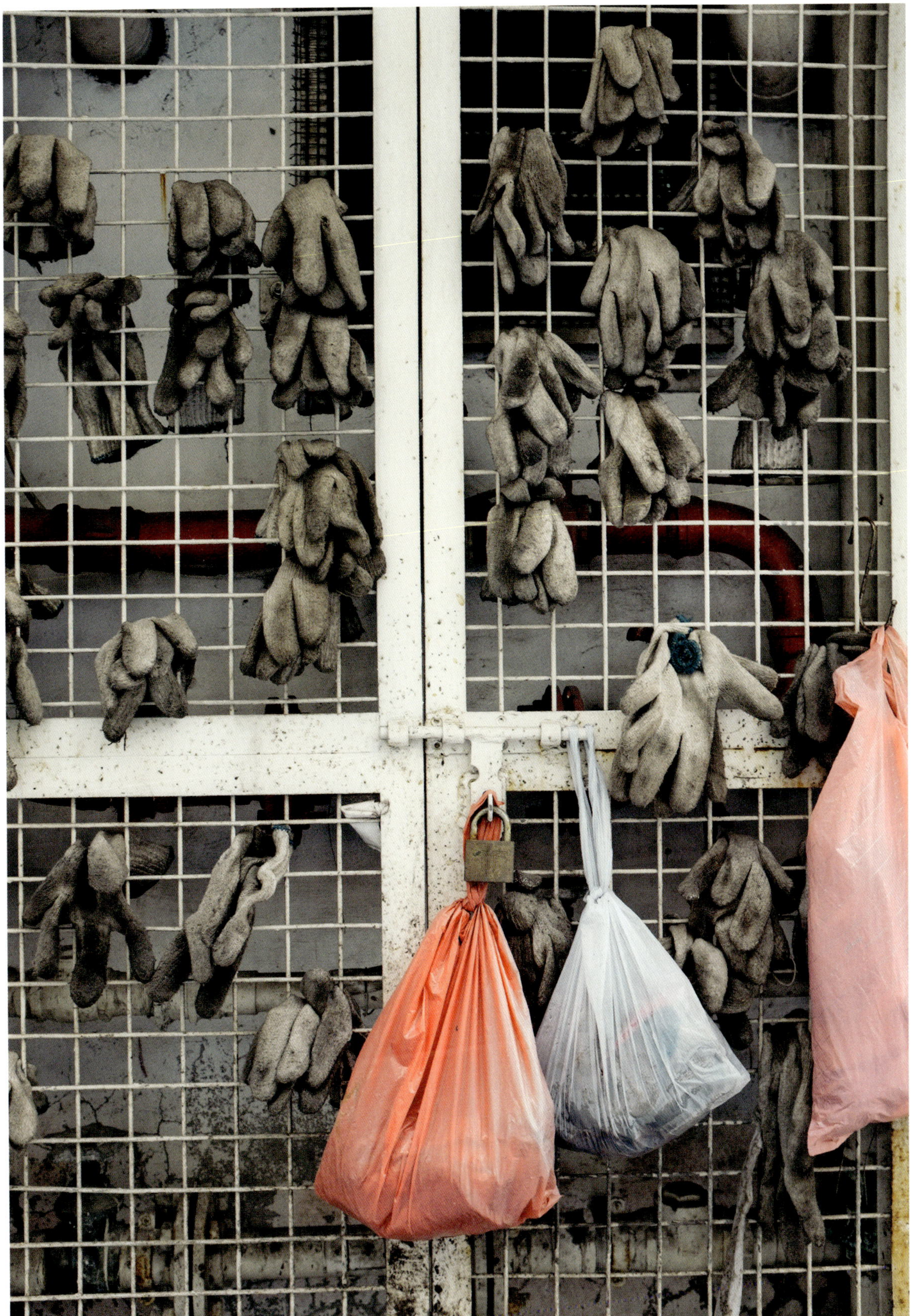

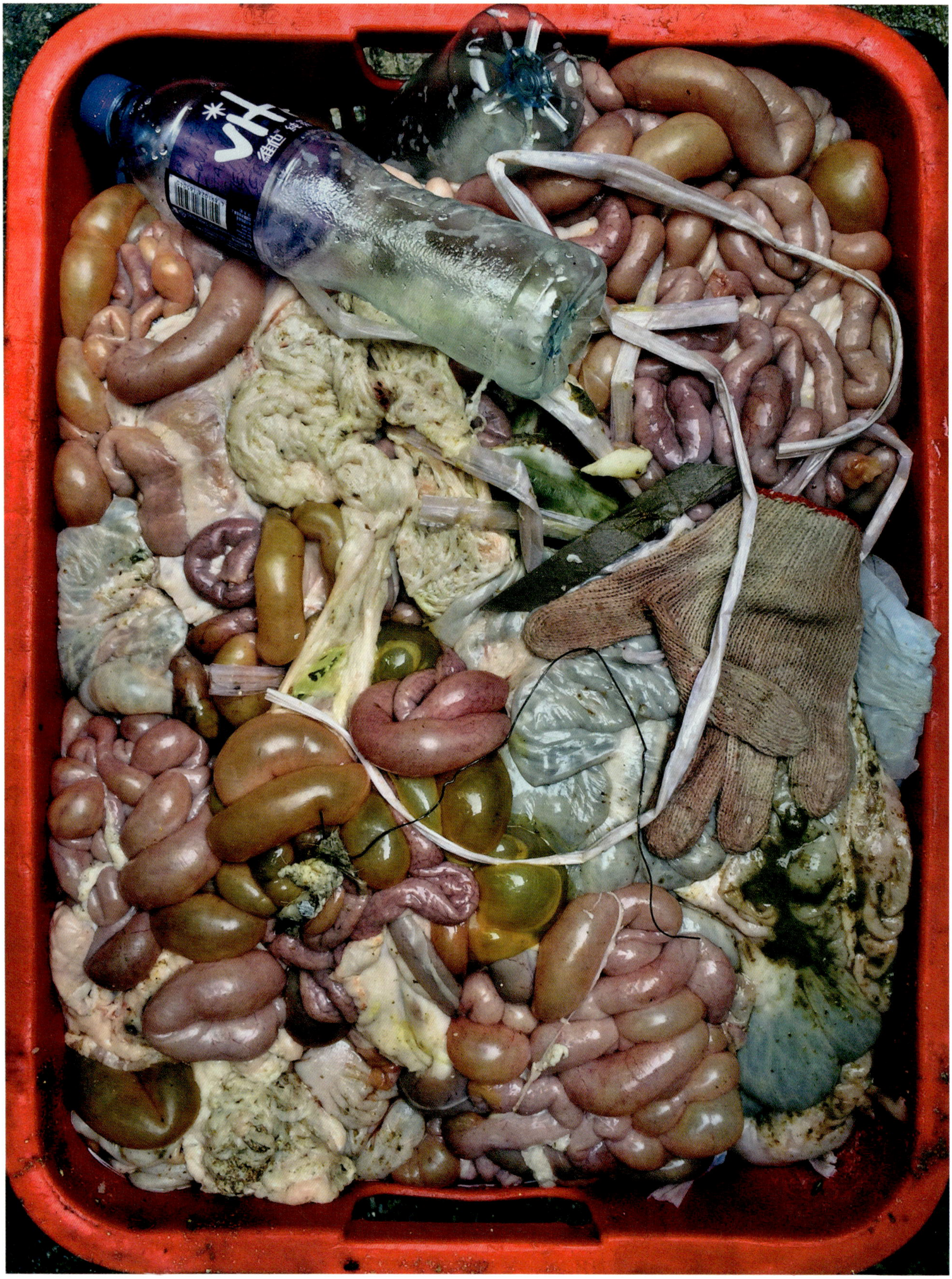

Informal Solutions #136

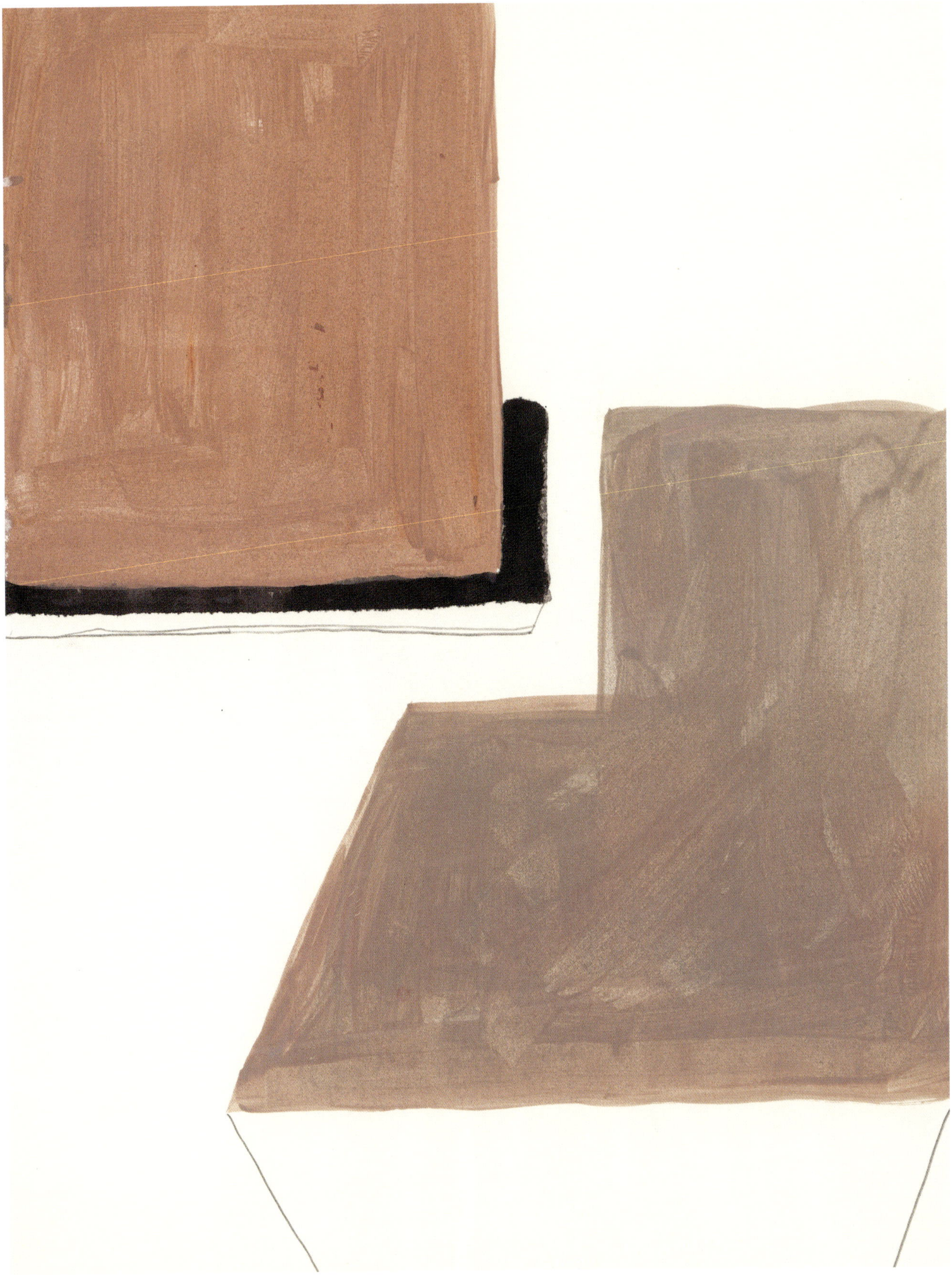

untitled, 2014, 25 × 19 cm, mixed media on paper

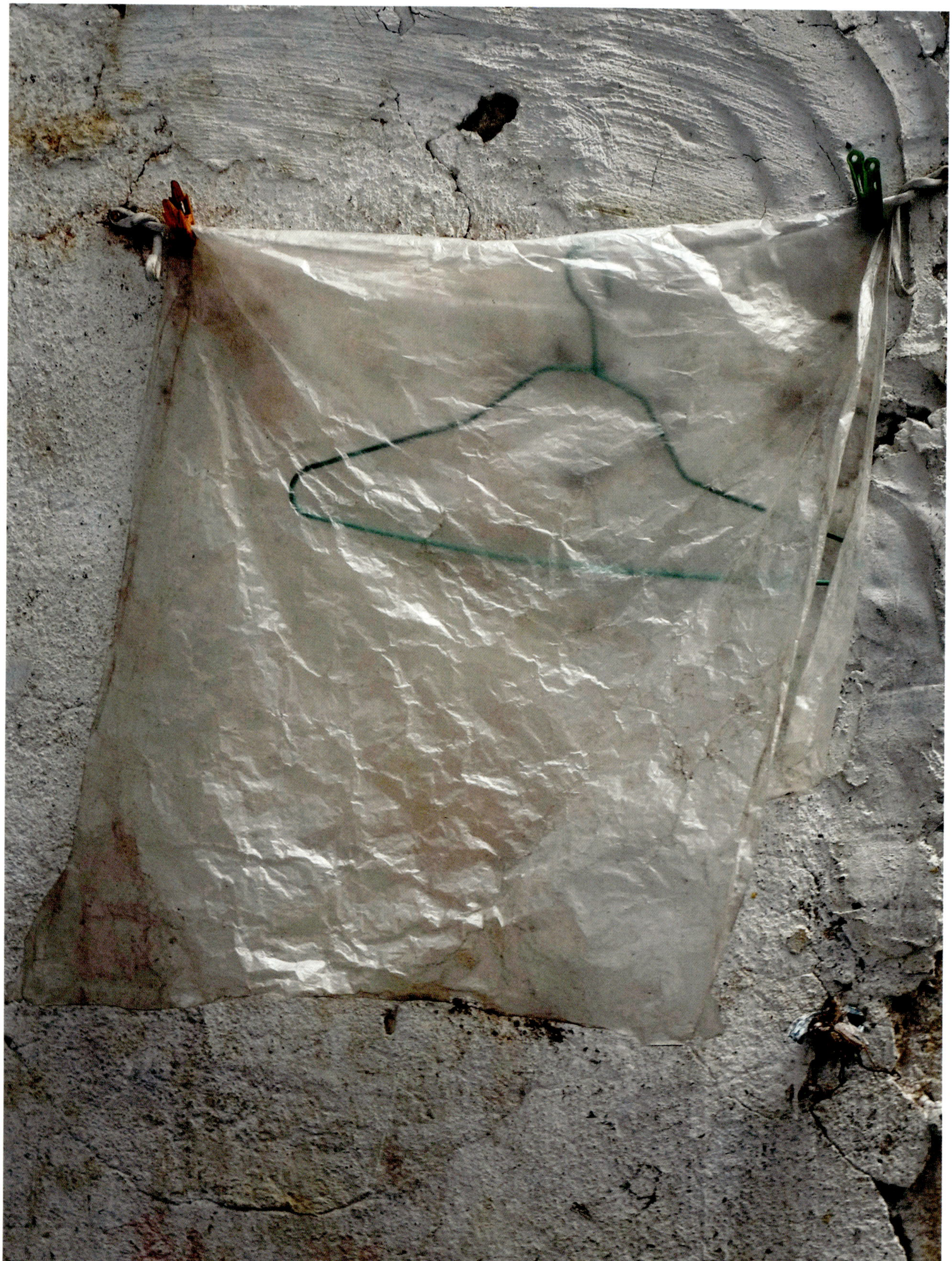

Informal Solutions #137

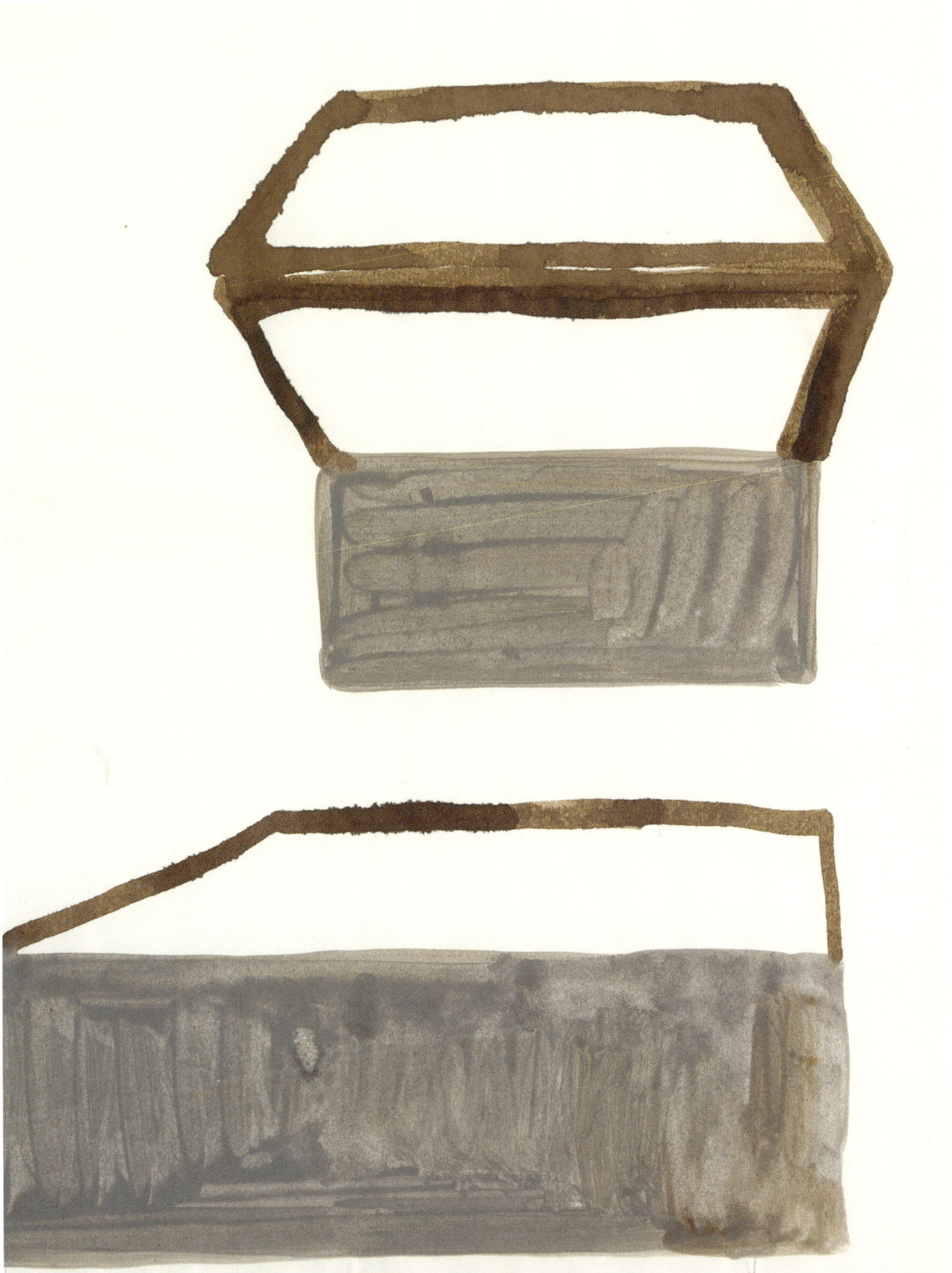

untitled, 2014, 25 × 19 cm, mixed media on paper

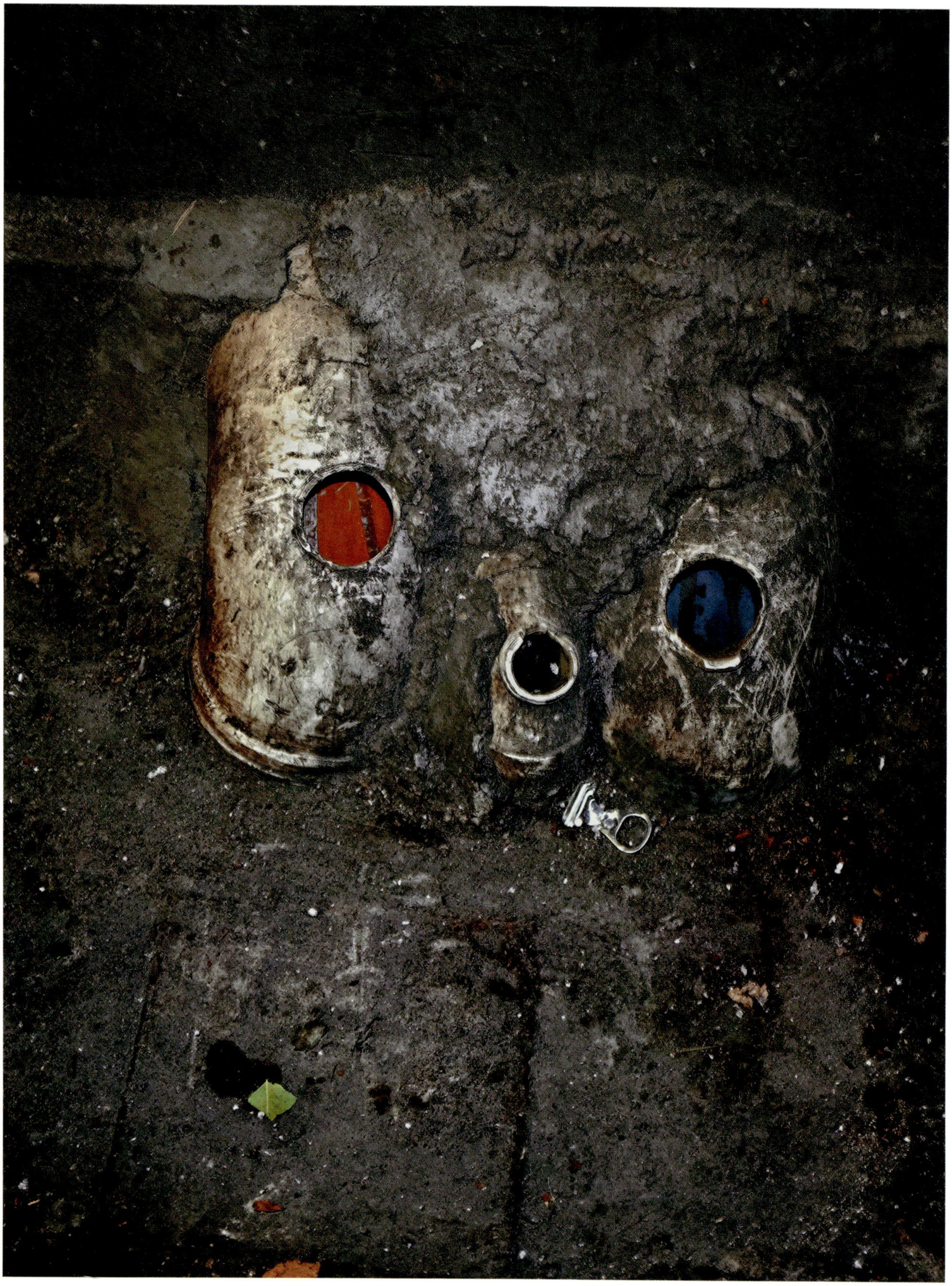

Informal Solutions #138

regardeuse (viewer), 2014, 25 × 19 cm, mixed media on paper

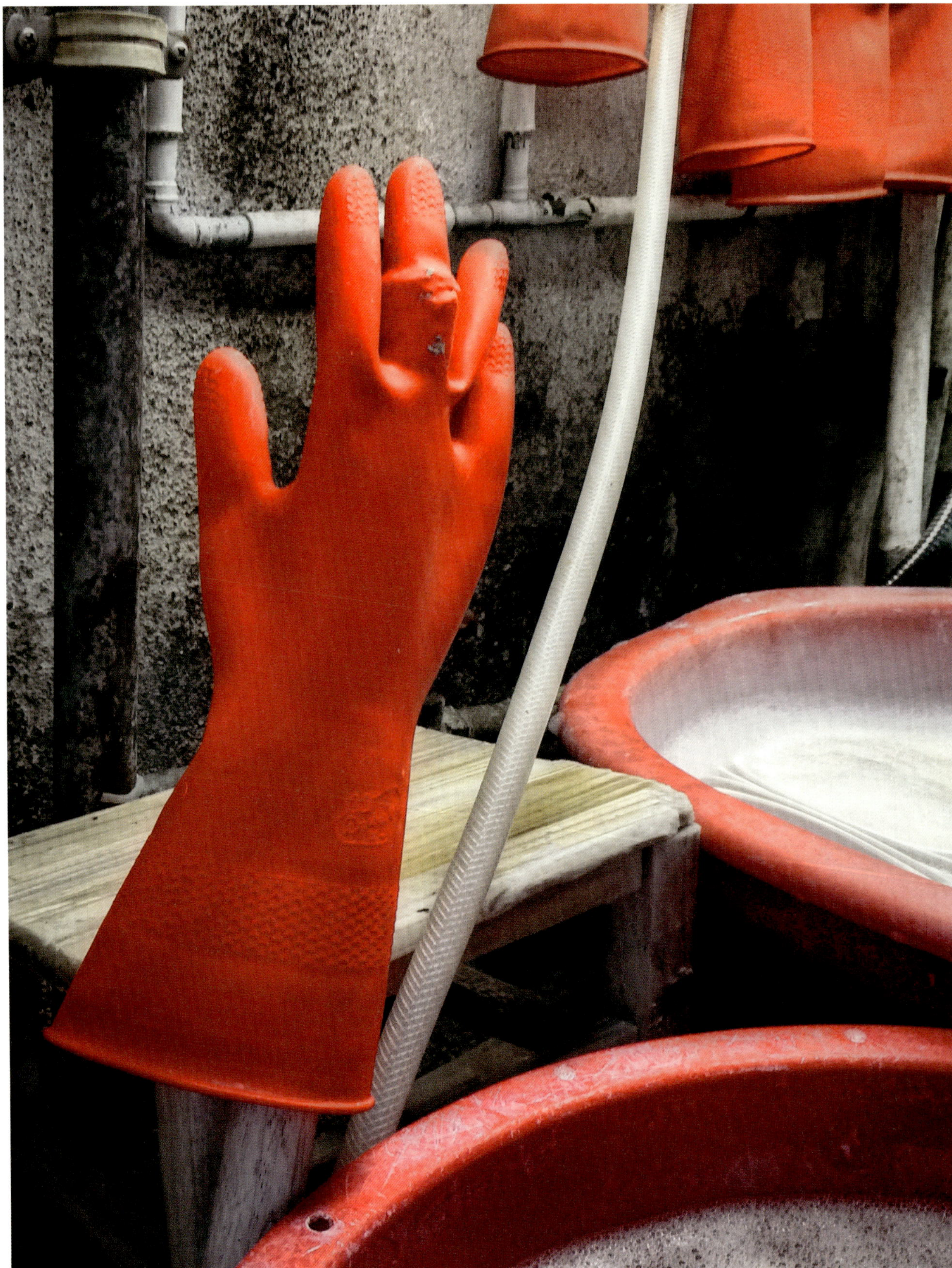

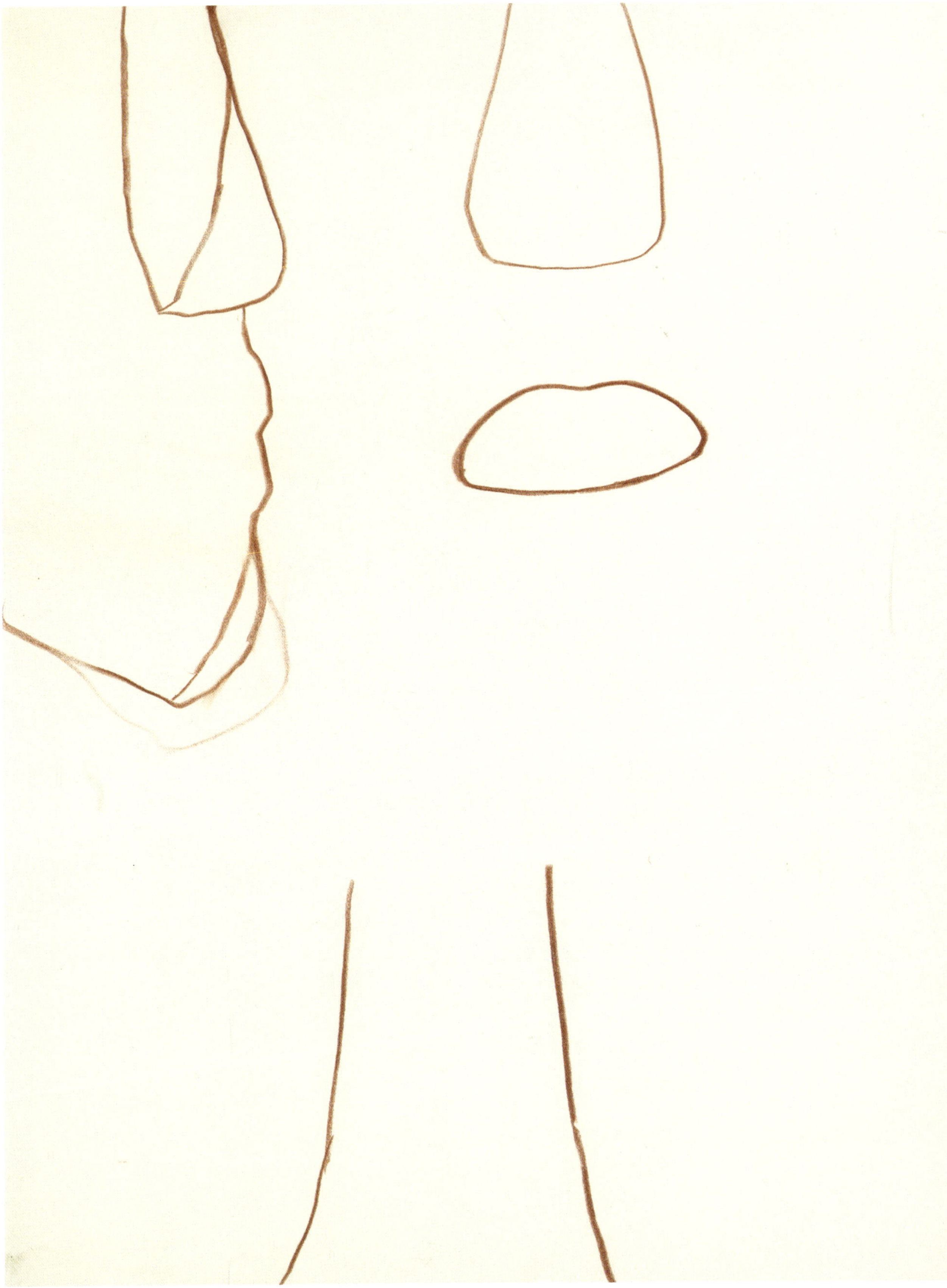

untitled, 2014, 25 × 19 cm, mixed media on paper

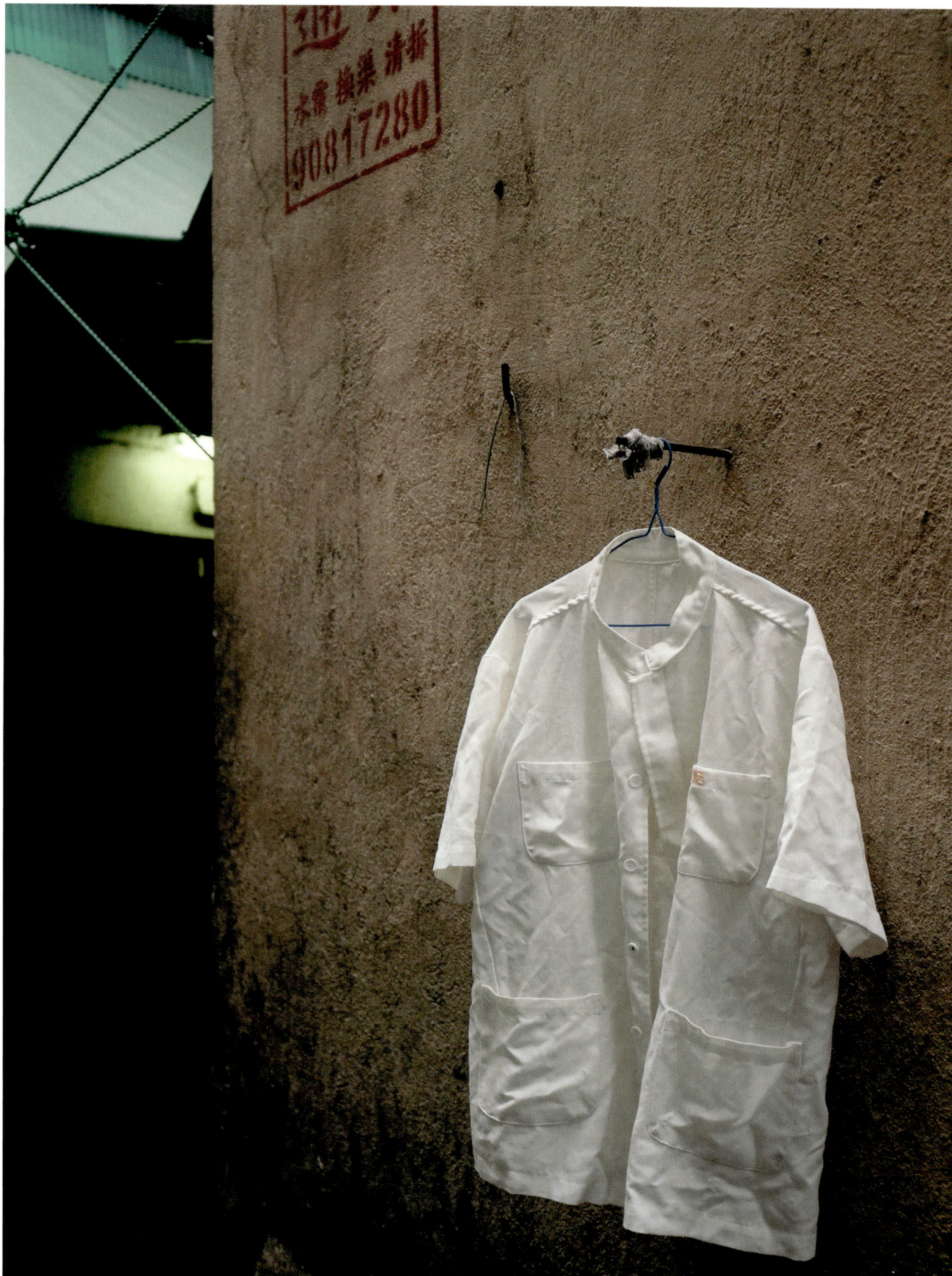
清拆
90817280

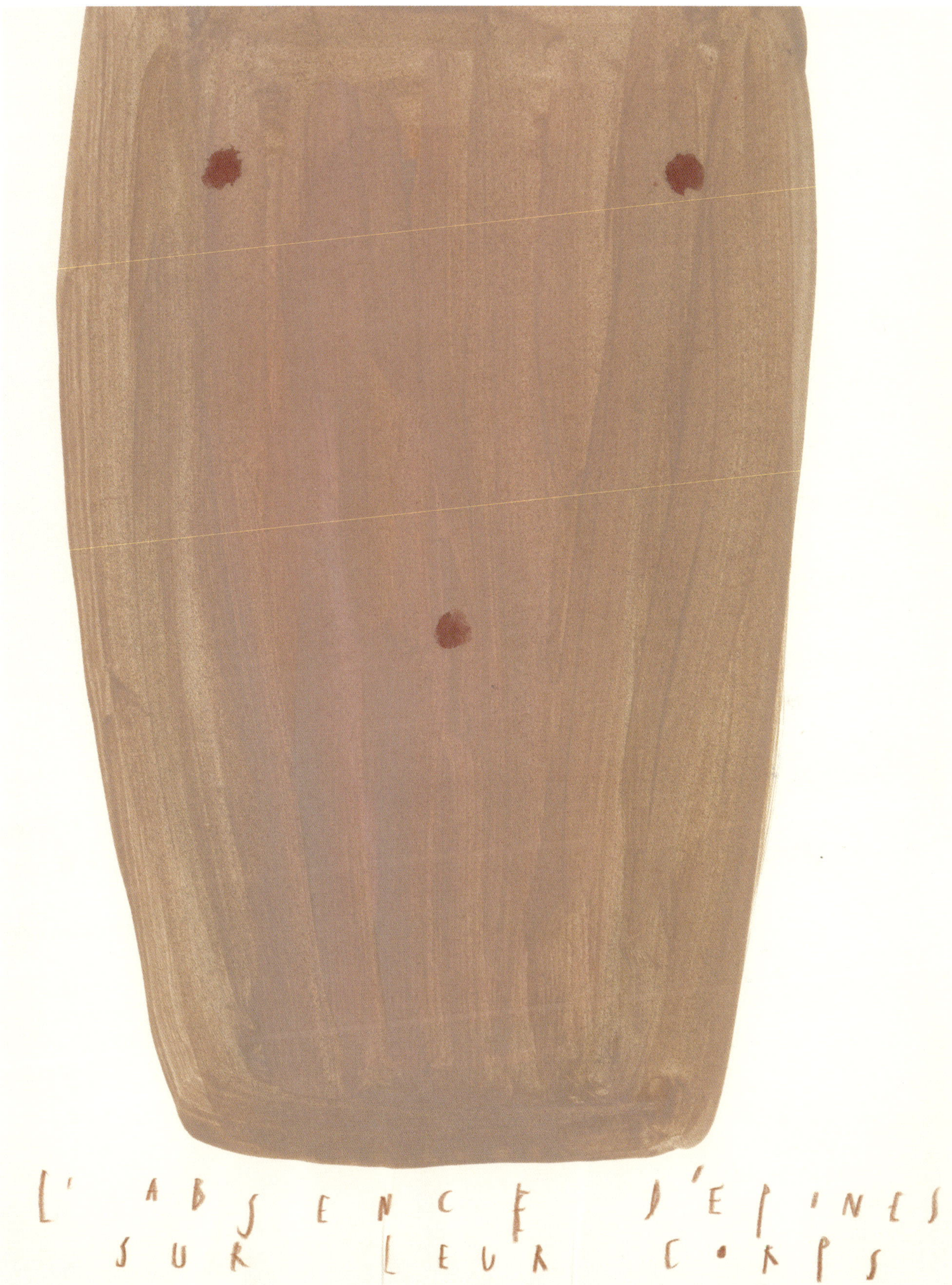

l'absence d'épines sur leur corps (the absence of thorns on their bodies), 2014, 25 × 19 cm, mixed media on paper

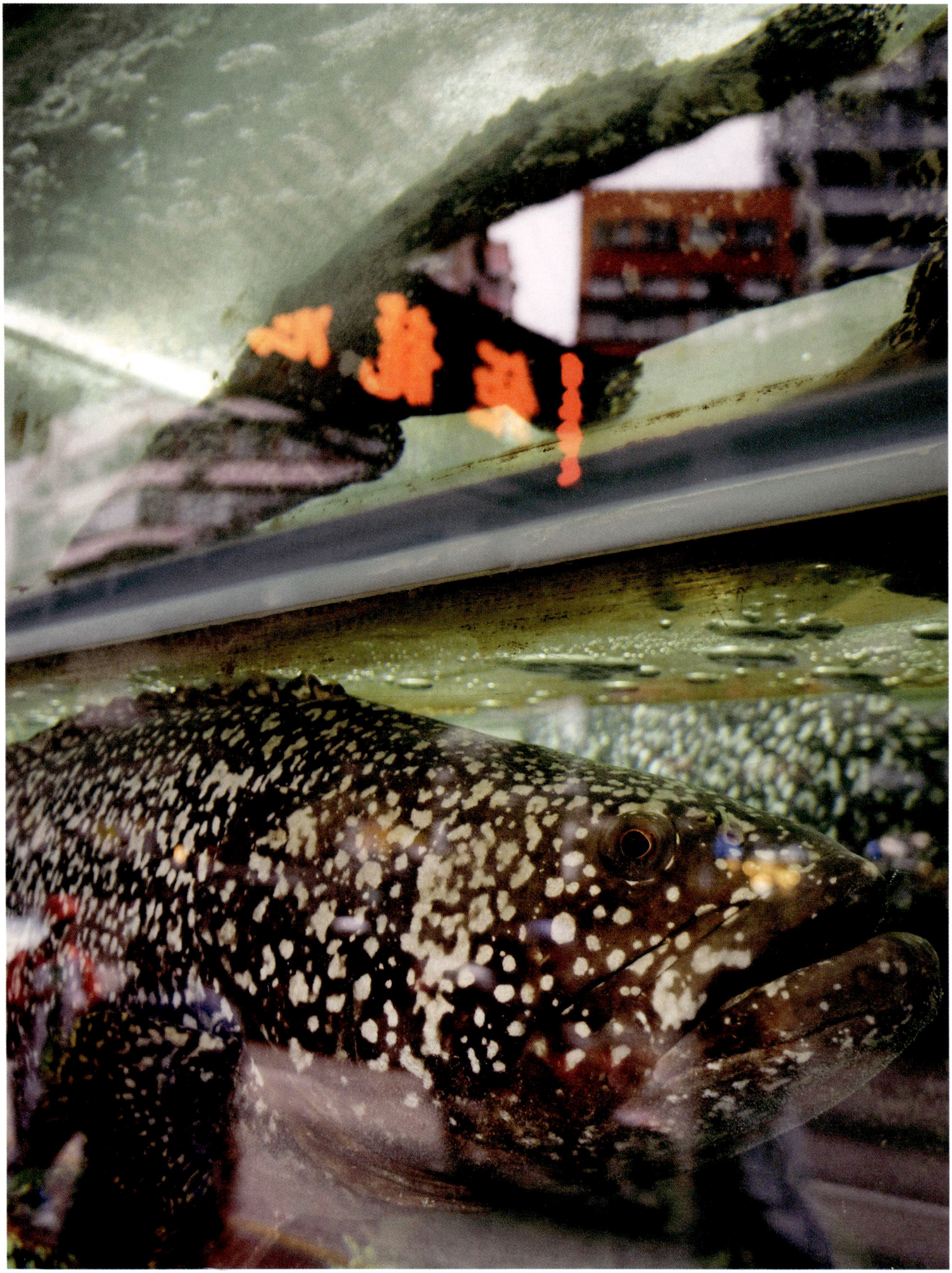

le grand œil vide du poisson trop solitaire (the big empty eye of the too lonely fish), 2014, 25 × 19 cm, mixed media on paper

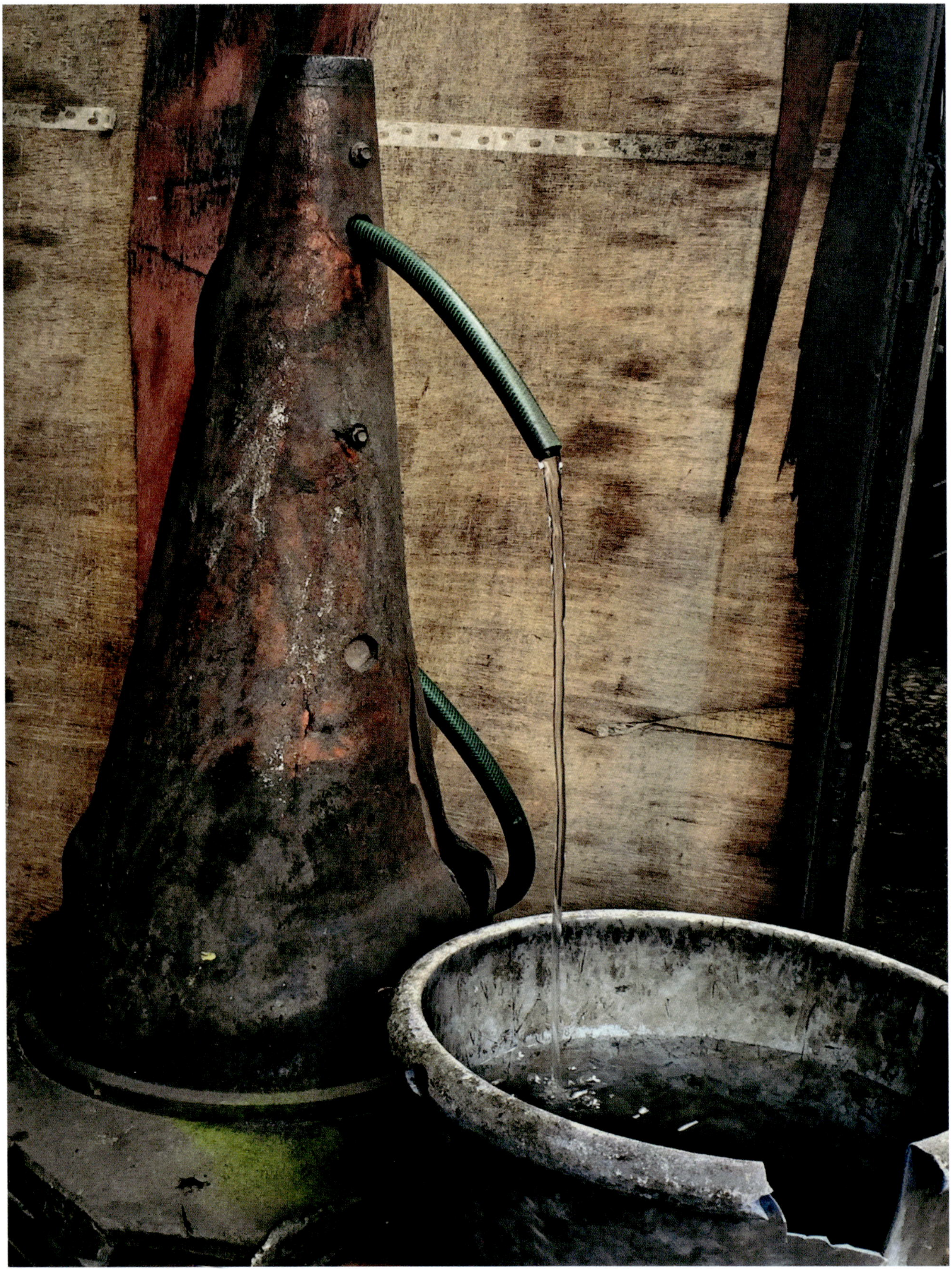

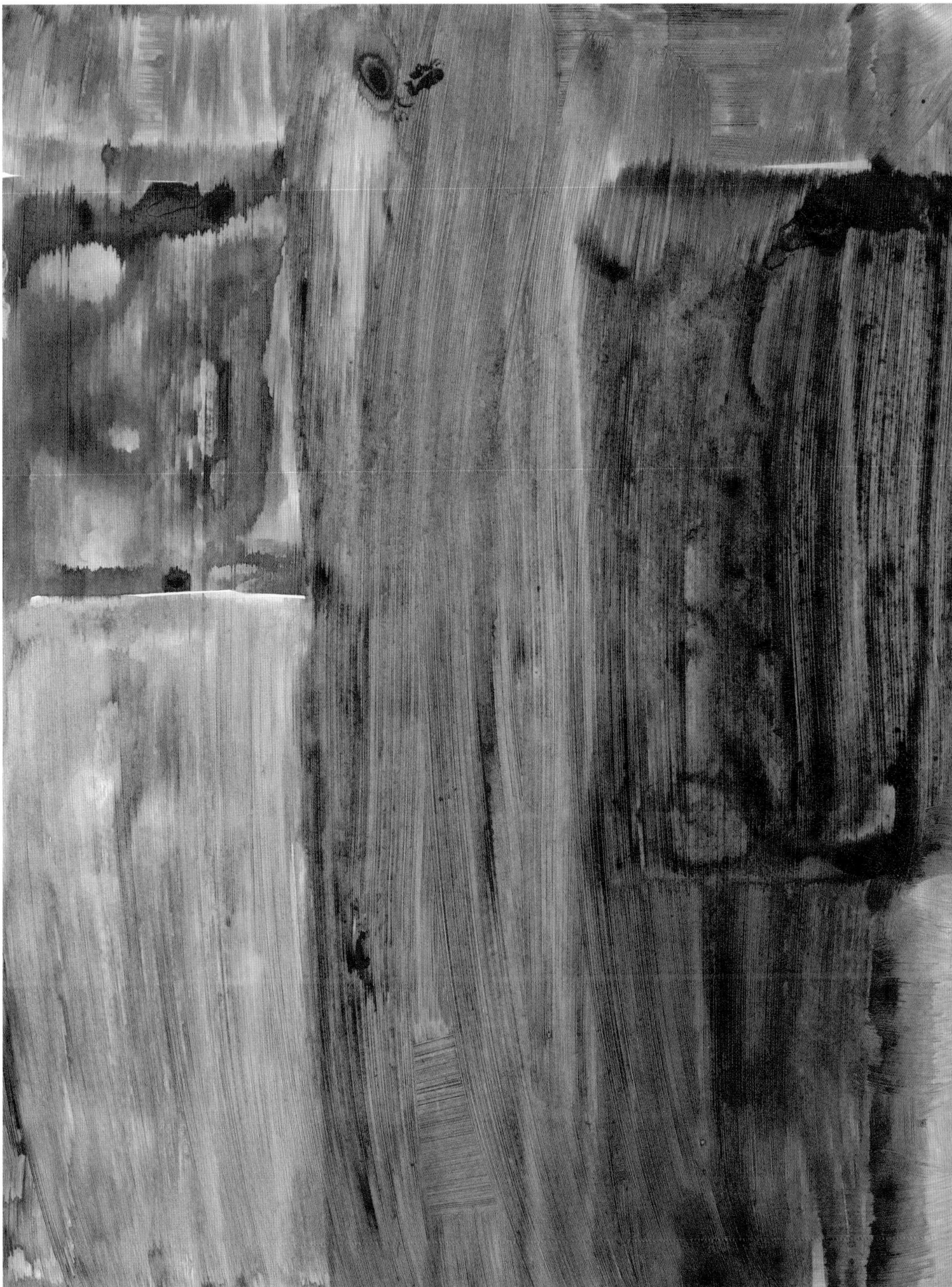

untitled, 2014, 25 × 19 cm, mixed media on paper

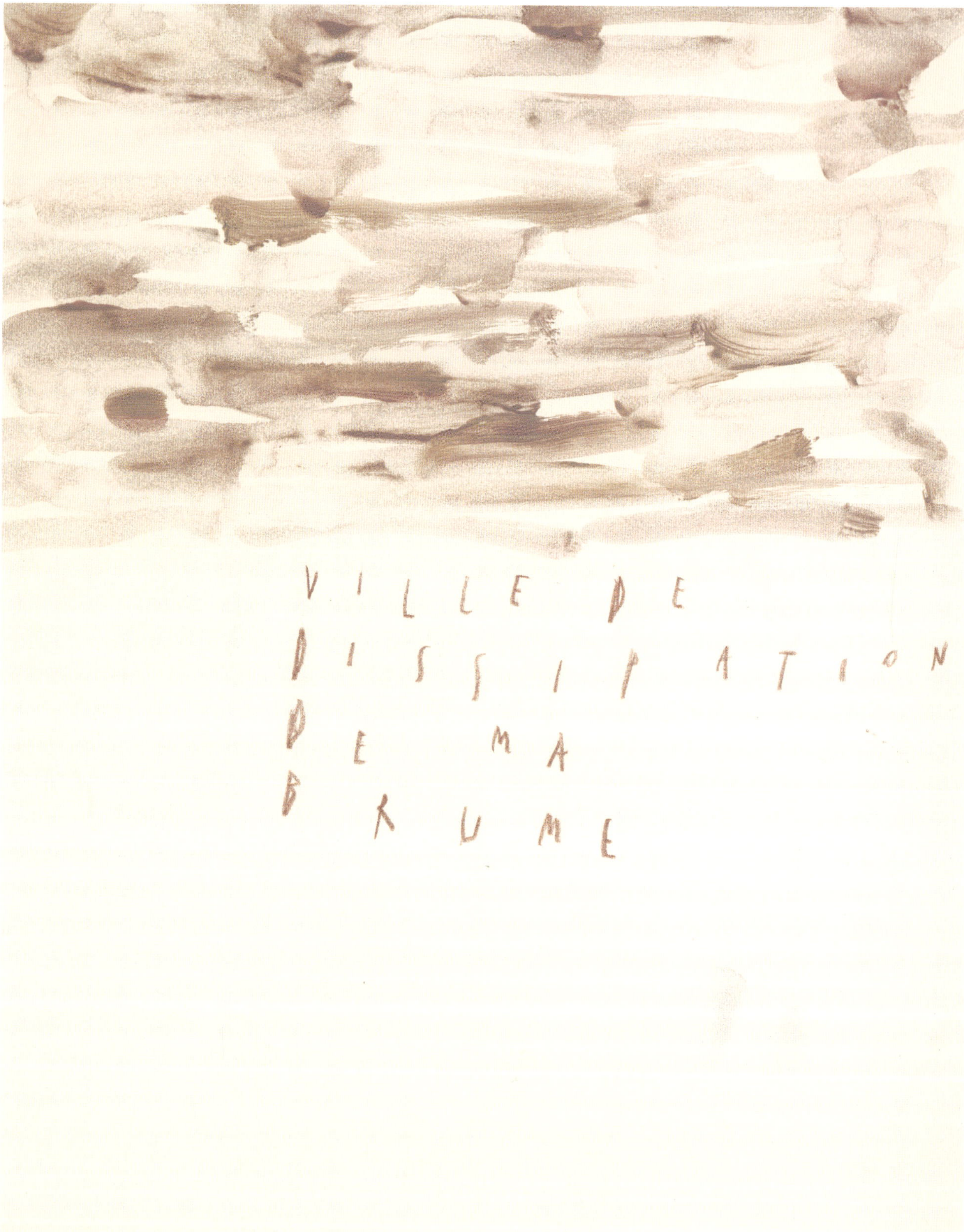

ville de dissipation de ma brume (the city where my fog dissipates), 2014, 25 × 19 cm, mixed media on paper

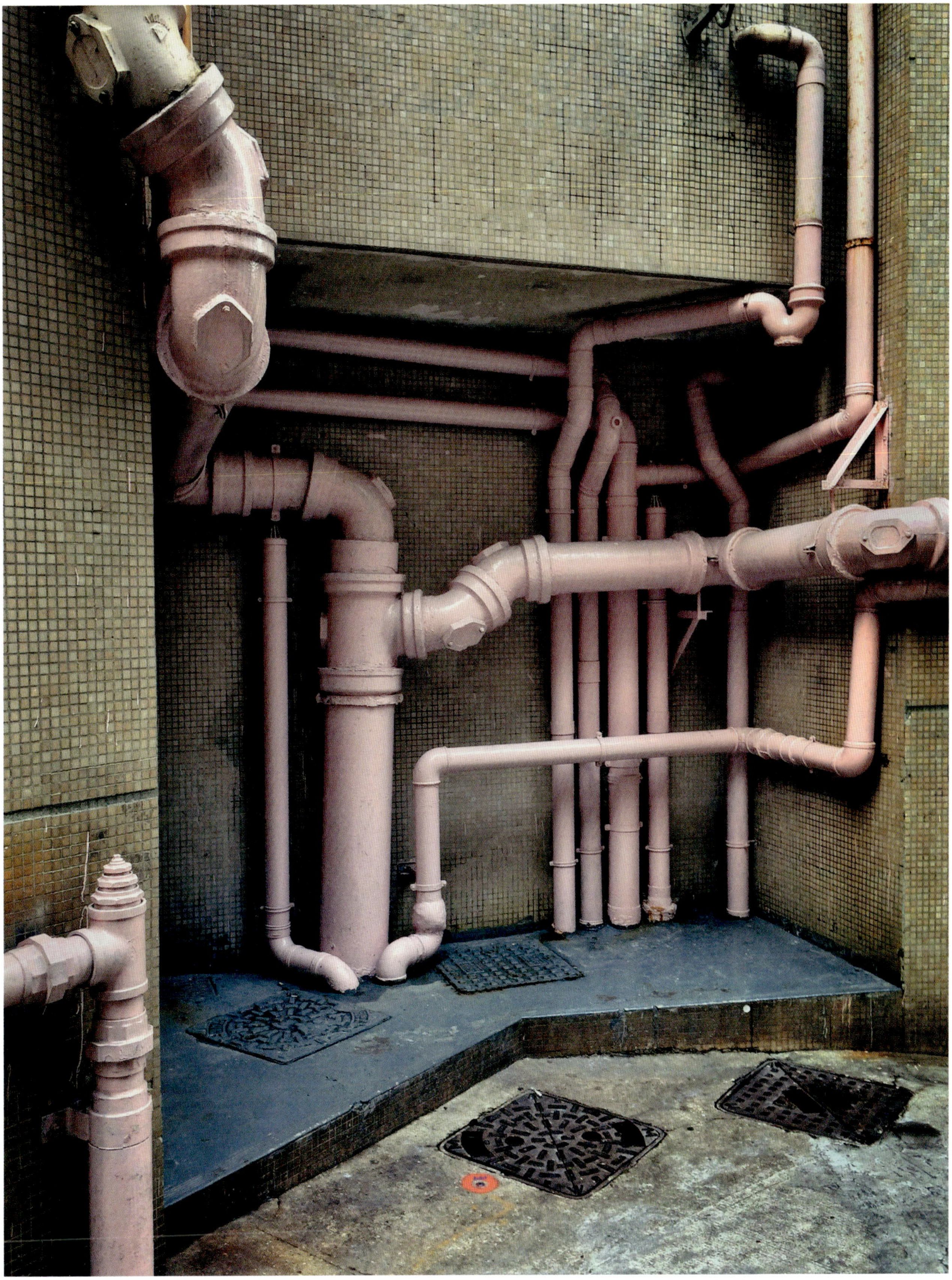

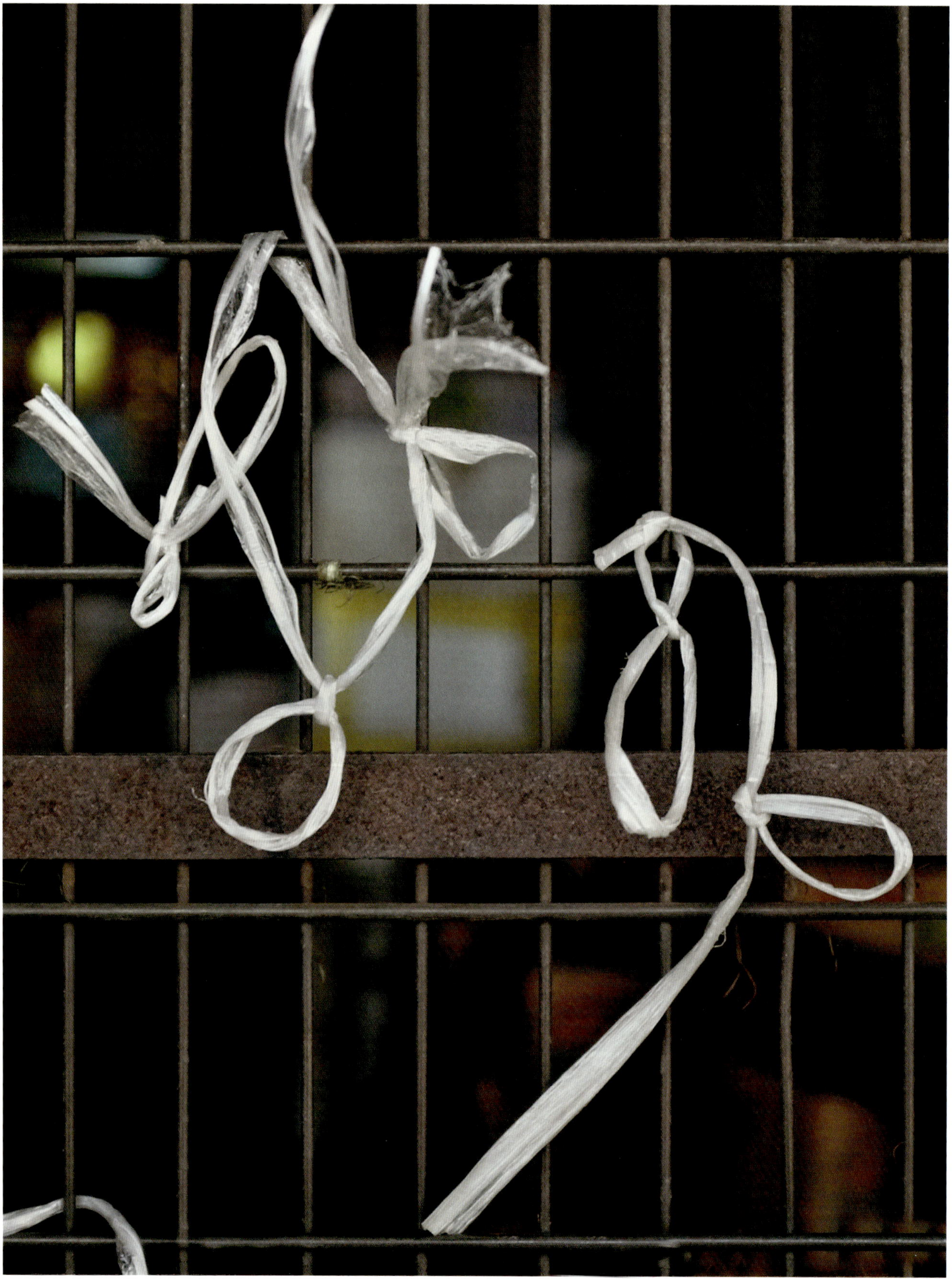

Informal Solutions #143

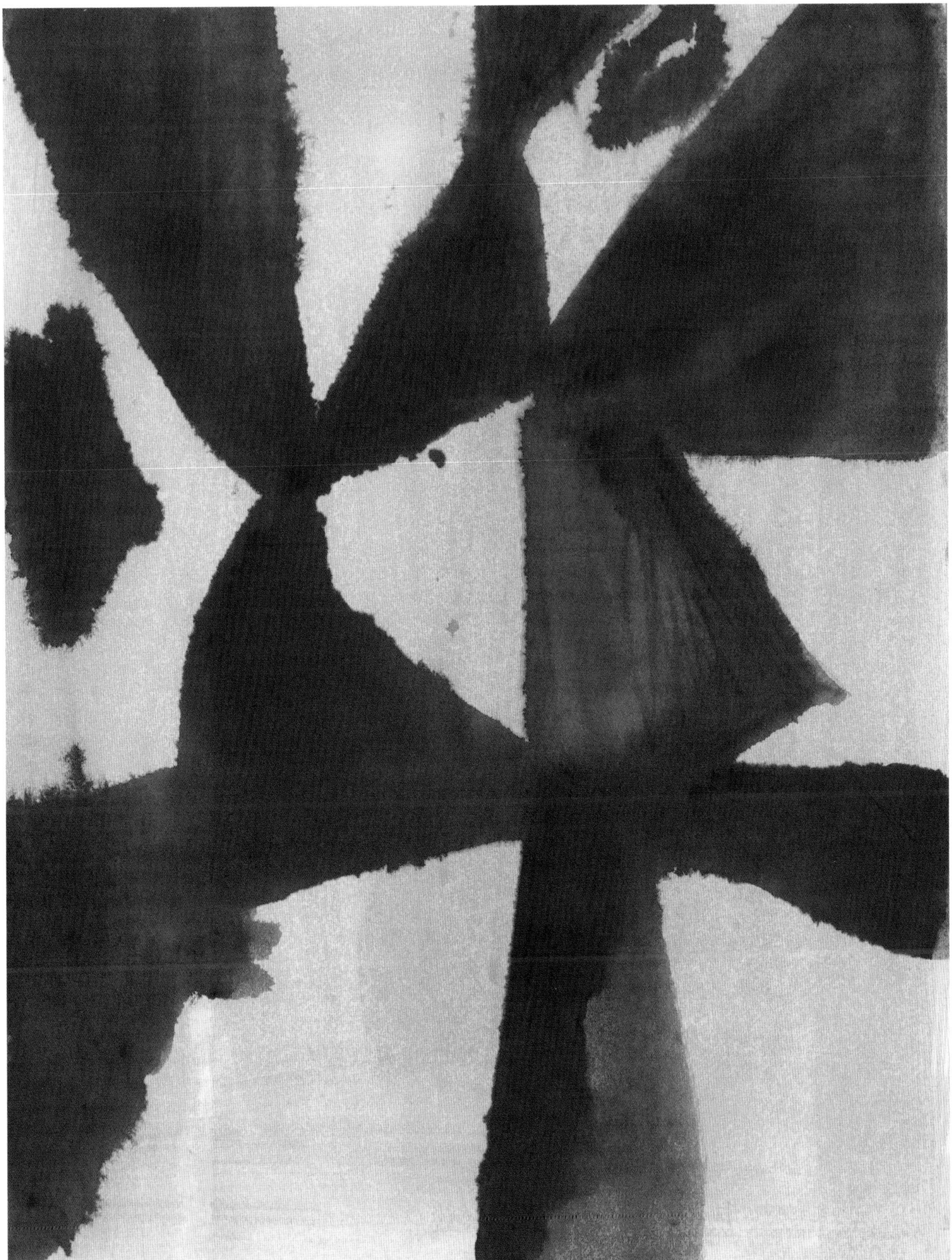

untitled, 2014, 25 × 19 cm, mixed media on paper

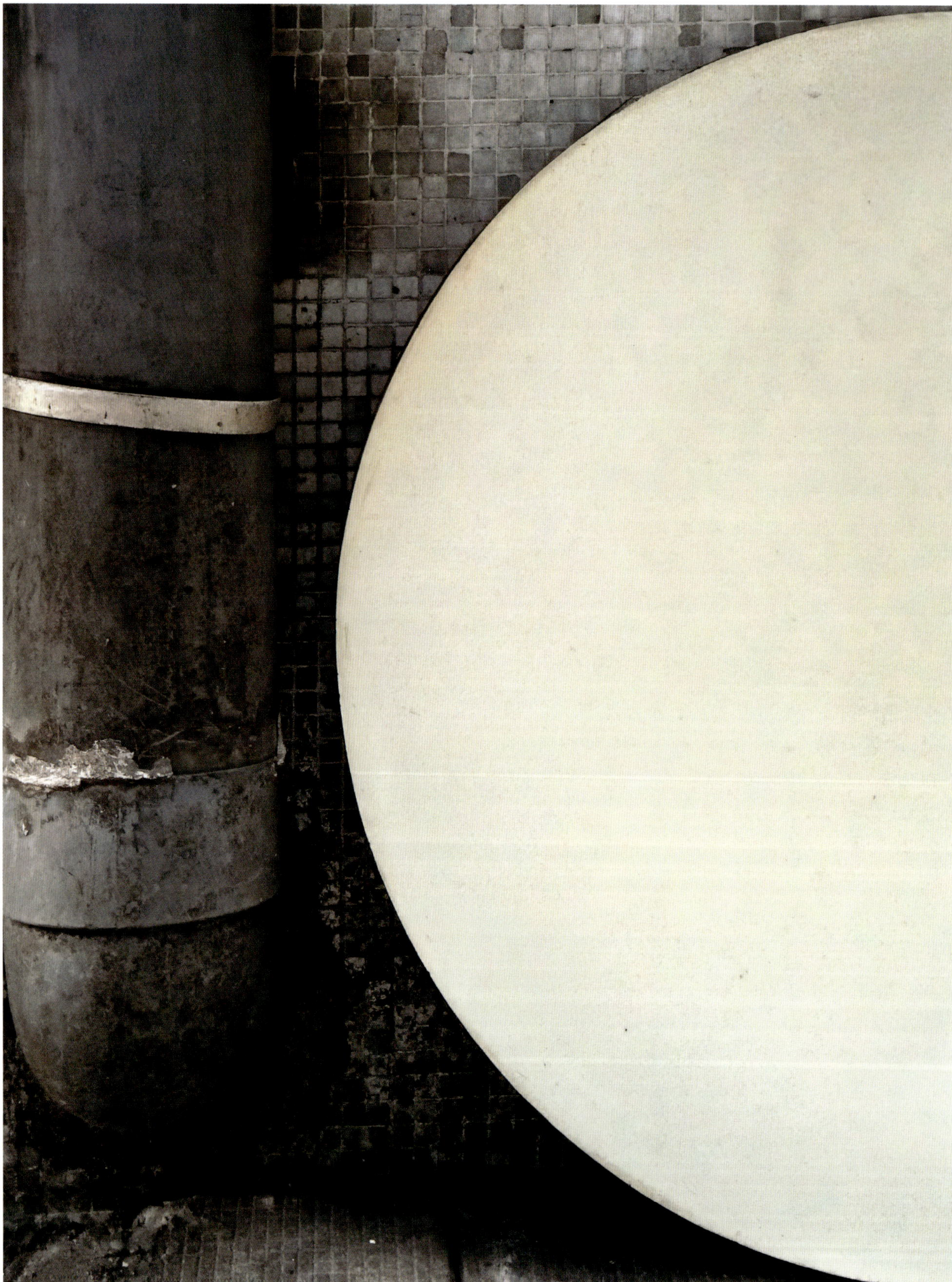

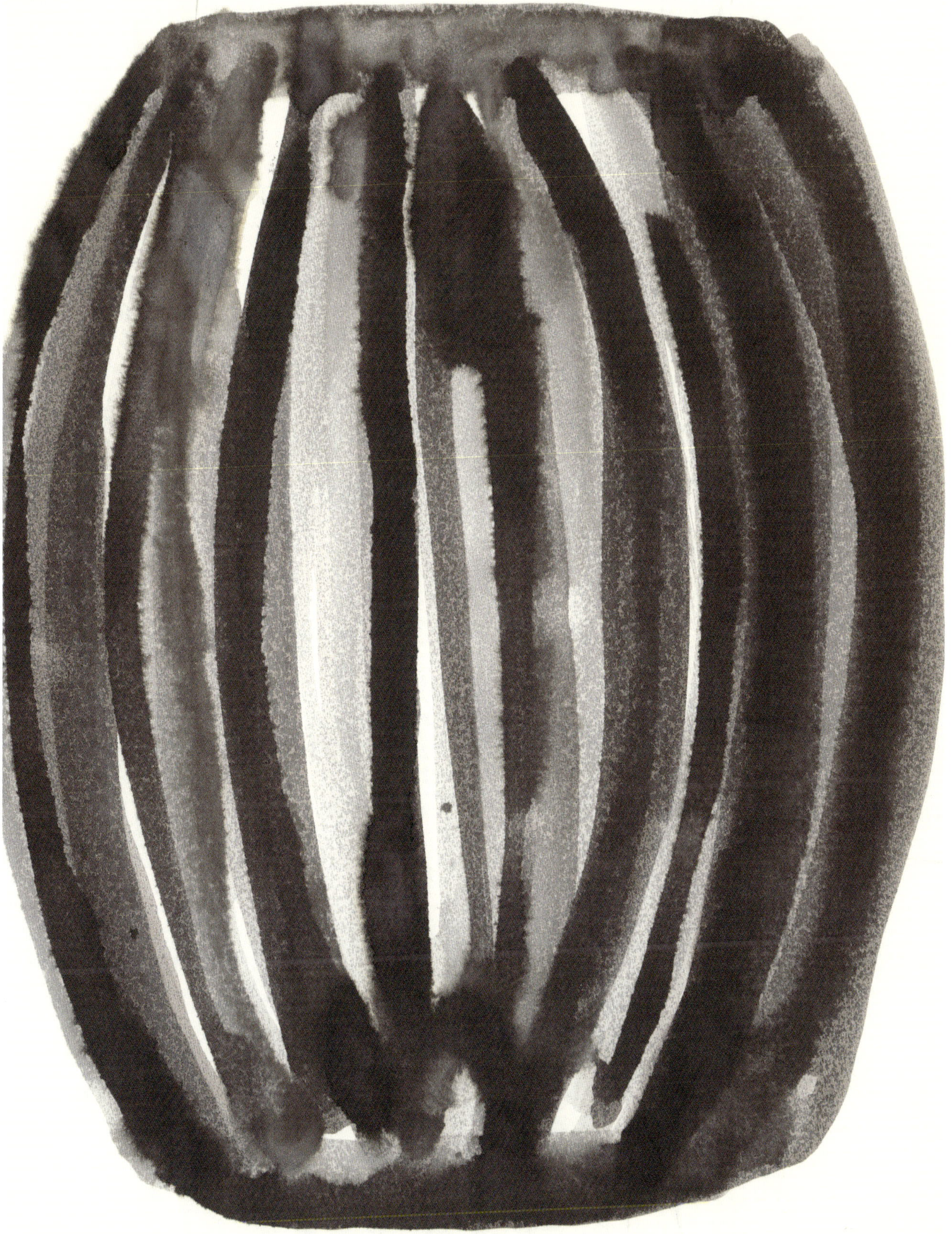

untitled, 2014, 25 × 19 cm, mixed media on paper

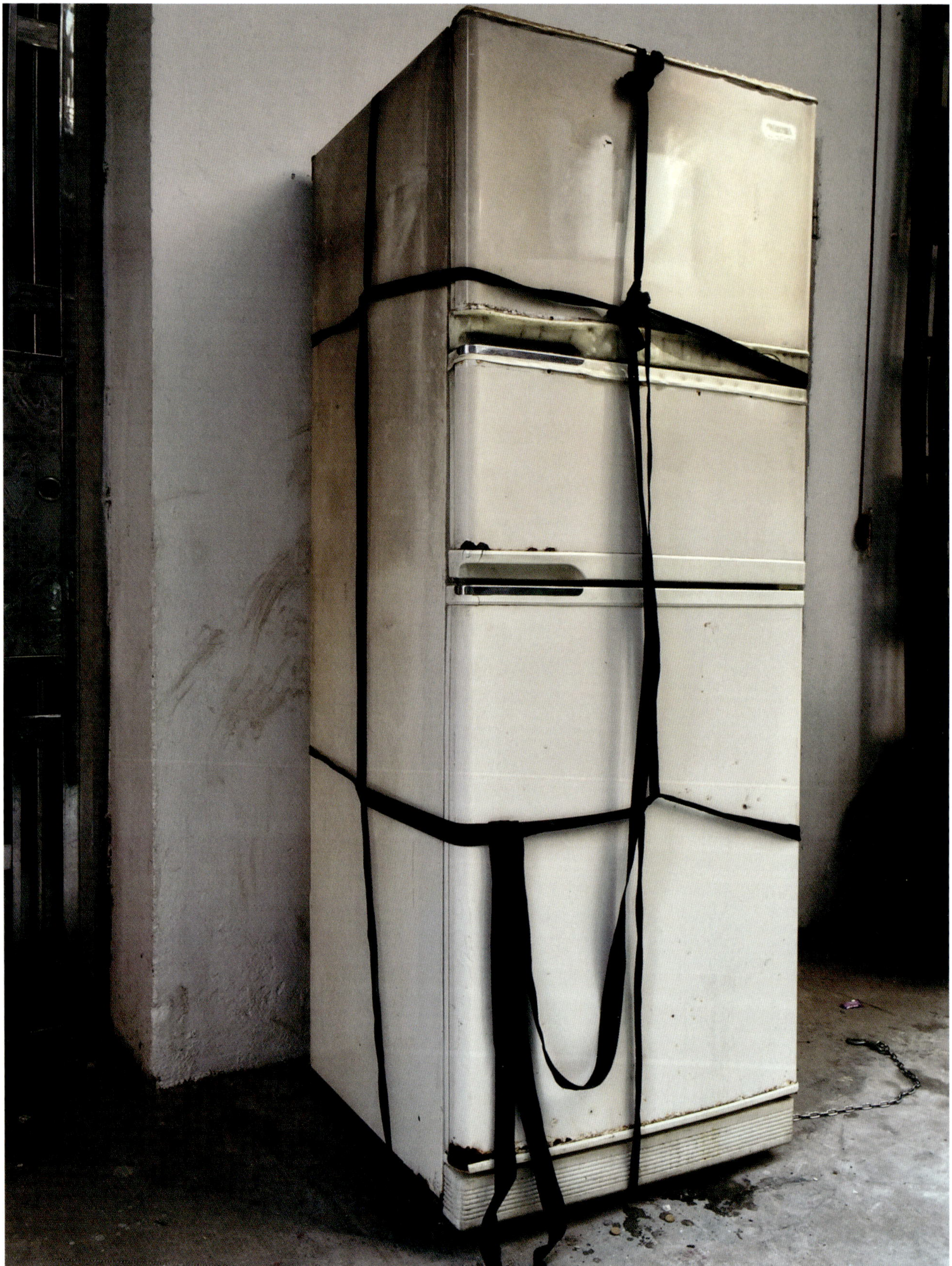

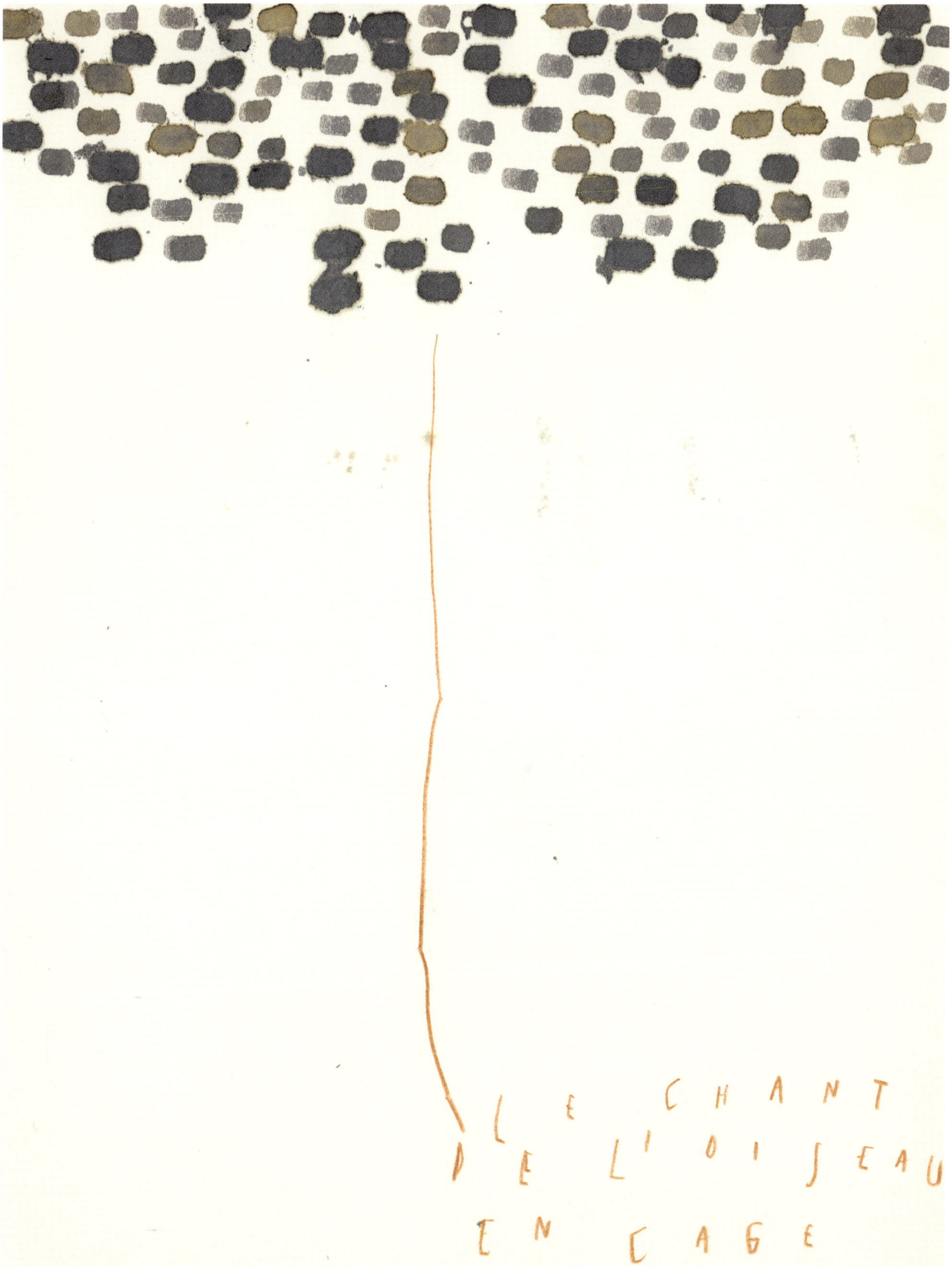

le chant de l'oiseau en cage (the song of the caged bird), 2014, 25 × 19 cm, mixed media on paper

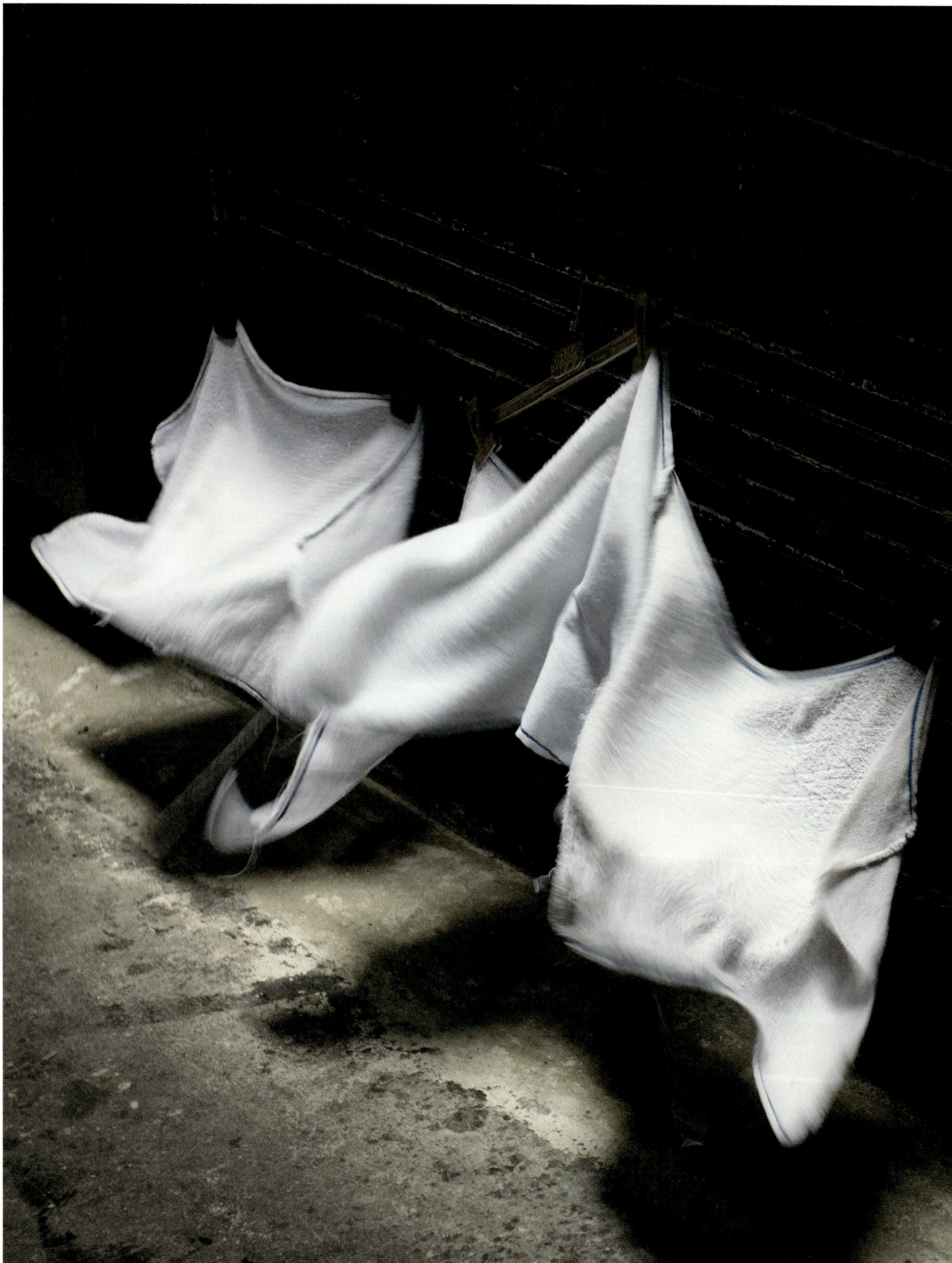

recadrer (reframing), 2014, 25 × 19 cm, mixed media on paper

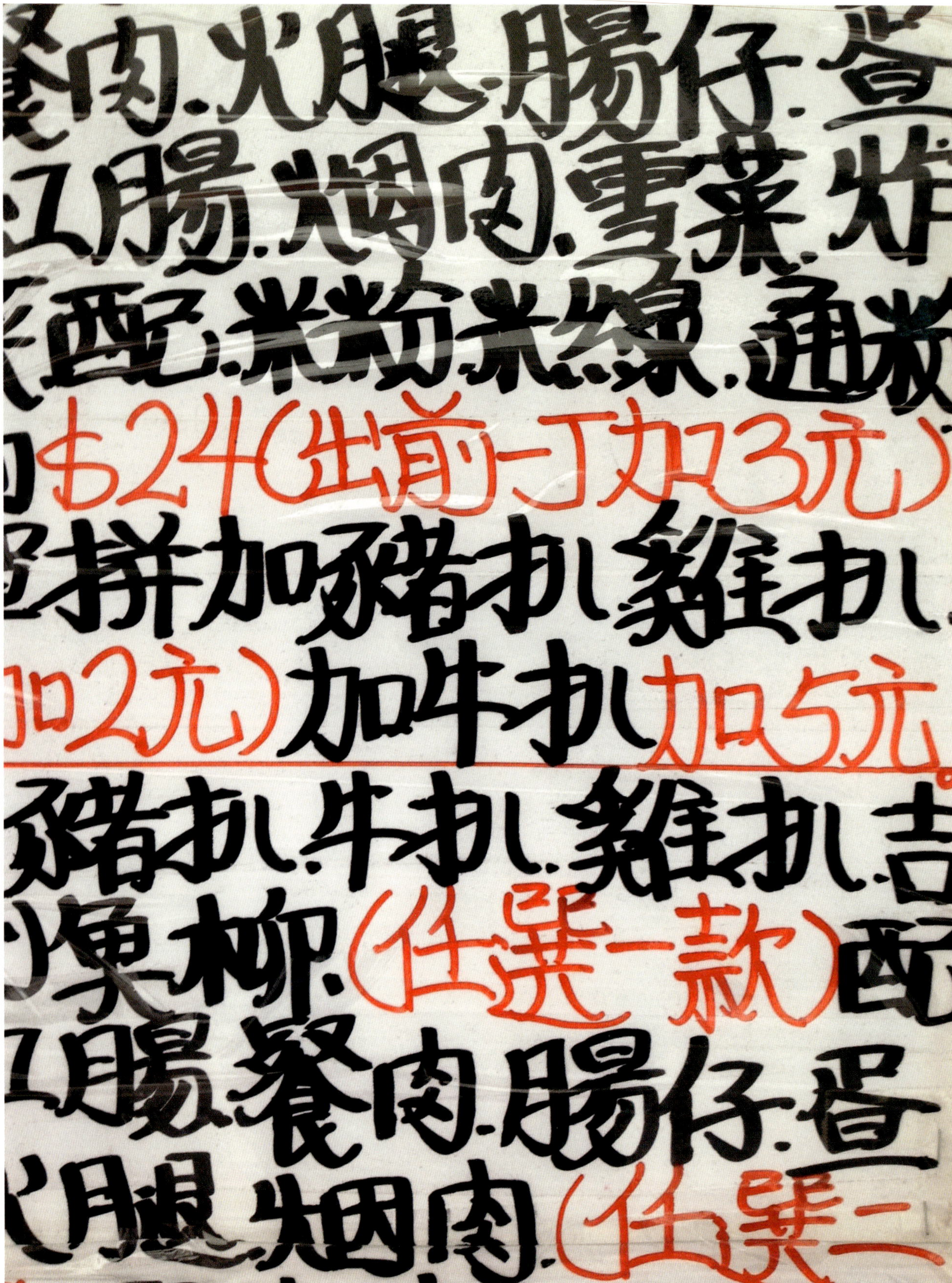
肉.火腿.腸仔.
腸.煙肉.雪菜.炸
西配.米粉.米線.通粉
$24(出前一丁加3元)
拼加豬扒.雞扒.
加2元)加牛扒(加5元
豬扒.牛扒.雞扒.吉
魚柳.(任選一款)
腸.餐肉.腸仔.
火腿.煙肉.(任選一

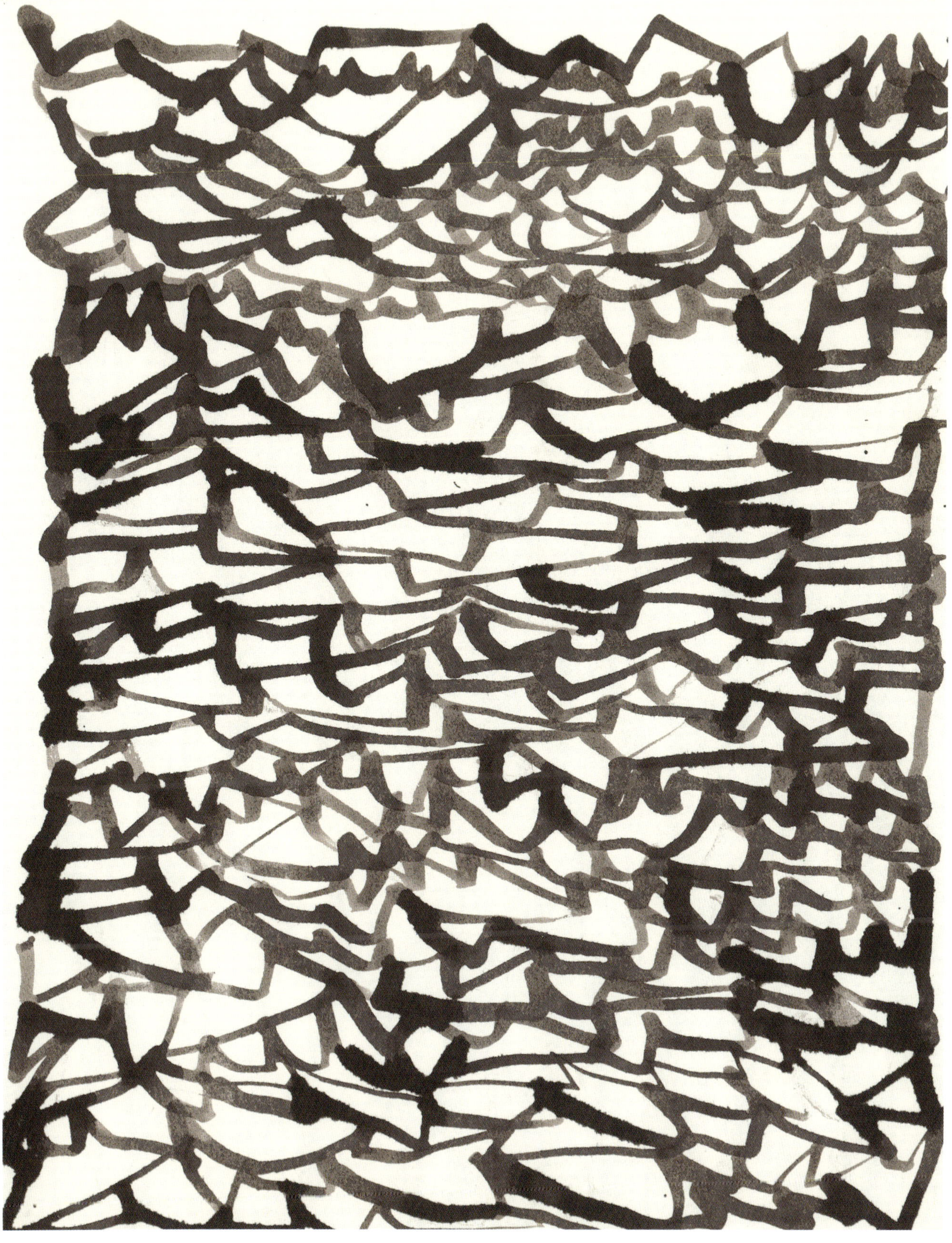

untitled, 2014, 25 × 19 cm, mixed media on paper

A dialogue between two artists that almost fell silent has been brought to the surface.

My thanks go to everyone, especially Arpaïs Du Bois and Gallery FIFTY ONE, Michael Wolf's close friend Marc Feustel for his text, Pierfrancesco Celada and Jasper Wolf for their support, as well as the brilliant team of Gautier Platteau.

In memory of Michael Wolf, who passed away in April 2019.

Barbara Wolf

COLOPHON

Photographs
© Michael Wolf, 2014
The Estate of Michael Wolf

Drawings
© Arpaïs Du Bois, 2014

Texts
Arpaïs Du Bois
Marc Feustel

Image research
Pierfrancesco Celada
Barbara Wolf

Image editing
Chau Digital, Hong Kong, China
die Keure, Bruges, Belgium

Translation
Helen Simpson

Copy-editing
Xavier De Jonge

Project management
Stephanie Van den bosch

Art direction
Natacha Hofman

Design
Tim Bisschop

Printing & binding
Trento, Italy

Publisher
Gautier Platteau

With special thanks to
Reg Herygers

ISBN 978 94 6494 120 3
D/2024/11922/30
NUR 653/646

HANNIBAL
BOOKS

www.hannibalbooks.be

www.photomichaelwolf.com
www.arpais.com
www.gallery51.com

FRONT COVER

Michael Wolf, *Informal Solutions #112, #93*

Arpaïs Du Bois, untitled

BACK COVER

Michael Wolf, *Informal Solutions #129, #108*

Arpaïs Du Bois, *sans les organes des anges (without the angels' organs)*

Arpaïs Du Bois, untitled